# TEST SCORES
# AND
# WHAT THEY MEAN

second edition

*HOWARD B. LYMAN*
*University of Cincinnati*

PRENTICE-HALL, INC., *Englewood Cliffs, New Jersey*

**This
2nd
Edition
Is Affectionately
Dedicated
to
2,
too**

P–13–903781–0
C–13–903799–3
Library of Congress Catalog Card Number: 71–121726
Printed in the United States of America

Current printing (last number):
10  9  8  7  6  5  4  3  2  1

PRENTICE-HALL INTERNATIONAL, INC., *London*
PRENTICE-HALL OF AUSTRALIA, PTY. LTD., *Sydney*
PRENTICE-HALL OF CANADA, LTD., *Toronto*
PRENTICE-HALL OF INDIA PRIVATE LIMITED, *New Delhi*
PRENTICE-HALL OF JAPAN, INC., *Tokyo*

# PREFACE

Standardized testing is a fascinating study. The number of tests being used increases by millions each year. New tests are constantly being published—and new applications for tests are constantly being found.

Back in 1963, when the first edition of *Test Scores and What They Mean* was published, I stated the belief that there was need for a book which could be used by people who have access to test results but who have had little training in the meaning of test scores. I thought that such a book would be most helpful to those people whose professional training had not included much about testing (even though they might make occasional or even frequent reference to test results): school teachers, psychiatrists, social workers, pediatricians, academic deans, and admissions counselors, among others. I suggested also that the book might be used in connection with courses in introductory psychology, educational psychology, counseling, psychological testing, educational measurement and evaluation, guidance, individual differences, and the like—in the training of psychologists, counselors, personnel workers, and others who may use tests often.

The reception given to the first edition was gratifying. The book was used as a text or supplementary text for a wide variety of courses in colleges and universities throughout the United States and Canada, and at some institutions elsewhere. It was translated into Japanese. At least one consulting firm urged personnel from client companies to consider its use. At least two test publishers advertised it in their own catalogs as a service to their respective customers. Reviews were generally favorable, as were the comments of professional colleagues. One Past President of the American Psychological Association wrote: "The book is a beautiful job of matching information to the need for it."

There have been some improvements in the testing field since 1963.

Test manuals are generally better. Test publishers seem to have made some technical improvements in their tests, their selection of norms groups, etc. And there has been a great increase in the use of sophisticated (and, generally, more accurate) electronic scoring services. It's even possible that there is some improved test interpretation. But the job is far from complete, for there is still too much test *misuse* and *misinterpretation*.

Criticism of standardized testing is louder than ever. Intelligence tests, critics maintain, do not measure creativity. The tests do not give unvarying results, and they are unfair to minority groups. Personality tests, they contend, are an unfair invasion of privacy. Although tests are being used in ever-increasing numbers, the critics are making ever-stronger adverse comments. My views on these and related issues form the basis for Chapter Eleven.

The difficulties with testing, of course, lie more with the users of tests and of test results than with the tests themselves. The evidence seems clear: more tests are going to be used by more people who have access to test results without knowing as much as they should about the meaning of test scores. Is it too much to hope that the critics may have the beneficial effect of encouraging greater responsibility in the use and interpretation of test information?

The second edition, like the first, is intended primarily for students of testing and for the test-naïve. For this reason, I have written informally in an effort to make the book interesting and intelligible to any intelligent adult.

My philosophy of testing is dynamic and still evolving. It has been influenced by my own teachers, both undergraduate and graduate: J. McVicker Hunt, Donald Lindsley, Donald G. Paterson, Howard P. Longstaff, C. Gilbert Wrenn, Walter Cook, W. S. Miller, E. G. Williamson, John G. Darley, Ralph F. Berdie, Herbert Sorenson, Robert North, Lysle Croft, and others. My views have developed through years of research with tests, through teaching and interacting with students in testing courses, and through consultation on testing problems with a wide variety of clients.

The most distinctive feature of the first edition was the original classification of types of test score. It has been retained almost unchanged. The conversion table which enables the reader to convert from one type of score to another (under certain assumptions) has been completely reset by the publisher to enable the reader to use it more easily. This table was used more widely by professional psychologists and counselors than any other feature of the first edition.

Most features of the first edition have been retained. Numerous *minor* changes have been made throughout the book in the interest of clarity, but there has been little change just for the sake of change.

There are two completely new chapters, "The Test Manual" and "Testing Today and Social Responsibility." In the former, I have tried to give the reader some idea of what a good test manual is like and some suggestions for reading the manual intelligently.

I am indebted to Dr. Robert Walker, of The Personnel Press (a subsidiary of Ginn and Company) for the idea of including such a chapter; and I am indebted to several test publishers (California Test Bureau, Consulting Psychologists Press, Educational Testing Service, Houghton Mifflin Company, Personnel Press, Science Research Associates, and The Psychological Corporation) for permission to use the illustrative material which made the chapter possible. It is an interesting commentary on the status of testing, I think, that I find it more difficult to *select* the material than to *find* the examples; i.e., I could easily have used other illustrations for every example in this chapter.

Chapter Eleven, "Testing Today and Social Responsibility," is a statement of some of the present concerns about testing. Here, I have discussed the cultural and racial fairness of tests, the charge that tests are an invasion of privacy, and other issues.

The bibliography has been updated and greatly expanded. New items include audio and video tapes, testing monographs, and books of readings.

The section on reliability has been almost completely rewritten in an effort to explain that concept in a manner that will be most meaningful to the beginning tester. In doing so, I have developed a five-dimensional model of reliability which I believe will make this important test attribute a little easier for the student to appreciate.

I want to thank the many users of the first edition of *Test Scores and What They Mean*, especially those who were thoughtful enough to express their comments. I want to thank Professor Saburo Iwawaki, who contributed many thoughts while preparing his excellent Japanese translation of the book. I want to thank my colleagues in Cincinnati (most especially Venus Bluestein, Goldine Gleser, Richard Melton, and Joan Bollenbacher) for permitting me to throw occasional questions their way while writing this manuscript. Thanks are due, too, to my wife, Pat, for her encouragement and her counsel, as well as for her typing of the manuscript. Thanks, too, to my own students for their free expressions of opinions—not always favorable—which have helped me to write intelligibly for future users of this book.

HOWARD B. LYMAN

# CONTENTS

# SCORE
# INTERPRETATION

## Chapter One

"When am I going to start failing?" a student asked me several years ago. Upon being questioned, he told me this story: "My high school teacher told me that my IQ is only 88. He said that I might be able to get into college because of my football, but that I'd be certain to flunk out—with an IQ like that!" I pointed out to Don that he had been doing well in my course. I found out that he had had a B+ average for the three semesters he had completed. I reminded him that the proof of a pudding lies in its eating—and that the proof of scholastic achievement lies in grades, not in a test designed to predict grades.

Last June, Don graduated with honors.

This little story, true in all essential details, illustrates many points; for example:

1. Was the test score correct? I suspect that an error was made in administering or scoring the test. Or, perhaps that score was a *percentile rank* instead of an *IQ*—which would make a lot of difference.

2. Regardless of the accuracy of the score, the teacher should not have told him the specific value of his IQ on the test.

3. The teacher went far beyond proper limits in telling Don that he would "... be certain to flunk out. ...." The teacher should have known that test scores are not perfect.

4. Furthermore, test scores do not determine future performance; demonstrated achievement is more conclusive evidence than is a score on a test intended to predict achievement. Both the teacher and Don should have known that!

If Don's case were unusual, I might have forgotten about it; however, mistakes in interpreting tests occur every day. Here are three other examples that come quickly to mind:

A college freshman, told that she had "average ability," withdrew from college. Her counselor had not added ". . . when compared with students in other topflight colleges." She reasoned that if she had only average ability compared with people in general, she must be very low when compared with college students; rather than face this, she dropped out of college. (There may have been other reasons, too, but this seemed to be the principal one.)

A high school student who had high measured clerical and literary *interests* was told that this proved that he should become either a clerk or a writer!

A personnel manager, learning that one of his best workers had scored very low on a test that eventually would be used in selecting future employees, nearly discharged the worker; ". . . the tests really opened our eyes about her. Why, she's worked here for several years, does good work, gets along well with the others. That test shows how she had us fooled!"

None of these illustrative cases is fictitious. All involve real people. And we will see a good many more examples of test interpretation throughout this book. Each one is based on a true situation, most of them drawn from my own experience in working with people who use tests.

No amount of anecdotal material, however, can show the thousands of instances every year in which the wrong persons are selected for jobs, admitted to schools and colleges, granted scholarships, and the like—merely because someone in authority is unable to interpret available test scores or, equally bad, places undue confidence in the results.

Nor will anecdotal material reveal the full scope of the misinformation being given to students and parents by teachers and others who are trying to help. Willingness to help is only the first step. There is also a lot to know about the meaning of test scores. Even the expert who works daily with tests has to keep his wits with him, for this is no game for dullards.

### Testing Today

What is testing like today?

The quality of tests has improved over the past forty years. Definite advances in testing have been noted even in the past decade: in novel approaches to achievement testing, in efforts at the measurement of creativity, in varied approaches to the measurement of interests, etc. Most test authors and test publishers are competent and service-motivated; they subscribe to ethical standards that are commendably high. Each year universities turn out greater numbers of well-trained measurements people. More and more teachers and personnel workers are being taught the fundamentals of testing. In spite of these and other positive influences, we still find a desperate need for wider understanding of what test scores mean.

Probably more than one million standardized tests per school day are being used in American schools alone! Add to this number the tests that are being given in industry, personnel offices, employment bureaus, hospitals, civil service agencies, etc.—add all of these in, and we can conclude that there is a great deal of testing being done.

Who will interpret the test scores? Often, nobody will. In literally millions of instances, the test scores never progress beyond the point of being recorded on a file card or folder; indeed, this seems to be the official policy of many personnel offices and school systems. In other instances, the scores are made available to supervisors or teachers; these people may, at their discretion, interpret the results.

Unfortunately, many people whose positions seem to give them legitimate access to test results have had little training in test interpretation. People who are going to have access to test scores have a strong moral obligation to learn what scores mean; however, many do not realize the extent of their ignorance. I should not have been surprised at the following incident:

> I was asking about some test scores made by Dickie Davis, a boy in whom I had a particular interest. As an eighth-grader in a large school system, he was being used in a research study and had taken an extensive test battery. The homeroom teacher, Betty Blenkove, must have been taught that tests should be kept secure; she extracted a key from her handbag, unlocked her desk, took out a ring of keys, selected one, and unlocked a storage closet; from the closet, she drew a folder out from underneath a stack of books. Miss Blenkove promptly read off a long list of scores made by young Dickie. "What tests are these?" I asked. She didn't know. "Do these scores compare Dickie with the national norms group, the local school norms group, or with just those in the research project?" She didn't know. Nor could she tell me anything about tests that Dickie had taken previously. She thought the counselor might have that information—or perhaps it was the principal's office—she wasn't sure.
>
> Now, I've known Miss Blenkove for years. I know that she is a good teacher, and I know that her students like her. But she was taught very little in college about the use of tests, and her work today keeps her busy. Consequently she finds it easy to pay no attention to the standardized tests taken by her students. She reasons that Hallie Halone, the counselor, knows more about tests and will take care of any test interpretation that needs to be done.
>
> Mrs. Halone is a certified school counselor and a good one. In tests and measurements, she has had only a little training because she had to take courses for a teaching certificate before she could start her counselor preparation. She wants to take more courses in measurement, but it is difficult now that she has family responsibilities. She tries to see her students as often as she can, but she has nearly 1,000 students to counsel.
>
> As you have suspected, many students are never given much information about their test results. Who has time?

This school system is a good one. Its policies are enlightened, and its personnel are interested in their students. Testing is not, after all, the school's most important activity. Good tests are selected, administered, scored, and recorded properly; and some teachers do a remarkable job of using the test results and in interpreting the results to their students.

The typical school system has few teachers who are well trained in testing, because most teachers have had little opportunity to take elective courses while in college. Only a very few states require even a single course in tests and measurements.

Even those teachers who have had a course have probably learned less about what test scores mean and how to interpret test results than they have about general principles of measurement and the construction of classroom tests.

Personnel workers in industry often have had no training in tests and measurements. Test interpretation in industry is even worse than in education —except for one thing: industry seldom gives tests for purposes of individual guidance. Rather, most tests are used as a basis for institutitonal decisions. (See the following section.)

Many people whose positions demand that they have access to test results have had no real training in what test scores mean. I hope that this book will help people with limited backgrounds in testing to attain a better understanding of test scores and test interpretation.

## INSTITUTIONAL AND INDIVIDUAL DECISIONS

Tests are often used as tools in reaching decisions. Some decisions are *institutional;* that is, the decisions are made in behalf of an institution (school, college, corporation, etc.) and such decisions are made frequently. Two examples of such institutional decisions are: which persons to select and which to reject, and where to place a particular examinee. Often tests can be extremely effective in such situations because they help the institution to reach a higher percentage of good decisions. And an occasional bad decision about an individual examinee is not likely to have any adverse effect on the institution. Tests can be used more effectively to predict the performance of a group than they can to predict the performance of an individual.

> Let us test a random sample of 1,000 fifth-grade pupils. Let me have the top fifty pupils, and you take the bottom fifty pupils. You may decide what these one hundred pupils are to be taught. You may have a team of experts to help you teach your pupils; I will teach mine myself. At the end of one semester, we will give both groups the same final examination. Regardless of the subject matter taught, I am sure that my group will be higher on the average. On the other hand, it is probable that some of your pupils will outscore some of mine—despite that tremendous original difference in ability. Which of your pupils will show this tremendous response to superior teaching? Which of my pupils will lag far behind the others? I doubt whether we can predict very accurately which ones these would be; however, we can have

considerable confidence in predicting that my group will have the higher average achievement.

A second general type of decision is the *individual* decision. Here, the individual must make a decision which will affect himself, or perhaps, a son or daughter. The individual has no backlog of similar decisions, and he may never have to reach a comparable decision again. The situation is unique insofar as the individual is concerned, and a wrong decision may have a lasting effect on him. Typical examples of individual decisions include: whether to accept a certain job offer, whether to go to college, which college to attend, which curriculum to study, which course to take, or which girl to marry. Tests sometimes help, but they are rarely so helpful as in institutional decisions; and they are always far less accurate in individual situations.

## TWO MEANINGS OF INTERPRETATION

These decision types, introduced by Cronbach and Gleser, suggest two distinct meanings for *test interpretation*. According to the first meaning, we need to understand test scores well enough to use them in making an institutional type of decision. The emphasis is on our personal understanding of the scores. Less skill is required for interpretation in this sense than when we must interpret the meaning of test scores to someone else. In this second meaning, test interpretation requires a thorough understanding of test scores plus an ability to communicate the results.

For the most part, I will make no effort to differentiate between these two meanings of interpretation; however, Chapter 9 is concerned almost entirely with the problem of telling other people what scores mean.

## A Pretest

As a pretest of your own ability to interpret test scores, try the following questions—typical of those asked by test-naïve teachers and personnel workers. If you answer the questions satisfactorily (answers at the end of this chapter), you will probably learn little from this book. If you cannot understand the questions, you certainly need this book! Let us see how you do.

1. **Why don't we use the raw score itself in test interpretation?**
2. **What is the difference between a percentile rank and a percentage-correct score?**
3. **Why are norms important?**
4. **How constant is the IQ?**
5. **What is the difference between reliability and validity?**
6. **Are tests fair to Blacks and to other minority groups?**

> 7. **What effect, if any, does the range of scores have on test reliability and validity?**
> 8. **Can tests measure native (i.e., inborn) intelligence?**
> 9. **How big must a difference in scores be in order to be called a "significant difference"?**
> 10. **How can test difficulty influence the apparent performance or improvement of a school class?**

Did you take the pretest? If not, go back and take it now—before reading the answers which follow.

## Answers to Pretest Questions

### 1. Why don't we use the raw score itself in test interpretation?

The raw score, based usually on the number of items answered correctly, depends so much on the number and difficulty of the test items that it is nearly valueless in test interpretation; however, because it provides the basis for all other types of scores, the raw score needs to be accurate. In other words, the raw score is basic—nothing can be more accurate than it is.

### 2. What is the difference between a percentile rank and a percentage-correct score?

A person's *percentile rank* describes his relative standing within a particular group: a percentile rank of 80 ($P_{80}$) means that a person's score is equal to or higher than the scores made by 80 percent of the people in some specified group. A *percentage-correct score*, on the other hand, tells us nothing about a person's relative performance. It tells us only the percentage of items answered correctly; for example, a percentage-correct score of 80 means that a person has answered 80 percent of the test items correctly. Confusion between these two basically different types of score sometimes results in considerable embarrassment.

### 3. Why are norms important?

Norms give meaning to our scores. They provide a basis for comparing one individual's score with the scores of others who have taken the test. Ideally the test publisher describes the norm group or groups as precisely as possible, so that the user may decide how appropriate they are for reporting the performance of individuals in whom he is interested. Local norms, developed by the user, may be more appropriate in some situations than any of the publisher's norms. Norms tables are used to translate raw scores into derived scores such as percentiles, standard scores, grade-equivalent scores, intelligence quotients, and the like.

### 4. How constant is the IQ?

Volumes could be written (and have been) on this topic. Even under ideal conditions (for example, a short time between testings on the same test for a highly motivated young adult), we would expect to find slight differences in IQ from testing to testing. In general, changes in IQ tend to be greatest: among young children; when a long time separates the first and subsequent testings; when different tests are used; and when there is a marked difference in motivational level of the examinee at the different test sessions. Changes of five IQ points are common even under good conditions.

On the other hand, most people change relatively little in IQ. Only rarely will individuals vary so much as to be classified as normal or average at one time and either mentally retarded or near-genius at some other time.

The IQ is only a type of test score. Any fluctuation or inaccuracy in test performance will be reflected in the scores and will help to cause differences in score.

**5. What is the difference between reliability and validity?**

*Reliability* refers to the consistency of measured performance. *Validity* refers to a test's ability to measure what we want it to. High reliability is necessary for reasonable validity, because a test that does not measure consistently cannot measure anything well; however, a test may be highly reliable without being able to do any specified task well.

**6. Are tests fair to Blacks and to other minority groups?**

It all depends, but—in general—no. All tests are certain to be culture-bound to some extent. Most intelligence tests tend to emphasize the sorts of material studied in school; school-related test items are more likely to be familiar to children from upper- and middle-class families. It is possible to construct a test that will result in higher scores for Blacks than for Whites, but such a test might not reflect the skills and knowledges that most people feel are included as part of intelligence. Any test that is worthwhile must *discriminate;* after all, this is just another way of saying that it will "reveal individual differences." But the intended discrimination should be on the basis of the characteristic being measured, not on the basis of race or ethnic background.

**7. What effect does the range of scores have on test reliability and validity?**

Variability has a great effect on both reliability and validity. Other things being equal, a greater range in scores makes for higher reliability and validity coefficients. The sophisticated test user bears this fact in mind when he reads reliability and validity coefficients in test manuals.

**8. Can tests measure native (i.e., inborn) intelligence?**

Only partly and indirectly. Any intelligence test (or aptitude or achievement test) does measure native ability—but only as it has been modified by the influence of the environment (including all training, experience, learning, etc.), and by the motivation of the examinee at the time he is tested. It is clearly a mistake to think of anyone's IQ as being purely inborn—or as being determined solely by his heredity.

**9. How big must a difference in scores be in order to be called a "significant difference"?**

This is a trick question. As we will see in subsequent chapters, there are statistics that give us some idea of how far apart a person's scores must be before we can be reasonably sure that they are truly different; however, no single statistic answers the question directly and satisfactorily.

**10. How can test difficulty influence the apparent performance or improvement of a school class?**

If a test is far too easy for a class, the pupils will obtain scores that are lower than they should be; we cannot tell how much better the pupils might have been able to do if there had been more items of suitable difficulty. If they are given a test of appropriate difficulty some time later, the pupils will appear to have made greater gains than we should expect; now they are not prohibited (by the very content of the test) from attempting items of reasonable difficulty, and there are fewer students with near-perfect scores.

There are many other facets to the problem of item difficulty. Some of these will be considered later in this book.

**How did you do?**

# THE LANGUAGE OF TESTING

*Chapter Two*

Can you be interested in something without being any good at it? Of course! And yet:

> A school counselor is reporting *interest* test results to a high school junior and his father: "John scored high on Computational and Mechanical. This means that he should go on to college and study mechanical engineering."

Maybe John will become a good mechanical engineer. Maybe not. No decision should be made solely on the basis of test scores—and most certainly not just on the results of some interest or preference inventory! What about his intelligence? His aptitudes? His grades in school? His motivation? His willingness to study hard and consistently? His ability to pay for college training? Many factors besides interest-test scores are involved in deciding whether anyone should go to college, or in the choosing of a vocational objective.

Interest and aptitude are not synonymous, but some test users do confuse them. And there are so many terms used in describing different kinds of tests that it is easy to become confused. In this chapter I will define and discuss a number of common testing terms.

## Maximum-Performance Versus Typical-Performance Tests

All tests may be classified as measuring either *maximum* or *typical performance*. Tests of maximum performance ask the examinee to do his best work; his ability, either attained or potential, is being tested. With tests of typical performance, we hope to obtain some ideas as to what the examinee is really like or what he actually does—rather than what he is capable of doing.

Included under maximum-performance tests are tests of intelligence, aptitude, and achievement. In all of these, we assume that the examinees are equally and highly motivated. To the extent that this assumption is not justified, we must discount the results. Since we rarely know how well persons were motivated while taking a test, we usually must accept the assumption or have the person retested.

> Private Peter Panner was in the army for several years before the start of World War II. During that time, he took so many tests (many of them experimental or research editions) that he paid little attention to them. Not infrequently he would loaf through a test, making no effort to obtain a good score. As World War II approached, he wanted to attend Officer Candidate School; he found that the army required a score of at least 110 on the *Army General Classification Test,* and that his score had been only 92. Peter was given permission to retake the test and scored well above the cutoff score of 110.

As noted in the previous chapter, at least three determinants are involved in every score on a test of maximum performance: innate ability, acquired ability, and motivation. There is no way to determine how much of a person's score is caused by any one of these three determinants—they are necessarily involved in every maximum-performance score; that is, a person's test score necessarily depends in part on his inborn potential as it has been modified by his life experiences (his education and training, his environment, etc.), and by his motivation at the time of testing.

*INTELLIGENCE TESTS*

Intelligence is an abstract concept. We all have ideas about its meaning, but there is little general agreement on its precise meaning. Just as you may have your own definition and I may have my own, so, too, does the author of each intelligence test have his own.

Intelligence tests reflect these differences in definition. Some include only verbal items; others contain much nonverbal material. Some stress problem-solving while others emphasize memory. Some intelligence tests result in a single total score (probably an IQ), whereas others yield several scores.

These varying emphases lead to diverse results. We should expect to find different IQ's when the same person is tested with different tests. We may be obtaining several measures of intelligence, but each time intelligence is being defined just a little differently. Under the circumstances, perhaps we should be surprised whenever different intelligence tests give us nearly the same results.

Intelligence goes under many names: mental maturity, general classification, scholastic aptitude, general ability, mental ability, college ability, primary mental abilities, etc. They all mean about the same as intelligence although they may differ somewhat in emphasis or application.

For most purposes, intelligence tests may be thought of as tests of general aptitude or scholastic aptitude. When so regarded, they are most typically used in predicting achievement in school, college, or training programs.

It should be obvious, too, that performance on intelligence tests is related to achievement. Even the ability to take an intelligence test depends on achievement (in reading, arithmetic, etc.) Because intelligence tests depend so much on what has already been learned, minority groups often score lower (on the average) than do upper- and middle-class American-born Whites.

Several ambitious federal programs are aimed at decreasing cultural differences in academic achievement: Project Head Start, Project Upward Bound, etc. At the present time, it is impossible to state definitively how successful these programs will be. (The reader may wish to see the differences of opinions along these lines in the 1969 volume of the *Harvard Educational Review*.)

### APTITUDE TESTS

All aptitude tests imply prediction. They give us a basis for predicting future level of performance. Aptitude tests often are used in selecting individuals for jobs, for admission to training programs, for scholarships, etc. Sometimes aptitude tests are used for classifying individuals—as when college students are assigned to different ability-grouped sections of the same course.

### ACHIEVEMENT TESTS

Achievement tests are used in measuring present level of knowledge, skills, competence, etc. Unlike other types of test, many achievement tests are produced locally. A teacher's classroom test is a good example. There are also many commercially developed achievement tests.

## Differentiating Types of Maximum-Performance Tests

The principal basis for differentiating between aptitude and achievement tests lies in their use. The same test may be used, in different situations, to measure aptitude and achievement. The purpose of the testing, whether for assessing present attainment or for predicting future level of performance, is the best basis for distinction.

As noted above, intelligence tests are often regarded as aptitude tests. Some intelligence tests could give us a fair indication of academic achievement—though they are rarely (if ever) used in this manner. And achievement tests obviously measure intelligence to some extent. In fact, when one city's school board briefly outlawed the use of intelligence tests in its system, teachers soon found a fair substitute: a reading achievement test.

With tests of maximum performance, we seldom have difficulty in understanding what we are measuring for. With aptitude tests, we are trying to predict how well people will do. With achievement tests, we are trying to measure their present attainment. With intelligence tests, although we may disagree on specific definitions, we are trying to measure level of intellectual capacity or functioning.

## Typical-Performance Tests

The situation is far less clear with tests of typical performance. There is less agreement about what is being measured or what should be measured. To start with, there is a tremendous proliferation of terms: adjustment, personality, temperament, interests, preferences, values, etc. There are tests, scales, blanks, inventories, indexes, etc. And there are Q-sorts, forced-choice methods, etc.—to say nothing about projective techniques, situational tests, and the like.

What does a score mean? It is very hard to say—even after having given the matter careful thought. In the first place, the scales of a typical-performance test are likely to be vaguely defined: what is *sociable* to one author may not be to the next. Then, too, the philosophy or rationale underlying typical-performance tests must necessarily be more involved and less obvious than the rationale for most aptitude and achievement tests.

Whereas a person's ability is more or less stable, his affective nature may change over a short period of time. And it is this aspect of the individual that we try to get at through tests of typical performance. We are trying to find out what a person is really like, how he typically reacts or feels.

With maximum-performance tests, we are certain at least that a person did not obtain a higher score than he is capable of; after all, one can't fake knowing more algebra or fake being more intelligent. The examinee can, of course, perform far beneath his capabilities—by simply not trying, by paying little attention, or by any of many other means. With typical-performance tests, though, a person usually can fake in either direction (higher or lower, better adjustment or poorer adjustment, etc.). With these tests, we do not want the examinee to do the best he can; instead, we want him to answer as honestly as he can. That is why the purpose of these tests often is disguised.

There would seem to be an assumption that an examinee was trying to answer honestly. Yet on some personality tests the authors have been concerned only with the response made, rather than with the examinee's reasons for having made it. Thus, the person who responds *Yes* to an item may do so honestly, or he may be trying to look better or to look worse than he really is; it makes no difference, for he resembles specified other people at least to the extent that he, too, made the same response.

## CRITERION-KEYING

Some typical-performance tests are said to be *criterion-keyed*, because their scoring keys have been developed through the performance of two contrasting groups, as:

> We decide to construct a *Progressivism and Liberalism Index* (*PALI*). After defining what we mean by progressivism and liberalism, we decide that an ultraconservative group—say, the James Burke Society (JBS)—should obtain very low scores if our test is valid; we decide, too, that members of the American Association for Civil Liberties (AACL) should obtain high scores. We write a large number of items that seem relevant and administer them to members of both groups. With the aid of statistics, we retain for our *PALI* those items that discriminate best between the JBS and the AACL, regardless of whether the result seems logical. We might, for example find more members of JBS than members of AACL answering *Yes* to: *Do you consider yourself a liberal individual?* Regardless of the real-life accuracy or inaccuracy of the responses, we still might retain this item—counting a response of *No* as one score point in the liberal direction.

Typical-performance tests which are criterion-keyed often seem superior to tests for which the scoring keys have been developed in other ways. Criterion-keyed tests sometimes are criticized because occasional items are scored in a way that seems to make little sense; the answer to this criticism is, of course, that the scoring system "works."

## FORCED-CHOICE ITEMS

Forced-choice is a term being heard with increasing frequency. An item is *forced-choice* if the alternatives have been matched for social acceptability, even though only one alternative relates to a particular criterion. The simplest form of forced-choice item has two alternatives, each seeming to be equally desirable:

> *Would you rather be:* (a) *honest;* (b) *loyal?*
> I would like to be both—and you would, too. Perhaps, though, some group (say, good bookkeepers) could be found statistically to answer (a) more often than less good bookkeepers.

Other forced-choice items may involve three or four alternatives, rather than only two. Forced-choice items have the advantage of being somewhat disguised as to intent, but they are not unanimously favored. They may be resented by examinees because of the fine discriminations demanded. When used in such a way that the items are scored for more than one variable, they result in an *ipsative* sort of score; i.e., the strength of each variable depends not solely on that variable but on its strength relative to the strength of others. In other words, if one variable goes up, another must go down.

With nearly all typical-performance test items, there is likely to be some ambiguity. Let us take the item:

> *I am a liberal.*
> *Strongly Agree   Agree   Don't Know   Disagree   Strongly Disagree*

If I had to answer this item, my reasoning might go something like this:

> What do they mean by *liberal?* I could say *Strongly Agree*, for I am strongly opposed to censorship. My political views are largely conservative, so I could answer *Disagree;* in fact, I am sure that some of my colleagues think that I ought to answer *Strongly Disagree*—considering my views on the _____ Bill. In honesty, I should not say that I *Don't Know*. But the truth is that I am sometimes liberal and sometimes not!

The indecisiveness of an examinee may be caused by the ambiguity of a term, or it may be a reflection of the individual's personality. In either case, the examinee may answer an item sometimes one way and sometimes another, and be perfectly sincere each time. (As we shall see in Chapter Three, such factors as these lower test reliability.)

*Use Caution!* There are other reasons, too, for viewing typical-performance tests with caution. The very nature of these tests is such that individualized meanings of the items become important. Let us take the item:

> *I am a liberal.   True   False*

This may be answered *True* by many conservatives who believe that they are more liberal than their friends; and some liberals, feeling that they are less liberal in their views than they would like to be, may answer the item *False*. (Note, however, that this would make no difference if the test were criterion-keyed.)

Furthermore, the motivational pattern of each examinee becomes of great importance. With maximum-performance tests, we want each examinee to do his best. The case is not so simple, though, with typical-performance tests. If the examinee has much to gain by showing up well, he may try to answer the items so that he will appear to be better than he really is. Similarly, he may try to appear more disturbed than he really is if that would be to his advantage. And he may do so either deliberately or subconsciously.

Still further, most typical-performance tests try to measure several different characteristics of the individual. A person who fakes, deliberately or not, along one scale of the test may inadvertently change his scores on other measured characteristics as well. For example, the person who tries to appear more *sociable* may inadvertently score higher on the *aggressive* scale, too.

Often test norms are based on the performances of groups of people (perhaps students) in nonthreatening situations. To compare the performance of a person under stress (of being selected for a job, of severe personal problems, or whatever) with the performance of such groups is rather unrealistic.

Typical-performance tests, of course, can be useful to skilled counselors; however, they rarely should be interpreted by people who have only limited backgrounds in testing and psychology. There are so many pitfalls to be aware of. The tests do have their place—but that place is not in the hands of the amateur.

For all of these reasons—and more—most psychologists feel that we can place much less confidence in typical-performance tests than in the maximum-performance tests with which we shall be principally concerned.

## OBJECTIVE—SUBJECTIVE—PROJECTIVE

Another way of looking at tests gives us a classification according to the form of response called for. One familiar classification is *objective* vs. *essay*. This classification is probably better stated as *objective* vs. *subjective*, and I would add *projective*. A little later I will mention a similar classification, one that I prefer even though it is less common.

An item is objective if the complete scoring procedure is prescribed in advance of the scoring. Thus multiple-choice and true-false tests are usually objective, for the test-writer can draw up a scoring key that contains the right (or best) answer for each item on the test. Except for mistakes or for difficulties in reading responses, we can be completely objective. When answered on special answer sheets, such items can even be scored by machine.

I dislike using *essay* as opposed to *objective*. An essay item is a specific type of item in which the examinee is asked to write an essay of greater or lesser length on an assigned topic; it is not broad enough to be considered a general type. *Subjective* is better, for it is more inclusive and indicates that some element of personal judgment will be involved in the scoring. Completion items are another example of subjective items, for the tester usually cannot anticipate every possible answer that may be scored as correct; however, completion items can be written so that there is very little subjectivity left to the scoring.

I have tried to stress objectivity of scoring. Any time we prepare a test, whether for classroom use or for national distribution, we must decide what items to write, what elements of information to include, what wording to use, etc. Inevitably there is some degree of subjectivity in test-making.

*Projective* items are, in a sense, subjective items—but they are something more. They are items which are deliberately made ambiguous to permit individualistic responses. The Rorschach inkblots, Allen's *Three-Dimensional*

*Personality Test*, Murray's *Thematic Apperception Test* are examples. Verbal material may be used projectively, too; Rotter, for example, presents the examinee with stems of sentences to be completed, thereby making him *project* his personality into the response. Typical of Rotter's items are:

> *I like to . . .*
> *One thing I dread is . . .*
> *My mother . . .*

### SELECT-RESPONSE—SUPPLY-RESPONSE

A similar classification, one which I prefer, is *select-response* vs. *supply-response*. This classification, it seems to me, is self-defining: if the examinee may select from among the alternatives given to him, the item is select-response; otherwise, it is a supply-response item.

### WRITTEN—ORAL

Another basis for test classification is found in the medium used for presenting the directions and the item material. Most typically, test items are printed or written and the examinee responds by writing his answers or by making marks that correspond to chosen answers. Directions sometimes are given orally, but most frequently are given both orally and in writing.

Rather few tests are oral; teacher-prepared spelling tests are the most common example. A few tests are available on sound recordings. There are tests for blind people, some of which were especially developed for them and others that are simply adaptations of tests for the sighted. There are trade tests; prepared for oral presentation and oral response, used almost exclusively in employment offices. And non-standardized oral exams are given in graduate school and other settings.

### STANDARDIZED—INFORMAL

*Standardized tests* are tests that have been developed, usually by specialists, for more extensive use than by the test-writer himself. The test content is set, the directions prescribed, the scoring procedure more or less completely specified. In addition, there are almost always norms against which we may compare the scores of our examinees.

*Informal tests*, on the other hand, refer primarily to tests written by the examiner for his own use. We are not concerned with such tests in this book; however, much that is said about standardized tests may have some application to informal tests, too.

### SPEED—POWER

*Speeded tests* are maximum-performance tests in which speed plays an important part in determining a person's score; however, a test may have a time limit and still not be speeded. If there is no time limit or if the time limit is so generous that most examinees are able to finish, the test is said to be a *power test.*

Most achievement tests should be power tests, for we are likely to be more concerned with assessing our examinees' levels of attainment than we are in finding out how rapidly they respond. Even here, though, there are exceptions: for example, an achievement test in shorthand or typing. We cannot say categorically whether speed or power is more important in aptitude and intelligence tests, for each has its place.

We have used power and speed as if they were separate categories. It would be more accurate to think of them as opposite ends of a continuum. Some tests are almost purely power (having no time limit), and other tests are almost purely speed (having items of such little difficulty that everyone could answer them perfectly if given enough time); but in between these extremes are many tests with time limits, some generous and some limited. Such in-between tests have some characteristics of both speed and power tests and are best classified as being one or the other, depending upon whether the time limit makes speed an important determinant of score.

### GROUP—INDIVIDUAL

This classification is perhaps most obvious of all. An *individual* test is one which can be administered to only one individual at a time. Common examples are individual tests of intelligence, such as the *Stanford–Binet* and the *Wechsler* tests. Some tests that involve special apparatus, such as manual dexterity tests, usually are administered individually; however, such tests can be administered simultaneously to small groups if proper conditions exist and if the examiner has multiple copies available.

*Group tests* can be administered to more than one individual at a time and usually can be administered simultaneously to a group of any size. Group tests are usually *paper-and-pencil* (the only materials involved), but not necessarily so. Individual tests frequently, but not always, involve materials other than paper and pencil.

### PAPER-AND-PENCIL—APPARATUS (PERFORMANCE)

When special equipment is needed, the test may be called an *apparatus* test or, sometimes, a *performance* test. I don't like this use of *performance*, for the term is already overworked—being a generic term for tested behavior (as . . . his *performance* on the test . . . ), as well as a term that is sometimes used in opposition to verbal (as on the *Wechsler* tests, which yield Verbal and Performance IQs).

### VERBAL-NONVERBAL

A *verbal test* has verbal items; that is, the items involve words (either oral or written). So-called *nonverbal* tests contain no verbal items; however, words almost always are used in the directions. Some writers prefer to use *nonlanguage* to describe tests that have no verbal items but for which the directions are given either orally or in writing; these writers would use nonverbal only for tests where no words are used, even in the directions.

### MACHINE-SCORED—HAND-SCORED

Until recently, *machine-scored* tests meant tests taken on special IBM answer sheets and scored on an IBM 805 Test Scoring Machine. Now, however, there are several types of scoring machines. The most common operate on one or more of three principles: (1) mark-sensing; (2) punched-hole; or (3) visual-scanning.

In mark-sensing, the scoring machine makes an electrical contact with a mark made with an exceptionally soft lead pencil. This is the basis for the IBM 805 Test Scoring Machine. It is also the basis for another IBM scoring system where special pencil marks are made on IBM cards. A special machine reads these marks and punches holes corresponding to them; these cards can then be scored either with special equipment or with standard IBM accounting or statistical machines.

In punched-hole scoring, the responses may have been made either with mark-sensing pencils, or with special individual card punchers. The test cards are then scored either with special equipment or with standard IBM machines.

Electronic scoring is the latest development; here the process involves visual-scanning with an electric eye. Regular No.2 pencils are used. Depending upon its complexity, the machine may be capable of scoring several different test parts simultaneously, of printing the scores on the answer sheets, of reading examinees' names from the answer sheets and preparing a roster, etc. The IBM 1230 and Digitek scoring machines operate electronically, as do special machines at several large scoring services.

These are the principal types of scoring, but not the only ones. There are many other scoring machines; for example, one which literally weighs the number of correct responses with tiny weights on the pan of a scale, another that records correct responses whenever a puff of air is allowed to penetrate a special roll of paper through a player-piano-like hole, etc. Neither of these is in common use. Many teaching machines use programs which are only progressively difficult test items.

With few exceptions, machine-scored tests could be *hand-scored*. Hand-scoring, although slower and more old fashioned, has some advantages—especially when nonstandardized tests are involved.

We need to use care in scoring tests, regardless of the method of scoring involved. Mistakes can be made under any system, and we cannot permit ourselves to be careless.

I once contracted with a professional scoring service to machine score several hundred interest tests. I noted that the service provided no check or verification of its results, so I hand-scored a small sample of the tests. Every one of these hand-scored answer sheets revealed scoring errors on three different interest areas. After correspondence with the director of the scoring service, I learned that his service had been using faulty scoring keys on this test for several years.

### CULTURE-FAIR

Some tests are said to be *culture-fair* or *culture-free*. The latter term should be avoided, for no test can be developed completely free from cultural influences. Some tests, though, are relatively independent of cultural or environmental influences and may be thought of as being fair to people of most cultures; however, these tests may do less well than others in measuring individuals within our own culture. By using items that are relatively culture-free, such tests may not measure anything very effectively within any given culture.

### HOW TO TELL

How can we tell what a test is like? We can learn something about available tests by reading the catalogs of the various test publishers. This is not necessarily safe, though, for:

A few years ago one small (and minor) test publisher listed an interest test under Aptitude in his catalog, "because," he told me privately, "it's the only interest test I have, and I didn't want to create a separate section for just one test."

This is admittedly an extreme example; however, test catalogs are created for the purpose of selling tests and are not the most objective source of information.

Nor are test titles the best means for telling what a test is. In the past, there have been many examples of tests with misleading titles; however, test publishers today are beginning to do a much better job of giving descriptive titles to their tests.

Test manuals are usually the best guides to test content, especially since the publication in 1954 of the American Psychological Association's *Technical Recommendations for Psychological Tests and Diagnostic Techniques*, revised in 1966 under the title of *Standards for Educational and Psychological Tests and Manuals*. A good manual describes the test and its development, gives norms for the test, and presents evidence of its validity and reliability. Of course, not even test manuals are objective enough to permit the test user to become careless (*see* Chapter Five).

The major reference for critical and objective reviews of most psychological tests is provided by the *Mental Measurements Yearbooks*, edited by Oscar K. Buros. At this writing, there are six bound volumes in the series: the *1938*,

*1940, Third, Fourth, Fifth,* and *Sixth;* all are needed, for they are essentially nonduplicative. Tests ordinarily are reviewed in a subsequent edition only when there is additional evidence to consider. Buros' *MMY*s are also an excellent source for references to articles about specific tests.

## This Book

Our book is concerned mainly with maximum-performance, objective, select-response, written, standardized group tests which may be power or speeded and hand- or machine-scored.

# BASIC ATTRIBUTES
# OF THE TEST

*Chapter Three*

What test should we use? Is Test B better than Test A? Questions like these are really outside the scope of this book. Even so, we should know a little about the characteristics of a good test. We at least should know what to look for when evaluating a test. (*See also* Chapter Five, "The Test Manual.")

Three main attributes will be considered here: *validity, reliability,* and *usability.* Validity refers to the ability of the test to do the job we want it to. Reliability means that a test gives dependable or consistent scores. Usability includes all such practical factors as cost, ease of scoring, time required, and the like. These attributes should never be considered as absolute, for they are relative to specific situations, uses, groups, etc.

## Validity

Validity is the most important single attribute. Nothing will be gained by testing unless the test has some validity for the use we wish to make of it. A test that has high validity for one purpose may have moderate validity for another, and negligible validity for a third.

> The hypothetical *Mechanical Applications and Practices Test (MAP)* has been found highly valid for predicting grades at the Manual Arts High School and for selection of machinists' apprentices. It has reasonable, but low, validity for predicting performance in a manual training course and for the selection of women for simple industrial assembly jobs. The *MAP* is of no value, though, in predicting academic grade-point averages, in selecting industrial sales representatives, or in selecting students to enter engineering colleges. The *MAP*, for some reason that is not immediately apparent, even relates negatively to success in real estate selling; the better salesmen tend to score lower on the test.

There are no fixed rules for deciding what is meant by high validity, moderate validity, etc. Skill in making such decisions comes through training and experience in dealing with tests, and we cannot go into much detail here. It will be seen that the study of a test's validity may be either primarily logical (face or content) or primarily empirical-statistical (criterion-related or construct).

### FACE VALIDITY

The term *face validity* means simply that the test looks as if it should be valid. Good face validity helps to keep motivation high, for people are likely to try harder when the test seems reasonable. In some situations, too, good face validity is important to public relations.

> According to a recent news item, one state senator has criticized his state's civil service examiners for using this (paraphrased) item in a test for hospital orderlies:
>
> *In what way are a moth and a plant alike?*
>
> The original item comes from an excellent and widely accepted standardized adult intelligence test and is one of a series of items calling for the examinee to detect the essential similarity between two seemingly dissimilar things. Taken by itself, the item has very poor face validity; after all, why should a hospital orderly have to know such a trivial fact as this?

Face validity is not nearly so important as other indications of validity.

### CONTENT VALIDITY

Somewhat similar, but more systematic and more sophisticated, is *content validity* (otherwise known as: logical validity, course validity, curricular validity, or textbook validity). Like face validity, content validity is nonstatistical; here, however, the test content is examined in detail.

> We may check an achievement test to see whether each item covers an important bit of knowledge or involves an important skill related to a particular training program. Or we may start off with a detailed outline of our training program and see how thoroughly the test covers its important points.

Content validity is most obviously important in achievement tests, but it can be important with other types, too (*see* Chapter Five).

### CONSTRUCT VALIDITY

*Construct validity* is probably the most important type in psychological theory. In general, construct validity is concerned with the psychological meaningfulness of the test.

Suppose that we decide to develop a *Social Extraversion Test* (*SET*) for high school students. We decide that one evidence of extraversion is to be found in participation in school activities. We give the *SET* to all of the students in our school and check the number of hours per week each student spends on school activities. The correlation coefficient between these two variables will be evidence of construct validity. [Correlation is explained in greater detail in Chapter Four.]

With construct validity, we predict the results which logically should be obtained if the test is valid. The prediction is stated concretely enough and precisely enough so that it can be tested statistically. In this way, we actually are checking the validity of both the test and its underlying theory.

The term *factorial validity* is sometimes used to indicate that a test is a relatively pure measure of some particular characteristic. Factorial indicates that the evidence for its purity comes from factor analysis, a mathematical technique for identifying the basic dimensions causing the interrelations found among sets of test scores.

A test is said to have high factorial validity if it seems to be a good measure of some dimension that has been isolated or identified through a factor analysis. The naming of the factor, of course, is not determined mathematically; rather, it depends on the subjective judgment of the researcher. If factorial validity is really validity at all, it presumably is a sort of construct validity.

Additional sophistication is needed for evaluating construct validities. The concept is mentioned here only for general information. The casual test user will want to study the concept further before attempting to evaluate tests where construct validation is involved.

## Criterion-Related Validity (Empirical Validity)

*Criterion-related validity* is implied whenever no adjective is used to modify *validity*. This sort of validity is most important in practical situations. How well does the test measure what we want it to? Empirical validity gives us the answer by indicating how closely the test relates to some criterion (i.e., to some standard of performance). When empirical validity is high, we can use the test for predicting performance on the criterion variable. Almost anything else can be forgiven if the test has very high validity.

Evidence for this type of validity is gained through a validity coefficient, a coefficient of correlation between the test and a criterion.

A correlation coefficient is a statistic which expresses the tendency for values of two variables to change together systematically. It may take any value between 0.00 (no relationship) and $+ 1.00$ or $- 1.00$ (each indicating a perfect relationship). Further information on this statistic will be found in Chapter Four.

## FACTORS INFLUENCING CRITERION-RELATED VALIDITY

Skill is required to interpret validity coefficients. In general, the higher the correlation between the test and the criterion, the better; however, many other factors have to be considered:

### 1. Test Variables Differ

Some tests lend themselves more naturally to validation studies than do others. For example, school grades are a natural criterion to use in validating a scholastic aptitude test. On the other hand, what would we use as a good criterion for an anxiety scale? Where good criteria are hard to find, we usually cannot expect high validity coefficients; sometimes in fact the test may be a better measure of the characteristic than the criterion is.

### 2. Criteria Differ

The criterion used in one validation study may be more important or more relevant to our purposes than the criterion used in another validation study.

> We want a test to help us in the selection of bookbinders. The *Health Analysis Form* correlates 0.65 with record of attendance; the Hand Dexterity Test correlates 0.30 with number of books bound during an observation period. Which test should we use? Should we use both? We would need more information, of course, but we would certainly want to consider which criterion (attendance record or production record) is more pertinent.

### 3. Groups Differ

For any number of reasons, the test which works well with one group may not do so with another group. The test which discriminates between bright and dull primary school pupils may be worthless when used with high school students because all high school students get near-perfect scores. Consider also:

> The *Aytown Advertiser* finds that the *Typographers Own Performance Scale* (*TOPS*) is very helpful in selecting good printers and in reducing turnover among printers, but that it is no good in selecting reporters and office workers. The *Beetown Bugle* finds that the *TOPS* is of little value in selecting its printers. (This is entirely possible, for the two newspapers may have different standards of quality, the labor markets may differ in the two cities, etc.)

### 4. Variability Differs

Validity coefficients are likely to be higher when the group of examinees shows a wide range of scores. A casual glance may tell us that John (a basketball center) is taller than Bill (who is of average height), but it may take a close look to tell whether Bill is taller than Tom (who is also of average height). In much the same way, a crude test can discriminate well if there are gross differences among those tested, but a much better test may not discriminate adequately if the group is highly homogeneous.

### 5. Additional Information

A validity coefficient must also be evaluated in terms of how much additional information it will give us. One test may correlate very high with a criterion variable, but still not help us much. This situation is likely to occur whenever the test also correlates very high with information we already have (e.g., scores from another test or previous school grades). In other words, the test will not be helpful unless it contributes something new to our understanding of the examinees. (Note: If this were not so, we could give several different forms of a valid test to each examinee and, eventually, get perfect validity; unfortunately, we would be getting only a very slight increase in validity in this manner by getting successive measures of the same characteristic.)

These five considerations are only illustrative of why we cannot assert flatly, "the higher the validity coefficient, the better." Other things being equal, the statement will be true; however, we must be sure that other things are equal.

Criterion-related validity may be either concurrent or predictive. Some writers have treated these as separate types of validity, but I believe that they are better described as being instances of empirical validity, for they differ only in time sequence. In concurrent validity, both test scores and criterion values are obtained at about the same time. In predictive validity, there is some lapse in time between testing and obtaining the criterion values.

### Reliability

Test reliability is very important to the test user, for it is necessary (but *not* sufficient) for good validity. In other words, a test can be highly reliable without necessarily being valid for any purpose of interest to us.

> A classroom teacher would have little confidence in the standardized achievement test in mathematics that placed Robbie in the top 10 percent of his class last month but places him at about the median today. The industrial personnel man would care little for the selection test which ranked Tavis Taylor in the bottom fourth of the applicants norms group a few weeks ago but ranks him in the top quarter of the same group today.

The teacher and the personnel man share the same concern: the doubtful reliability of their respective tests. And the validity of any test is limited mathematically by the test's reliability.

By test reliability, we refer to the *reproduce-ability* of a set of test results. In other words, a test with high reliability is one that will yield very much the same relative magnitude of test scores for a group of people under differing conditions or situations.

> Note that it is the *relative size* of score—not the exact same scores. If everyone's scores were to change by the same (or proportional) amount under the two conditions, the reliability would still be perfect.

Any factor that tends to exert a varying or changeable influence on a set of test scores has an adverse effect on the reliability of the test. We say that such factors contribute to the *error variance* of the test.

Test scores, of course, can never be perfectly reliable. One's *obtained score* (i.e., the score he receives on the test) is made up of two elements: *true score* + *error score*. Neither the true score nor the error score is measurable for any individual. However, we know that the error score is variable (by definition) and that it may be either positive or negative. According to measurement theory, this error component tends to average out over a large number of people; and thus the mean error score equals zero, and the mean true score equals the mean of obtained scores.

Even though the mean error score is thought to average out to zero over a large number of cases, the error component of individual scores may be large or small, and plus or minus. It is the error variance that keeps a test from being perfectly reliable. If the error component of each person's score were zero, error variance would equal zero—and, of course, each obtained score would equal the corresponding true score.

If we were able to know the exact value of the error variance in a distribution of scores (even if we could not tell the amount of the error component in each person's score), we would still be able to tell just how much confidence we could place in each person's obtained score.

Unfortunately, we can never tell just how much error variance is present in a set of test scores. We can, however, estimate how much error variance there is. And that is essentially what we are doing when we compute reliability coefficients (i.e., correlation coefficients between two versions of the test scores of the same group of individuals). There are different types of reliability coefficients, each of them telling us something—but not everything —about the reliability of the test scores.

When we read test manuals, we need to look carefully at the reliability coefficients reported. We can sometimes get a good estimate of how stable and consistent we may expect results from a test to be. There are some sources of error variance, however, which are not included in any estimates of reliability. Thus, any reliability coefficient is likely to be higher than it should be, for it is accounting for only some of the sources of error. On the other hand, it should be noted that all sources of error are operating to keep any validity coefficient from being unrealistically high.

What are some of the sources of error variance? It seems to me that we can consider them reasonably well using a five-dimensional model; i.e., by considering five different categories. But remember that *anything* which affects scores differentially increases the amount of error variance and lowers the reliability.

> My apologies in advance: this outline is not so precise as I should like. Unfortunately, neither is the domain of test reliability! A good classification scheme is one that offers non-overlapping categories which collectively provide a place for every single item. This scheme falls far short of the ideal, but I believe that it may be helpful to the person new at testing who wishes to understand reliability a bit better. If nothing else, it may help one to realize why the concept of reliability is one which intrigues (and perplexes) the experts.

### Examinee-Incurred

Some error variance is contributed more by the examinee himself than by anything else. For example: the motivation of the examinee at the times he is tested—to the extent that motivation varies—the resulting test scores will be unreliable. But the individuals may also vary in other significant ways: in physical health, mental alertness, stamina, competitive spirit, willingness to ask questions when directions are incompletely understood, ability to follow directions, efficiency of work habits, etc. These are just suggestive of the near-infinite ways in which the examinee himself may introduce variable influences that will tend to lower test reliability.

None of the common methods of estimating test reliability gets at any of these examinee-incurred influences; however, we try to minimize these influences whenever we have charge of a testing session—by trying to insure that all individuals are ready, willing, and desirous of doing their best on the test. We cannot, of course, completely eliminate this type of error variance. All we can do is to try to keep it minimal.

### Examiner-Scorer Influence

This source of error variance can be, and often is, negligible. Variable errors attributable to the examiner and scorer of most standardized paper-and-pencil tests are seldom of great magnitude; however, they can be. Variable error is introduced, for example, if the examiner does not follow the standard test directions: perhaps by giving too much or too little time, or perhaps by giving more help than is permitted in the directions. In their efforts to have their students do as well as they can on a standardized achievement test or an intelligence test, teachers sometimes invalidate the test by giving extra help, pointing out errors, allowing more time, etc. An overly strict or rigid or angry examiner may reduce the test's reliability, for this non-standard behavior will be reacted to differentially by the various examinees. Examiner influences almost certainly have the most adverse effects on the scores of young and inexperienced examinees. It seems likely that relatively mature, test-wise examinees who are well-motivated can withstand a great deal without being too badly affected. Typically, the person who administers a standardized paper-and-pencil test contributes little to error variance if he follows the directions for giving the test.

The examiner is likely to be a major contributor to error variance when the test is administered individually. The literature is full of research showing that there are large differences in the test results obtained by different examiners; and this, of course, is just another way of saying that error variance may be relatively great in a set of results from such tests unless the tests are given by skilled examiners.

But notice that we have included the *scorer* element as part of this source of variable error. If the test is capable of objective scoring, there can be perfect scorer reliability. Only when there is an element of subjectivity in the grading of tests does scorer reliability become a factor—as, for example, in the scoring of individual tests of intelligence and of personality. Where there is subjectivity of scoring, the test manual should give consideration to scorer reliability.

### Test Content

Some of the most common reliability coefficients are those relating to test content. A test, being a sample of the items that might have been written from the same universe of content, offers a major source of error variance. In other words, the scores obtained by a group of examinees might have been markedly different if a different set of questions had been asked. When there are alternate forms of a test, we may obtain an estimate of content reliability by administering both forms to the same group of people and determining the correlation between the two sets of scores.

Provided the test is not highly speeded, evidence of content reliability may be obtained from one administration of a single form of a test. One common way of doing this is through the use of an internal-consistency measure such as one of the Kuder–Richardson formulas; these formulas involve detailed assumptions about the test items and total score, but the assumptions are reasonable to make about many tests. The use of an appropriate formula gives a good estimate of the test's content reliability.

Also common is the use of a split-half (sometimes called odd-even) reliability coefficient.

> We score each person's paper twice: once for the odd-numbered items only and once for the even-numbered items only. We find the correlation between the odd-item and even-item scores; however, this correlation coefficient is an underestimate of the test's reliability, for longer tests tend to be more reliable than shorter ones—and we have correlated two half-length tests. Fortunately

we can estimate the full-length test's reliability from a formula (the Spearman–Brown prophecy formula).

Both the internal-consistency and the split-half approaches make many assumptions that we will not go into here. However, one precaution does seem in order: neither approach may be used when speed is an important factor in determining a person's test score.

A clerical test consists of pairs of numbers which the examinee must mark as being $S$ (exactly the same) or $D$ (different in some way). The score is the number of items correctly marked in five minutes. The items have almost no difficulty; without a time limit, anyone could obtain a perfect score. Few examinees make any errors. If we split this test into odd and even halves, we will usually have exactly equal scores. Computing a split-half or internal-consistency reliability coefficient for this test would be ridiculous, for the coefficient would be spuriously high. On tests such as this, examinees differ in the speed with which they can do the tasks, not in their ability to do the work that is called for.

If other things are equal, longer tests are more reliable than short ones. We should expect this to be true, for the test's content is a more adequate sample of the universe of possible content.

Consider a major national golf tournament, one which lasts several days. A relatively unknown golfer often leads at the end of the first day, but the eventual winner is usually a well-known personality. Although any golfer in the tournament may have a single "hot" round, it is the expert who can be depended upon in the long run. In the same way, chance plays a relatively greater role in influencing test scores on short tests than on longer ones.

**Situation-Induced**

By the test situation, I am referring to those aspects of the total testing picture that are not clearly attributable elsewhere.

At a testing conference a few years ago, one participant inquired: "What is the effect on test reliability of a sudden, pre-season unexpected blizzard?" Would there be any effect on the test scores of a class of children being tested under such a condition? Certainly there would be, but it would be impossible to estimate just how much. Little redheaded Susie Sierra may be worried that her mother won't be able to get to the school to pick her up. Freckle-faced Timmy Tolpin may be stimulated to do his very best work as he looks forward to some after-school sledding. But Timmy's steady-minded sister, Rosie, probably would do just about the same as she would have done under normal weather conditions.

We don't mention it so often as we should, probably, but testing conditions can make a great deal of difference in test results. Such conditions as: ventilation, noise level, sound distractions, lighting, overcrowding, writing surface, etc.—all *can* (but usually don't) have a major adverse effect on reliability.

> Take "writing surface" for example. Suppose a highly speeded test is being taken by a group of high school students or by a group of job applicants. Suppose further that some examinees have those pencil-rutted, hand-carved desktops; some have to take the test while balancing lapboards; and some have good, roomy, smooth desks on which to take their tests. Is there any question as to whether some of the examinees will be unable to do their best work? Obviously, then, the writing surface will contribute considerable error variance in this situation.

Cheating is another variable error. The examinee is helped by an indeterminate amount (perhaps even by a negative amount) by his cheating.

These influences, although potentially important, are hard to estimate—and do not enter into any of the common reliability coefficients. Most of these testing-condition influences are subject to control by the examiner if he plans carefully in advance of the testing session. (Although the examiner certainly can't control the weather!)

In all fairness, too, it should be remembered that most of these situational influences can be overcome by reasonably experienced and highly motivated examinees. Conversely, of course, they produce more unreliability with younger, less experienced, and less confident examinees.

### Time Influences

The fifth type of contribution to error variance is probably the best known of all: time influences. *Temporal reliability* is estimated by giving the same test to the same group at two different times, and by correlating scores made on the first and second administrations of the test. A reliability coefficient obtained in this fashion estimates the contribution to error variance of the passage of time. Coefficients of stability are almost always reported in test manuals, and are reasonably well understood by most test users. Still, there are some points which do need to be taken into consideration.

If the second administration is given very shortly after the first, some people may remember specific items—and this will influence the results. With some kinds of tests, the difficulty level of the items is changed considerably once a person has taken the test, as, for example, when much of the difficulty depends on having the examinee figure out how to work some type of problem. If the time interval between testings is very long, real changes may have taken place in the examinees and test scores should be different; in such situations, the ability of the test to reflect these real changes in the people will result in a spuriously low reliability coefficient, because the changes in score are not the fault of the test. For example:

> Fourth-grade pupils are tested at the beginning and retested at the end of the school year; all pupils will have learned something, but some will have learned much more than others. Inexperienced machinists, retested after six months on the job, will show the same sort of pattern—some men having changed appreciably, some having changed little. People undergoing psychotherapy between first and second testing may show markedly different scores.

### INTER-RELATIONSHIP OF SOURCES OF ERROR VARIANCE

We noted earlier that these sources are not unrelated. By now it should be clear that some of the considerations could have been classified under categories other than the one I used.

But it is also true that some reliability coefficients take several sources of error variance into consideration. For example, some test manuals report test-retest reliability coefficients with alternate forms of the test being used—clearly taking cognizance of both content and temporal influences.

In general, test publishers do a better job of reporting on content and temporal influences than on the others. More attention should be paid to reporting examiner-scorer reliability studies. Although the effects of examinee-incurred and situation-induced influences are much more difficult to assess, some test publishers could do a better job of urging examiners to attend fully to their importance.

### FACTORS AFFECTING RELIABILITY

Thousands of pages have been written on test reliability; however, we will do little more here than suggest a few of the factors which influence reliability.

#### 1. Length Increases Reliability

The longer the test, the more reliable it will be—provided other factors are held constant (for example, that the group tested is the same, that the new items are as good as those on the shorter test, and that the test does not become so long that fatigue is a consideration).

#### 2. Heterogeneity Increases Reliability

The variability of the group tested is also important in evaluating any reliability coefficient. If everything else is the same, higher reliability coefficients will be found for groups which vary more in ability.

> We are going to demonstrate the temporal reliability of a *Reading Speed Test (RST)*. From our school system, we select at random, one pupil from each grade, one through nine. We test each child in this sample; one week

later, we test them all again. Inasmuch as speed of reading increases markedly through these grades, we should have a tremendous range in scores—and the differences among pupils should be so great that order of score is not likely to change from one administration of the test to the next. The reliability coefficient, then, would prove to be very high. If, on the other hand, we were to select a small group of average-ability second-graders and test them twice (as above) on the *RST*, we should find a very low reliability coefficient; these pupils probably would not differ much in their initial scores—and order of score might very well change on the second testing, thereby reducing the reliability coefficient.

We need to study carefully the publisher's description of the group used and the conditions of testing in any reliability report.

### 3. Shorter Time, Higher Reliability

The length of time between the two testings in a test-retest reliability coefficient is of obvious importance. As we would expect, reliability is higher when the time between the two testings is short. This is why IQs change most when there is a long period of time between testings.

### COMPARING VALIDITY AND RELIABILITY

Validity is established through a statistical comparison of scores with values on some outside variable. Any constant error in the test will have a direct adverse effect on the test's validity.

We want to select power sewing machine operators. We use a test which contains many difficult words that are not related to sewing machine operation. Since this extraneous factor will influence each individual's score in a consistent fashion, the hard words will reduce the test's validity for our purpose. (Note that the reliability is not necessarily reduced.)

No outside variable is involved in reliability, for reliability is not concerned with what a test measures—only with the consistency with which it measures. As noted above, irregularities in testing procedures have a direct and adverse effect on reliability; indirectly, they may reduce validity as well. (Note: these irregularities are known as variable errors. Variable here simply means nonconstant. In most other places throughout this book, variable is a general term referring to any characteristic, test, or the like, which may assume different values.)

### Usability

The third basic attribute of a test is *usability*. We include here all the many practical factors that go into our decision to use a particular test. Let me give one more imaginary example.

We are wondering whether to use the *Lyman Latin Verb Test* (*LLVT*) or the *Latin Original Verb Examination* (*LOVE*) in our high school Latin course. Since both tests are hypothetical, we may give them any characteristics we desire. My *LLVT*, therefore, has perfect reliability and validity. The *LOVE*, although not perfect, does have respectable validity and reliability for our purposes. We'll probably decide to use the *LOVE* in spite of the *LLVT*'s perfection, for the *LLVT* takes two weeks to administer and an additional week to score, can be given to only one examinee at a time, costs $1000 per examinee, and can be administered and scored by only one person. The *LOVE*, on the other hand, can be given to a group of students simultaneously, has reusable test booklets which cost only ten cents per copy (answer sheets cost three cents apiece), and can be scored by a clerical worker in two or three minutes.

Under usability, we deal with all sorts of practical considerations. A longer test may be more reliable, even more valid; however, if we have only a limited time for testing, we may have to compromise with the ideal. If the preferred test is too expensive, we may have to buy another one instead (or buy fewer copies of the first test), and so on.

I am not suggesting that validity and reliability are important only in theory. They are vitally important. After all, there is no point in testing unless we can have some confidence in the results. Practical factors must be considered, but only if the test has satisfactory reliability and validity.

# A FEW
# STATISTICS

*Chapter Four*

It is too bad that so many people are afraid of or bored by statistics, for statistics is a fascinating subject with a lurid history. Professional gamblers are among many who have found the study very profitable. More important right here, I suppose, is the fact that elementary statistics is easy to understand. If you have completed ninth-grade mathematics, you should have little trouble in grasping the basic fundamentals.

**Introduction**

Some of the points in this chapter will be a little clearer if we start off with a concrete example.

Fifty men who applied for jobs at the Knifty Knife Korporation took the *Speedy Signal Test*. They obtained the following scores (where one point was given for each correct answer):

| AA | 38 | AK | 35 | AU | 34 | BE | 32 | BO | 30 |
|----|----|----|----|----|----|----|----|----|----|
| AB | 43 | AL | 36 | AV | 36 | BF | 37 | BP | 30 |
| AC | 36 | AM | 37 | AW | 33 | BG | 29 | BQ | 36 |
| AD | 31 | AN | 35 | AX | 35 | BH | 33 | BR | 25 |
| AE | 25 | AO | 37 | AY | 37 | BI | 35 | BS | 42 |
| AF | 28 | AP | 31 | AZ | 33 | BJ | 34 | BT | 38 |
| AG | 38 | AQ | 34 | BA | 35 | BK | 31 | BU | 41 |
| AH | 35 | AR | 34 | BB | 35 | BL | 32 | BV | 27 |
| AI | 31 | AS | 26 | BC | 41 | BM | 34 | BW | 37 |
| AJ | 35 | AT | 28 | BD | 33 | BN | 30 | BX | 32 |

*CONTINUOUS AND DISCRETE VARIABLES*

We treat test scores as if they were *continuous*. Continuous values are the results of measuring, rather than counting. We cannot have absolute accu-

*34*

racy, for we might always use still finer instruments to obtain greater precision. We can measure relatively tangible variables such as length and weight with considerable accuracy, but we find it harder to measure accurately such intangibles as intelligence, aptitude, and neuroticism. The principle is the same, though: absolute precision of measurement is not possible with any variable. The degree of accuracy depends on the nature of the variable itself, the precision of the instrument, and the nature of the situation.

> See how this works with *length*. In discussing the size of my office, I may use dimensions accurate to the nearest foot. I may note my desk size to the nearest inch. I measure the height of my children to the nearest quarter-inch. My model builder friends do work that is accurate to the nearest one sixty-fourth inch, and scientists working on our rockets and satellites need far greater precision.

Some variables can be expressed only as discrete values. Here we count, and complete accuracy is possible: number of volumes in the public libraries of Ohio, number of students in each classroom at Aiken High School, number of seats in each Cincinnati theater, etc. The tipoff, usually, is in the phrase "number of." When the variable can be expressed only in that way, we nearly always have a discrete variable.

If we think of a test as only a collection of questions and of test scores as only the number of items correct, we will have to consider test scores as discrete values. We do often obtain our scores by counting the number of correct answers; however, we usually want to consider the test scores as measures of some characteristic beyond the test itself.

> We are not satisfied with thinking of AA merely as having answered correctly thirty-eight items on his *Speedy Signal Test* (*SST*). Rather, we want to consider this 38 as an indication of some amount of the ability underlying the test.

Any test is only a sample of the items that might have been included. We hope that the test is a representative sample of this universe (or population) of all possible items. The universe of possible items for most tests is almost infinite, for we could not possibly write all of the items which would be relevant. We find it helpful to think of any psychological or educational test as being a rather crude instrument for measuring whatever characteristic (ability, knowledge, aptitude, interest, etc.) is presumed to underlie the test. Although not everyone agrees, most test authorities treat test scores as continuous. And we shall do so in this book, for continuous scores can be handled mathematically in ways that discrete values cannot.

### THE HISTOGRAM

Let us return to our example of the fifty applicants for employment at the Knifty Knife Korporation. We may show the results graphically by marking

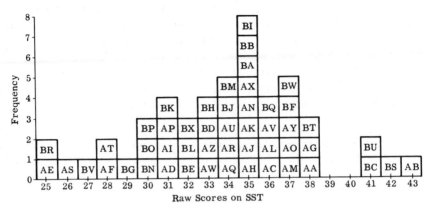

Fig. 4.1

off all possible score values (within the range actually made) along a horizontal line. This horizontal line, called the *abscissa*, will serve as the baseline of our graph. If we use a tiny square to represent each applicant, we will have a graph like that shown in Figure 4.1. Since these scores are continuous, we let each of those little squares occupy the space of one full unit; that is, each square occupies a space from 0.5 below the stated score value to 0.5 above the stated score value. AA's score was 38; his square is placed so that it extends from 37.5 to 38.5 (the real limits of the score), thereby having half of its area above and half below 38.0 (the midpoint of the score). We can tell the number of cases (the frequency) falling at any specified score by counting the number of squares above it or, even more simply, by reading the number on the ordinate (the vertical axis) of the graph at a height level with the top of the column. This is called a *histogram*.

When we draw a graph to show a set of scores, we ordinarily make no effort to retain the identity of the individuals. We are less interested in knowing AA's score or AB's score than we are in portraying the general nature of the scores made by the group. We are likely to be interested in general characteristics such as the shape of the distribution, the scores obtained most frequently, the range in scores, etc. Ordinarily, therefore, we would be more likely to draw the histogram in one of the ways shown in Figure 4.2. Here we have no need for individual squares; instead, we draw columns (each one unit wide) to the height required to show appropriate frequency.

### FREQUENCY DISTRIBUTION AND CLASS INTERVALS

We sometimes find it convenient to group adjacent scores together. For example, we might measure the length of each of one hundred objects to the

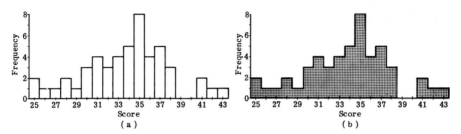

**Fig. 4.2**

nearest inch, but prefer to group the measurements into intervals of six inches or one foot when showing them graphically.

We often do this same thing when graphing test results. For the sake of illustration, we will take the same fifty test scores reported on page 34 and arrange them into a frequency distribution as in Table 4.1. At the left, we have retained the original score values—each unit, therefore, is equal to one score value. At the right, however, we have arranged the scores into class intervals which are two score values wide. Ordinarily we would use either individual score values or class intervals, not both. The essential information is contained in columns 1 and 4 or columns 5 and 8. The remaining columns are included only for the guidance of the reader.

In the last paragraph, we encountered two new terms: *frequency distribution* and *class interval*. A frequency distribution is any orderly arrangement of scores, usually from high to low, showing the frequency with which each score value (or class interval of scores) occurs when some specified group is tested. A class interval is the unit used within a frequency distribution (although we rarely call it a class interval if the unit is only a single score value). The use of class intervals provides a means of grouping together several adjacent score values so that they may be treated as alike for computational or graphing purposes. We assume that all of the cases in a particular class interval fall at the midpoint of that interval except when we're computing the median or other percentiles (where we assume that the cases are spread evenly across the interval). The midpoint seems self-descriptive: it is that value which lies halfway between the real limits of the interval.

When used with test scores, class intervals must be of the same width (size) throughout any given distribution. We cannot use class intervals two score values wide at one place and five score values wide at another place in the same distribution.

Usually, when selecting a class interval width we select an odd number, so that the midpoints of our class intervals will be integers (whole numbers).

**Table 4.1**

Speedy Signal Test Scores of the Fifty Knifty Knife Korporation Applicants

| (1) SCORE EX-PRESSED AS: | (2) REAL LIMITS OF SCORE | (3) MIDPOINT OF SCORE | (4) FREQUENCY (f) | (5) CLASS INTERVALS OF 2 | (6) REAL LIMITS OF INTERVAL | (7) MIDPOINT OF INTERVAL | (8) FREQUENCY (f) |
|---|---|---|---|---|---|---|---|
| 43 | 42.5-43.5 | 43.0 | 1 | 43-44 | 42.5-44.5 | 43.5 | 1 |
| 42 | 41.5-42.5 | 42.0 | 1 | | | | |
| 41 | 40.5-41.5 | 41.0 | 2 | 41-42 | 40.5-42.5 | 41.5 | 3 |
| 40 | 39.5-40.5 | 40.0 | 0 | | | | |
| 39 | 38.5-39.5 | 39.0 | 0 | 39-40 | 38.5-40.5 | 39.5 | 0 |
| 38 | 37.5-38.5 | 38.0 | 3 | | | | |
| 37 | 36.5-37.5 | 37.0 | 5 | 37-38 | 36.5-38.5 | 37.5 | 8 |
| 36 | 35.5-36.5 | 36.0 | 4 | | | | |
| 35 | 34.5-35.5 | 35.0 | 8 | 35-36 | 34.5-36.5 | 35.5 | 12 |
| 34 | 33.5-34.5 | 34.0 | 5 | | | | |
| 33 | 32.5-33.5 | 33.0 | 4 | 33-34 | 32.5-34.5 | 33.5 | 9 |
| 32 | 31.5-32.5 | 32.0 | 3 | | | | |
| 31 | 30.5-31.5 | 31.0 | 4 | 31-32 | 30.5-32.5 | 31.5 | 7 |
| 30 | 29.5-30.5 | 30.0 | 3 | | | | |
| 29 | 28.5-29.5 | 29.0 | 1 | 29-30 | 28.5-30.5 | 29.5 | 4 |
| 28 | 27.5-28.5 | 28.0 | 2 | | | | |
| 27 | 26.5-27.5 | 27.0 | 1 | 27-28 | 26.5-28.5 | 27.5 | 3 |
| 26 | 25.5-26.5 | 26.0 | 1 | | | | |
| 25 | 24.5-25.5 | 25.0 | 2 | 25-26 | 24.5-26.5 | 25.5 | 3 |

Note that when we used 2 as our class interval width in Table 4.1 our midpoints were not whole numbers (e.g., the midpoint of the class interval 43–44, is 43.5). This always happens when a class interval is not an odd number of score values in width. As a general rule, we try to make our intervals of such a width that we will have a total of about fifteen intervals—somewhat more, perhaps, when we have a great many scores, and somewhat fewer when we have very few scores. Some imprecision is introduced by using intervals. Using fewer and larger intervals makes statistical computations easier, but also less precise. Having about fifteen intervals seems a reasonable compromise for precision and computational ease.

We must now differentiate score limits and real limits. Score limits are simply the extreme integral score values included in a given class interval. Real limits are the upper and lower extremities.

> A class interval of 21–25 means that 21 and 25 are the score limits; scores of 21, 22, 23, 24, and 25 are included in this interval. The real limits extend from the real lower limit of the lowest score (20.5) to the real upper limit of the highest score (25.5). As a check to see that the interval is five units wide: $25.5 - 20.5 = 5.0$; as a double check, note that five different integral score values (21, 22, 23, 24, and 25) fall within the interval.

In drawing a histogram, we make the sides of the upright columns extend to the real limits of each score (or class interval). The height of each column depends on the frequency (the number of people making each score); thus we can tell the number of people who made any specified score by reading the number on the ordinate opposite the top of the column.

### FREQUENCY POLYGON

Another type of graph that may be used for the same purpose is the frequency polygon. A dot is placed above the midpoint of each score value (or each class interval) at a height corresponding to the number of people making that score. Each of these dots is connected with the two adjacent dots by straight lines. In addition, the distribution is extended one unit (i.e., either one score value or one class interval) beyond the highest and lowest scores obtained. This means that there will be lines to the baseline at each extreme, thereby completing the figure and making our graph a polygon (a many-sided figure).

Figure 4.3 is a frequency polygon showing the test scores of the fifty Knifty Knife Korporation applicants; we have used class intervals that are two score values wide and show the information in columns 5 and 8 of Table 4.1.

It can be shown mathematically, although we will not do so here, that a histogram and a frequency polygon showing the same data and drawn to the same scale, are identical in area. This is important, for it is customary when drawing graphs to make area proportional to frequency of cases.

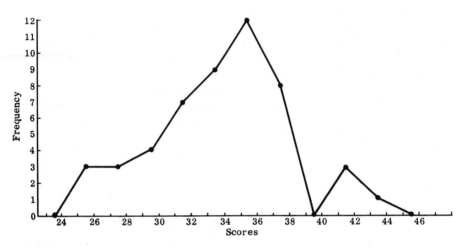

**Fig. 4.3**

(The fact that height is also proportional to frequency results from our having score units equally spaced along the abscissa.)

We may use the histogram and the frequency polygon interchangeably except when we need to compare the distributions of two or more groups. In such instances, we nearly always use the frequency polygon since it will be easier to read.

Figure 4.4 shows the distribution of the fifty Knifty Knife applicants compared with the distribution of fifty-two present employees of the Knifty Knife Korporation.

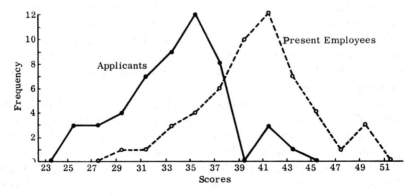

**Fig. 4.4**

[Please note: if the number of cases were not very nearly the same in each of the groups, we would have to use percentages (rather than frequencies) on the ordinate so that the areas under each polygon would be the same and a direct visual comparison could be made.]

## Descriptive Statistics

Graphs are very helpful in giving us a general impression of a distribution. After a little practice, we can learn a great deal from a graph. Descriptive statistics, however, provide a more precise means for summarizing or describing a set of scores. Descriptive statistics include measures of position (including central tendency), measures of variability, and measures of covariability.

### MEASURES OF POSITION (OTHER THAN CENTRAL TENDENCY)

Measures of position are numbers which tell us where a specified person or a particular score value stands within a set of scores. In a graph, any measure of position is located as a point on the baseline.

#### 1. Rank

*Rank* is the simplest description of position—first for the best or highest, second for the next best, third, etc., on to last. Its assets are its familiarity and its simplicity; however, its interpretation is so dependent on the size of the group that it is less useful than one might think at first. We use it only informally in describing test results.

#### 2. Percentile Rank

*Percentile rank* is a better position indicator because it makes allowance for difference in size of group. Percentile rank is a statement of a person's relative position within a defined group—thus a percentile rank of 38 indicates a score that is as high as or higher than those made by 38 percent of the people in that particular group. Percentile ranks are widely used as a type of test score and will be considered in detail in Chapter Six.

### MEASURES OF CENTRAL TENDENCY (AVERAGES)

A measure of central tendency is designed to give us a single value that is most characteristic or typical of a set of scores. Three such measures are fairly common in testing: the mean, median, and mode. Each of these may be located as a point along the baseline of a graph.

#### 1. Mean

The most common measure of position and of central tendency is the *arithmetic mean* (usually called simply the mean). This is nothing more than the average we learned about in elementary school. But average is a generic term and may refer to any measure of central tendency. The mean is the preferred measure for general use with test scores. Besides certain mathematical advantages, the mean is widely understood and easy to compute. We use the mean unless there is good reason to prefer some other statistic.

In grade school we learned to find the mean by adding up all the scores and dividing by the number of scores. Stated as a formula, this becomes:

$$\bar{X} = \frac{\Sigma X}{N}, \text{ where}$$

$\bar{X} =$ the mean of Test $X$

$\Sigma =$ "add the values of"

$X =$ raw score on Test $X$

$N =$ number of cases (number of persons for whom we have scores).

### 2. Median

With income data, we are likely to have one very high salary (or, at best, a very few high salaries) and many more lower salaries. The result is that the mean tends to exaggerate the salaries (that is, it pulls toward the extreme values) and the median becomes the preferred measure. The *median* is that value above which fall 50 percent of the cases and below which fall 50 percent of the cases; thus it is less likely to be drawn in the direction of the extreme cases.

Income data are usually positively skewed, having many low values and a few very high values. This same sort of distribution, shown in Figure 4.5(a), is frequently found when a test is too difficult or when the examinees are not well prepared. Figure 4.5(b) is negatively skewed, the sort of distribution we are likely to get when a test is too easy for the group tested. The mean gives us an erroneous impression of central tendency whenever a distribution is badly skewed, and the median becomes the preferred measure.

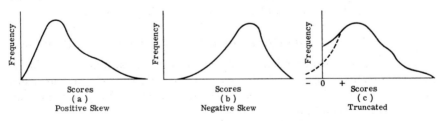

Fig. 4.5

Three Nonsymmetrical Distributions.

The median is also preferred whenever a distribution is truncated (cut off in some way so that there are no cases beyond a certain point). In Figure 4.5(c), the distribution is truncated, perhaps because of a very difficult test on which zero was the lowest score given; the dotted line suggests the distribution we might have obtained if the scoring had allowed negative scores.

Since the median is the fiftieth percentile (also the second quartile and the fifth decile), it is the logical measure of central tendency to use when percentile ranks are being used.

### 3. Mode

The third type of average used with test scores is the *mode*. The mode is the most commonly obtained score or the midpoint of the score interval having the highest frequency.

The mode is less often usable in connection with further computations than either the mean or the median. It is very easily found, however, and we can use it as a quick indication of central tendency. If the scores are arranged in a frequency distribution, the mode is equal to the midpoint of the score (or class interval) which has the highest frequency. If a distribution of scores is graphed, the mode is even more quickly found—it will be the highest point of the curve, as shown in Figure 4.6. Sometimes there are two modes (bimodal) or even more (multimodal) to a distribution. Graphs (c) and (d) in Figure 4.6 are both bimodal, even though the peaks are not quite of equal height.

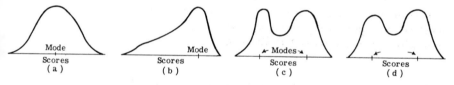

Fig. 4.6

The Mode.

### COMPARISON OF THE CENTRAL TENDENCY MEASURES

Let us recapitulate quickly.

The mean is the best measure of central tendency to use in most testing situations. We use it unless there is some good reason not to. It is widely understood and fairly easily computed. It fits logically and mathematically into the computation of other statistics. On the other hand, the mean should not be used when the distribution of scores is *badly* skewed or truncated, because it is not a good indicator of central tendency in such situations.

The median fits logically into the percentile scale. Its use is preferred whenever distributions are badly skewed or truncated. It involves fewer mathematical assumptions than the mean. Although less widely used than the mean, it is easily understood.

The mode is less widely used than either the mean or the median. It provides a quick and easy estimate of central tendency, but it is not especially useful in connection with test scores.

There are still other measures of central tendency, but none is commonly used in testing.

Any measure of central tendency can be located as a point along the abscissa of a graph.

### MEASURES OF VARIABILITY

It is possible for two distributions of scores to have similar (even identical) central tendency values and yet be very different. The scores in one distribution, for example, may be spread out over a far greater range of values than those in the other distribution. These next statistics tell us how much *variability* (or dispersion) there is in a distribution; that is, they tell us how scattered or spread out the scores are. In graphic work, each of these measures can be represented by a distance along the baseline.

#### 1. Range

The *range* is familiar to all of us, representing as it does the difference between highest and lowest scores. The range is easily found and easily understood, but is valuable only as a rough indication of variability.

It is the least stable measure of variability, depending entirely on the two most extreme (and, therefore, least typical) scores. It is less useful in connection with other statistics than other measures of variability.

#### 2. Semi-Interquartile Range

This statistic defines itself: *Semi* (half) *inter* (between) *quartile* (one of three points dividing the distribution into four groups of equal size) *range* (difference or distance); in other words, the statistic equals one-half the distance between the extreme quartiles, $Q_3$ (seventy-fifth percentile) and $Q_1$ (twenty-fifth percentile).

We use the semi-interquartile range as a measure of dispersion whenever we use the median as the measure of central tendency. It is preferred to other measures when a distribution of scores is truncated or badly skewed. It is sometimes useful when describing the variability of a set of scores to nonprofessionals. The formula for the semi-interquartile range is:

$$Q = \frac{Q_3 - Q_1}{2}, \text{ where}$$

$Q$ = semi-interquartile range
$Q_3$ = third quartile, the seventy-fifth percentile ($P_{75}$)
$Q_1$ = first quartile, the twenty-fifth percentile ($P_{25}$).

### 3. Average Deviation (Mean Deviation)

Another statistic which has been used to express variability is the *average deviation* or *mean deviation*. Its chief advantage is the simplicity of its rationale, for it is simply the mean absolute amount by which scores differ from the mean score; however, it is more difficult to compute than some better measures of variability and is seldom used today. It is mentioned only because there are occasional references to it in testing literature.

### 4. The Standard Deviation

Although it lacks the obvious rationale of the preceding measures of variability, the *standard deviation* is the best such measure. It is the most dependable measure of variability, for it varies less than other measures from one sample to the next. It fits mathematically with other statistics. It is widely accepted as the best measure of variability, and is of special value to test users because it is the basis for: (1) standard scores; (2) a way of expressing the reliability of a test score; (3) a way of indicating the accuracy of values predicted from a correlation coefficient; and (4) a common statistical test of significance. This statistic, in short, is one which every test user should know thoroughly.

*The standard deviation is equal to the square root of the mean of the squared deviations from the distribution's mean.* (Read that last sentence again—it is not really that hard!) Although more efficient formulas exist, the standard deviation may be computed from the following formula:

$$s_x = \sqrt{\frac{\Sigma(X - \bar{X})^2}{N}}, \text{ where}$$

$s_x =$ standard deviation of Test $X$

$\sqrt{\phantom{x}} =$ "take the square root of"

$\Sigma =$ "add the values of"

$X =$ raw score on Test $X$

$\bar{X} =$ mean of Test $X$

$N =$ number of persons whose scores are involved.

What does the standard deviation mean? After we have found it, what is it all about? As a measure of variability it can be expressed as a distance along the baseline of a graph. The standard deviation is often used as a unit in expressing the difference between two specified score values; differences expressed in this fashion are more comparable from one distribution to another than they would be if expressed as raw scores.

The standard deviation is also frequently used in making interpretations from the normal curve (described in detail later in this chapter). In a normal distribution, 34.13 percent of the area under the curve lies between the mean and a point that is one standard deviation away from it; 68.26 percent of the area lies between a point that is one standard deviation below the mean and a point one standard deviation above the mean. In nonnormal distributions (and perfect normality is never achieved), the figure will not be exactly 68.26 percent, but it will be approximately two-thirds for most distributions of test scores. In other words, approximately two-thirds of the area (and two-thirds of the cases, for area represents number of persons) will fall within one standard deviation of the mean in most distributions; approximately one-third of the cases will be more than one standard deviation away from the mean.

### MEASURES OF COVARIABILITY

Measures of *covariability* tell us the extent of the relationship between two tests (or other variables). There is a wide variety of correlation methods, but we shall consider only two of them here: the Pearson product–moment correlation coefficient and the Spearman rank–difference correlation coefficient.

*Correlation* is the degree of relationship between two (or, in specialized techniques, even more) variables. A correlation coefficient is an index number expressing the degree of relationship; it may take any value from 0.00 (no relationship) to + 1.00 (perfect positive correlation) or − 1.00 (perfect negative correlation). Let us take three extreme (and impractical) examples to illustrate correlation.

In Figure 4.7(a) we see a perfect positive correlation. Ten students have taken a math test. Their scores are shown as Number Right across the abscissa and as Percent Right along the ordinate. Each dot in this scatter diagram represents one student's score according to both number right and percent right. Since there is a perfect correlation, the dots fall along a straight line. Since the correlation is positive, the dots proceed from lower left to upper right.

In Figure 4.7(b) we see a perfect negative correlation. Here we have the same ten students with their test scores as Number Right (across the abscissa) and Number Wrong (along the ordinate). The dots fall along a straight line, but proceed from upper left to lower right as is characteristic of negative correlations.

There is no regular order to the dots in Figure 4.7(c) for this is a correlation coefficient of 0.00—no correlation at all, either positive or negative. Once again, the Number Right is shown along the abscissa, but this time we have shown Height of Student along the ordinate. Apparently, there is no tendency for math scores and heights to be related.

We will never encounter a perfect correlation in actual practice. Only rarely are we likely to encounter any correlation coefficients above 0.90 except as reliability coefficients (*see* "Reliability" in Chapter Three). Validity coefficients (*see* "Validity" in Chapter Three) are much more likely to run between about 0.20 and 0.60 depending upon the test, the criterion, and the variability in scores within the group tested.

Figure 4.8 shows a correlation coefficient of approximately 0.50. This is

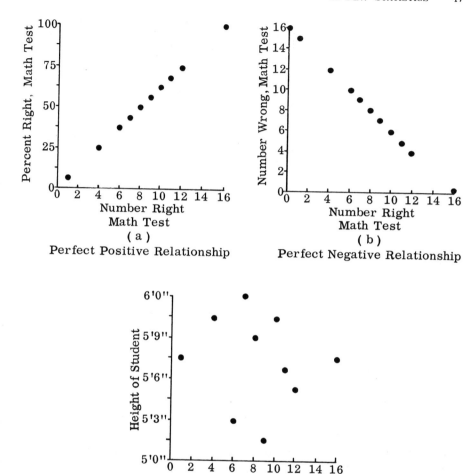

**Fig. 4.7**

Scatter Diagrams Showing Different
Relationships Between Two Variables.

the sort of scatter diagram we might reasonably expect to find for the correlation between a test and its criterion; in fact, such a correlation may be
a reasonably good validity coefficient. Note, however, that we would not
be able to predict specific criterion values very efficiently from the test
scores. If we could, there would be very little variation in scores within any

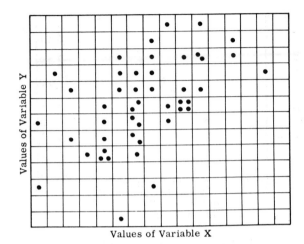

**Fig. 4.8**

Scatter Diagram Showing Correlation
Coefficient of Approximately 0.50
Between Variable *X* and Variable *Y*.

one of the columns; or, stated differently, all scores in any column would tend to be located very close together.

Although the correlation coefficient states the extent to which values of one variable tend to change systematically with changes in value of a second variable, correlation is not evidence of causation. Two variables may be related without either one causing change in the other.

Here is simple illustration of the principle that correlation is not proof of causation—an example that is not original with me, although I do not recall the source:

> Among elementary school pupils, there is a positive correlation between length of index finger and mental age. In other words, the longer the index finger, the higher the mental age. Before you start using length of index finger as a test of intelligence (or begin to stretch your child's finger), wait a minute! Do you suppose that higher intelligence causes the longer finger, or vice versa? Neither, of course. Among elementary school children, higher chronological ages result both in higher mental ages and in longer fingers.

As mentioned earlier, we shall consider here only the Pearson product–moment correlation coefficient (*r*) and the Spearman rank–difference correlation coefficient (*rho*, $\rho$). The product–moment correlation is computed when both variables are measured continuously and certain specified assumptions can be made. The rank–difference correlation may be employed when the data are expressed as ranks, rather than scores; rank coefficients (there are others besides Spearman's) are somewhat less efficient, but often are reasonably good estimates of $r$. The formulas for these two types of correlation are given here only for the sake of illustration.

$$r_{xy} = \frac{\Sigma(X - \bar{X})(Y - \bar{Y})}{N s_x s_y}, \text{ where}$$

$r_{xy}$ = product–moment correlation coefficient
$\Sigma$ = "add the values of"
$X$ = raw score on Variable $X$
$\bar{X}$ = mean of Variable $X$
$Y$ = raw score on Variable $Y$
$\bar{Y}$ = mean of Variable $Y$
$N$ = number of pairs of scores
$s_x$ = standard deviation of Variable $X$
$s_y$ = standard deviation of Variable $Y$,

and:

$$\rho = 1 - \frac{6\Sigma D^2}{N(N^2 - 1)}, \text{ where}$$

$\rho$ = rank–difference correlation coefficient
$\Sigma$ = "add the values of"
$D$ = difference between a person's rank on
      Variable $X$ and Variable $Y$
$N$ = number of cases.

Although there are special correlation techniques where this is not true, most correlation methods demand that we have pairs of scores for each individual.

We want to find a validity coefficient of the hypothetical *Industrial Index* by correlating its scores with criterion values (number of units produced during a four-hour period of work). We have test scores for seventy-nine men and criterion information on seventy-four men. The greatest number on whom we could possibly compute our correlation coefficient would be seventy-four; however, if some of the seventy-four men did not take the test we will have an even smaller number with which to work.

As noted in Chapter Three, correlation coefficients are widely used in testing to express validity (where test scores are correlated with criterion values) and reliability (where two sets of scores for the same test are correlated).

## The Normal Probability Curve

So far we have been discussing obtained distributions of test scores. Now it is time to consider a theoretical distribution: the normal probability distribution, the graphical representation of which is known to us as the *normal curve* (*see* Figure 4.9). We will never obtain a distribution exactly like it, for it is based on an infinite number of observations which vary by pure chance. Nevertheless many human characteristics do seem to be distributed in much this way, and most tests yield distributions which approximate this model when given to large numbers of people.

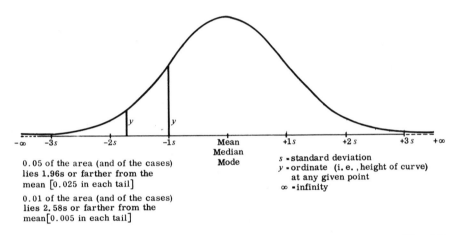

0.05 of the area (and of the cases) lies 1.96s or farther from the mean [0.025 in each tail]

0.01 of the area (and of the cases) lies 2.58s or farther from the mean [0.005 in each tail]

s = standard deviation
y = ordinate (i. e. , height of curve) at any given point
∞ = infinity

**Fig. 4.9**

The Normal Probability Curve.

We find it convenient to treat variables as if they were normally distributed when our results are not grossly asymmetrical, because all the properties of this mathematical model are known. If different obtained distributions approach this same model, we have a better basis for comparisons than we would have otherwise.

The normal curve is important, then, because: (1) it is a mathematical model whose properties are known completely; (2) it is a model that is approached by the distributions of many human characteristics and most test scores; (3) it is relevant to an understanding of certain inferential statistics; and, (4) it gives a basis for understanding the relationship between different types of test score.

*POINTS TO KNOW*

Chart 4.1 and Figure 4.9 constitute a summary of information about the normal probability curve that every test user should know. These points are worth remembering—even if we have to memorize them!

---

**Chart 4.1**

*IN THE NORMAL PROBABILITY CURVE:*

1. The curve is bilaterally symmetrical; i.e., the left and right halves are mirror images of each other. (Therefore the mean and median have the same value.)
2. The curve is highest in the middle of the distribution. (Therefore the mode is equal to the mean and the median.)
3. The limits of the curve are plus and minus infinity. (Therefore, the tails of the curve will never quite touch the baseline.)
4. The shape of the curve changes from convex to concave at points one standard deviation above and one below the mean.
5. About 34% (34.13%) of the total area under the curve lies between the mean and a point one standard deviation away. (Since area represents number of cases, about 34% of the examinees have scores which fall between the mean and a point one standard deviation away.)
6. Nearly 48% (47.72%) of the area (nearly 48% of the cases) lies between the mean and a point two standard deviations away.
7. Nearly 49.9% (49.87%) of the area (and the cases) lies between the mean and a point three standard deviations away.
8. About 68% (68.26%) of the area (and the cases) lies within one standard deviation (plus and minus) of the mean. (This was found by doubling the 34% in Item 5, above. In the same way, the percentages in Items 6 and 7 may be doubled to find the percentage of area or cases lying within two and three standard deviations of the mean, respectively.)
9. A known mathematical formula describes the curve exactly.
10. Tables exist giving all sorts of information: height of the ordinate at any distance (in standard-deviation units) from the mean, percentage of total area between any two points, etc.

---

## Inferential Statistics

*Inferential statistics* (sometimes called sampling statistics or probability statistics) tell us how much confidence may be placed in our descriptive statistics. Whereas descriptive statistics are values used to summarize a set of values, inferential statistics are used to answer the question "So what?" about descriptive statistics. They can be used to tell whether a descriptive statistic that is based on only a sample of cases is probably a close estimate of the value we would find for the entire population, whether the observed difference between means for two groups is best explained as probably due to chance alone, etc.

### STANDARD ERRORS

Space will not permit us to go into much detail on inferential statistics; however, we must develop one concept thoroughly: the *standard error* (especially, the standard error of measurement and the standard error of estimate).

Every descriptive statistic has its standard error, although some are rarely used and a few have not yet been worked out by statisticians. A standard error may be thought of as an estimate of the standard deviation of a set of like statistics; it expresses how much variation we might expect if we were to compute the same statistic on many more sample groups just like the one we are working with.

Although the formulas for the different standard errors vary somewhat according to the statistic, most standard errors become smaller (which is what we want) when the number of cases is large and when there is little variability in a set of scores (or a high correlation between sets of scores).

### 1. Standard Error of the Mean

We will illustrate the standard error concept with the *standard error of the mean*, which is found through the formula:

$$SE_{\bar{x}} = \frac{s}{\sqrt{N-1}}, \text{ where}$$

$SE_{\bar{x}} =$ standard error of the mean of Test $X$

$s =$ standard deviation of Test $X$

$\sqrt{\phantom{--}} =$ "take the square root of"

$N =$ number of cases.

Let us say that we give the *Task Test* to each man in one hundred different samples of fifty employees each; for each sample, men are selected randomly from among the 8000 working at the same job at Giant Enterprises. We compute the mean for each of these one hundred samples. We compute a standard deviation for this distribution of one hundred means by using each mean exactly as if it were a raw score. The standard error of the mean $(SE_{\bar{x}})$, based on only one sample, gives us an estimate of this standard deviation of a set of means. This $SE_{\bar{x}}$ tells how much the mean is likely to vary from one sample to the next.

Suppose now that we have only one random sample of fifty men. The mean is 85.0; the standard deviation is 28.0; the standard error of the mean is 4.0. We want to estimate the mean of the 8000 Giant Enterprises workers. Our sample mean is an unbiased, honest estimate of the mean of the population (here, our 8000 men); but we do not know whether our sample mean is higher or lower than the population mean. At least theoretically the value of the population mean is fixed and invariable at any given point in time, even though we don't know what its value is.

It can be shown that when a large number of random samples of the same size are selected from a population, the means of the samples tend to be distributed normally with a grand mean which is equal to the population's mean; the $SE_{\bar{x}}$ is an estimate of what the standard deviation of that distribution would be.

*Go back to page 50 and look at the normal curve, Figure 4.9.*

The situation now is this: we may consider our sample mean as one observation in a normal distribution having a standard deviation of 4.0. How close is our sample mean of 85.0 to the population mean?

Since 68 percent of the area of a normal curve is within one standard deviation of the mean, there are about sixty-eight chances in one hundred that our mean is no more than one standard deviation away from the population mean. It follows that we may be about 68 percent confident that the population mean is not more than one $SE_{\bar{x}}$ from the sample mean: 85.0 $\pm$ 4.0, or between 81.0 and 89.0.

Through similar reasoning, we might have about 95 percent confidence that the population mean has a value not more than $\pm 1.96\ SE_{\bar{x}}$ away from the sample mean; or 99 percent confidence that the population mean is not more than $\pm 2.58\ SE_{\bar{x}}$ away from the sample mean.

### 2. Standard Error of Measurement

We use a similar line of reasoning when we use the *standard error of measurement* $(SE_{\mathrm{meas}})$. This statistic indicates how much we would expect a person's score to vary if he were examined repeatedly with the same test (assuming that no learning occurs).

The standard error of measurement is a way of expressing a test's reliability in an absolute sense; that is, not in general or relative terms as with a reliability coefficient (*see* Chapter Three), but in terms of score units. As test users, we should not have to compute this statistic ourselves—unless, of course, we want to verify that the $SE_{\mathrm{meas}}$ for our group is comparable to that reported by the test publisher. The formula is:

$$SE_{\mathrm{meas}} = s_x\sqrt{1 - r_{xx}},\ \text{where}$$
$$SE_{\mathrm{meas}} = \text{standard error of measurement}$$
$$s_x = \text{standard deviation of Test } X$$
$$\sqrt{\ \ } = \text{``take the square root of''}$$
$$r_{xx} = \text{a reliability coefficient for Test } X.$$

Let us take an example:

Yung Youngdahl gets a score of 73 on an aptitude test. How close is this obtained score to Yung's true score? We use the $SE_{\mathrm{meas}}$ in much the same way we did the $SE_{\bar{x}}$ to set up confidence limits for his true score. Thus, we may have about 99 percent confidence that his true score lies between $73 \pm 2.58\ SE_{\mathrm{meas}}$.

Actually, measurement theory describes the distribution of obtained scores about the theoretical true score, rather than about the obtained score; however, we are not very wrong if we interpret the $SE_{\mathrm{meas}}$ as suggested in the preceding paragraph.

Following this line of reasoning, the counselor can set up whatever confidence limits seem reasonable. If he wants to be extremely certain of the level of any score that he attributes to a counselee, he may use the 99 percent confidence limits—as noted above; however, very often we are more interested in suggestions that may be gained from the various tests we've had the counselee take. In such instances, I have found it helpful to use something like a 90 percent confidence interval. This, it seems to me, is a good compromise between being too rigid and too lenient. Actually, I use $\pm 1.6\,SE_{\text{meas}}$ (which is closer to 89 percent than to 90 percent) instead of $\pm 1.65\,SE_{\text{meas}}$, because of easier multiplication.

If we use this 90 percent confidence interval with Yung Youngdahl's score of 73, we would say that we are about 90 percent certain that his true score falls within the interval: $73 \pm 1.6\,SE_{\text{meas}}$. Let's assume that the test is known to have a standard error of measurement of 2.5. We'd multiply: $1.6 \times 2.5 = 4.0$. Thus, the confidence interval would be $73 \pm 4$, or 69 to 77. We could have reasonable confidence that Yung's true score falls within that interval. (We can convert this information to a percentile band by finding the percentile ranks for the raw scores of 69 and 77. The concept of the percentile band is developed further in Chapter Six.)

The standard error of measurement is extremely important for test users to grasp. It is something we need to keep in mind at all times. If we assume that a person's obtained score is necessarily his true score, we will make all kinds of misinterpretations.

Jim and Jack Johnson are brothers. Jim's IQ, found on a group test taken in the second grade, was 108. Jack's IQ, found on the same test when he was in the second grade, was 111. Jim's score was interpreted as average, but Jack's score was described as above average. According to many IQ classifications, we might very well describe these two IQs in this fashion. We should note, however, that no test scores are infallible, and that it is entirely possible that the theoretical true scores of Jim and Jack on this test would place them in the reverse order.

Those of us who teach know the difficulty we often have in deciding exactly where to draw the line between *A* and *B* grades, *B* and *C* grades, etc. It is probable that true appraisals (if they were available) of our students would reverse the grades of many borderline students. This same situation exists with *every* type of score.

### 3. Errors, Not Mistakes

It is important to realize that when we speak of *error* here, we are speaking of the error that is inherent in any measurement. It is something with which we must cope whenever we have a continuous variable (described on pages 34–35).

Mistakes must be guarded against. But the error of measurement we are considering here is always with us in testing. We cannot eliminate measurement error, but we can estimate how much error is present. We can eliminate mistakes, but we cannot estimate their extent when they are present (*see* "Reliability," pages 25–32).

Because of certain similarities, the standard error of measurement is often confused with the standard error of estimate, the last standard error that we shall consider.

### 4. Standard Error of Estimate ($SE_{yx}$)

The purpose of the *standard error of estimate* is to indicate how well test scores predict criterion values. Correlation coefficients give us the basis for predicting values of a criterion from our knowledge of obtained test scores. The $SE_{yx}$ shows how much predicted criterion values and obtained criterion values are likely to differ.

With a perfect correlation ($\pm 1.00$), we can predict perfectly; the $SE_{yx}$ will equal 0.00, for there will be no difference between predicted and obtained criterion values. With no correlation between the test and the criterion, we can assume that everyone will fall at the mean on the criterion, and we will be less wrong in doing this than we would be in making any other sort of prediction. But the $SE_{yx}$ now will be as large as the standard deviation; let us see why.

At the left below is a formula for the standard deviation; at the right below is a formula for the standard error of estimate.

$$s_y = \sqrt{\frac{\Sigma (Y - \overline{Y})^2}{N}} \quad \text{and} \quad SE_{yx} = \sqrt{\frac{\Sigma (Y - Y')^2}{N}}, \text{ where}$$

$s_y$ = standard deviation of $Y$, our criterion variable

$SE_{yx}$ = standard error of estimate (predicting values of criterion $Y$ from known scores on Test $X$)

$\sqrt{\phantom{x}}$ = "take the square root of"

$\Sigma$ = "add the values of"

$Y$ = obtained value on the criterion variable

$\overline{Y}$ = mean criterion value

$Y'$ = predicted criterion value (the criterion value most likely to be associated with a specified score on Test $X$; determined statistically by formula)

$N$ = number of individuals whose scores are used in the study.

The standard deviation is based on differences between obtained values and the mean ($Y - \overline{Y}$), whereas the standard error of estimate is based on differences between obtained values and predicted values ($Y - Y'$); otherwise, the formulas are identical. And, as we noted above, our best prediction is that everyone will fall at the mean when there is no correlation between test and criterion. In that event, everyone's $Y'$ value is $\overline{Y}$, and the $SE_{yx}$ and the standard deviation will be the same.

In other words, our predictions are no better than chance if they are based on a correlation coefficient of 0.00. Our predictions become more accurate as the correlation between test and criterion increases. And, as noted, our predictions become completely accurate when the correlation between test and criterion is $\pm 1.00$. (Accuracy here means that obtained criterion values differ little from the predicted criterion values.)

We interpret the standard error of estimate in very much the same way we interpret a standard deviation. An illustration may be helfpful:

> We know that the *Widget Winding Test* correlates positively with the number of widgets produced during a one-hour observation period. We find a $SE_{yx}$ of 6.0 based on the correlation between *WWT* scores and criterion values (that is, number of widgets produced). Now we have *WWT* scores on 2000 more men (who seem to be very much like those on whom the correlation was based). We want to predict how many widgets each man will produce during the one-hour observation period.
>
> Hiram Hinkley and ninety-four others earned the same *WWT* score, so we predict (from formulas that we can find in almost any statistics text) that all of these ninety-five men will earn the same criterion value, 44. If all of the assumptions for use of the correlation coefficient were met, and if the present group is very much like the earlier group, we will find the $SE_{yx}$ very helpful to us. In all likelihood, the criterion values obtained by these ninety-five men will tend to be normally distributed with a mean of about 44.0 and a standard deviation of about 6.0.
>
> In the same way, eighty-eight other men have predicted criterion values of thirty-seven widgets. In all likelihood, their obtained criterion values will tend to be normally distributed with a mean of 37.0 and a standard deviation of about 6.0.
>
> If all of the assumptions are met, we may expect that there will be a normal distribution of criterion values (a separate distribution for each *WWT* score), that the mean of each distribution will be the predicted criterion value, and that the standard deviation of each distribution will be given by the $SE_{yx}$.
>
> But what about Hiram? It is true that his criterion value is more likely to be 44 than anything else; however, his actual obtained criterion value could be much lower or much higher. For individuals, we must expect occasional performances that differ markedly from what is predicted.
>
> Hiram will have a criterion value that belongs in that normal distribution which has a mean of 44.0 and a standard deviation of 6.0—at least, these are the assumptions we must make. In actual fact, the assumptions are only approximated. Hiram's obtained criterion value is most likely to be 44, and the chances are approximately: two in three that it is within $\pm 1 SE$ of 44 ($44 \pm 6$), or 38–50; ninety-five in one hundred it is within $\pm 2 SE$ of 44 ($44 \pm 12$), or 32–56; and so on, the normal probability distribution stating the likelihood that Hiram's obtained criterion value will lie between any limits that we may specify.

In this way, we can set up a confidence interval for each individual's predicted criterion value. This interval represents a band of values extending out from the predicted value—a band within which the obtained criterion value has a stated probability of falling.

Standard errors of estimate (and the confidence intervals based on them) are rather large. That this is so may become more clear when we look at this next formula, another one for $SE_{yx}$. Although different in appearance from the one given earlier, it gives the same results.

$SE_{yx} = s_y\sqrt{1 - r_{xy}^2}$, where

   $r_{xy}$ = correlation coefficient between Test $X$ and Criterion $Y$;

   i.e., a validity coefficient,

   and other symbols are as previously defined.

The expression, $\sqrt{1 - r_{xy}^2}$, is sometimes called the coefficient of aliena-tion and indicates the lack of relationship between two variables. Let us take several different values of $r$ and see what their coefficients of alienation are:

When $r = 0.00$, coefficient of alienation $= 1.00$
  "    " $= 0.20$,    "    "    "  $= 0.98$
  "    " $= 0.40$,    "    "    "  $= 0.92$
  "    " $= 0.60$,    "    "    "  $= 0.80$
  "    " $= 0.866$,   "    "    "  $= 0.50$
  "    " $= 1.00$,    "    "    "  $= 0.00$.

In other words, a correlation coefficient of 0.20 increases our accuracy of prediction by only 2 percent $(1.00 - 0.98)$; an $r$ of 0.60 only 20 percent; and an $r$ of 0.866 only 50 percent. In this sense, we need an $r$ of 0.866 to effect a 50 percent increase in efficiency over chance.

Nevertheless, it is this coefficient of alienation that, when multiplied by the criterion's standard deviation, gives us the standard error of estimate. Thus, $SE_{yx}$ will be 0.98 as large as the standard deviation when $r$ is 0.20; 0.80 as large when $r$ is 0.60; 0.50 as large when $r$ is 0.866, etc.

This seems to present a very discouraging picture. After all, we rarely get validity coefficients anywhere near as high as 0.866. We are much more likely to have validity coefficients of from about 0.20 to about 0.60—and with validity coefficients of such size, we still have a great deal of error in predicted values.

We do need very high correlations for predicting specific values with much accuracy; however, we can make general predictions very effectively with the modest-sized validities which we typically find. Consider the following exam-ple, adapted from The Psychological Corporation's *Test Service Bulletin No. 45:*

In a given company, seventy-four stenographers were given The Psycho-logical Corporation's *Short Employment Tests (SET)*. Each stenographer was rated by a supervisor as low, average, or high in ability. The validity coefficient (based on these ratings) was just 0.38, so there would be little predictive efficiency, according to the standard error of estimate.

**Table 4.2\***

*Percent of Stenographers in Each Third*
*on SET-Clerical Who Earned Various Proficiency Ratings*

| SET-CLERICAL TEST SCORE | PROFICIENCY RATING | | |
|---|---|---|---|
| | LOW | AVERAGE | HIGH |
| Upper Third | **18** | **33** | **50** |
| Middle Third | **29** | **36** | **28** |
| Lowest Third | **53** | **31** | **22** |
| Total Percent | 100 | 100 | 100 |
| No. of Stenographers | 17 | 39 | 18 |

*\*Adapted from The Psychological Corporation's Test Service Bulletin No. 45, "Better than Chance" (1953). (Used with permission.)*

Let us see what happens if we try to predict which girls will fall into which criterion categories—instead of the specific criterion values we were concerned with in earlier examples. Table 4.2 shows for each criterion category the percentage of girls in each third on the Clerical part of the *SET*. Wesman, author of the *Bulletin*, states:

By chance alone, the percent of upper, middle, and low scorers in each of the rated groups would be the same—in this case, $33^1/_3$ per cent. The boldface numbers in the table would consist of nine 33's. Note how closely this expected per cent is approximated for those ranked average in proficiency, and for those in the middle third on test score; the percentages in the middle row and those in the middle column run between 28 and 36. Note also that at the extremes—the four corner numbers—the prediction picture is more promising. Among those *rated* low, there are almost three times as many people from the lowest third on the test as there are from the top third. Among those rated high, the per cent from the top third on the test is almost two and one-half times as great as the per cent from the bottom third. The personnel man would do well to be guided by these data in selecting future stenographers, even though the validity coefficient is just 0.38.

\*      \*      \*

The data in the above example are based on relatively small numbers of cases (which is typically true of practical test situations) and the per cents found in each category are consequently somewhat unstable. The validity coefficients based on groups of such sizes are, of course, also less stable than coefficients based on large numbers of cases. The wise test user will make several validity studies using successive groups. Having done so, he may take an average of the validity coefficients from these studies as being a more dependable estimate of the validity of the test in his situation.[1]

## Expectancy Tables

Table 4.2 is an *expectancy table*—that is, a table showing the relationship between test-score intervals and criterion categories. Typically, intervals of  test scores are shown at the left of the table, the number of intervals depending partly on number of cases involved and partly on the degree of differentiation desired for the situation; criterion categories are usually shown across the top of the table, the number of categories here also depending on the number of cases and on the degree of differentiation desired.

Into the individual cells of the table are placed either the number of cases or the percentage of cases which fall into that score interval and criterion category; most people prefer to use percentages, feeling that this practice is easier to interpret.

A similar technique, again from a Psychological Corporation *Test Service Bulletin*, is shown in Table 4.3. Basically, it is a bar graph—focusing our attention on those clerical workers, among sixty-five tested, who were rated as average or better by their supervisors. The number of workers involved is not very large, but there is certainly reason to believe that the company is more likely to find satisfactory clerical workers among high-scoring individuals than among lower-scoring individuals.

**Table 4.3**

*Expectancy Table and Graph Showing Percentage expected to rate Average or Better in Office Clerical Tasks on the Basis of Scores on the General Clerical Test.*
(N = 65, Mean Score = 136.1, S.D. = 39.1, r = 0.31)

| General Clerical Test Scores | No. in score group | No. rated average or better | % rated average or better | |
|---|---|---|---|---|
| 200–up | 5 | 5 | 100 | |
| 150–199 | 18 | 15 | 83 | |
| 100–149 | 31 | 23 | 74 | |
| 50–99 | 11 | 6 | 55 | |
| Total | 65 | | | 0%  20%  40%  60%  80%  100% |

[1] The Psychological Corporation, *Test Service Bulletin No. 45* (1953).

Although still not too widely used in test interpretation, the expectancy table is an excellent device to use when communicating test results to laymen. It is easy to understand and to explain to others. It directs attention to the purpose of testing by comparing test scores with criterion performance. [Note also the similarity to "Norms," in Chapter Five.]

Furthermore, the expectancy table is. an aid in test interpretation that shows a realistic outlook so far as criterion results are concerned. A common misinterpretation of test scores goes something like this: "This score means that you will fail in college." No test score (except, perhaps, a final examination in some course!) means any such thing. The expectancy table encourages an interpretation of this sort: "In the past, students with scores like yours have seldom succeeded at our college; in fact, only two students in ten have had satisfactory averages at the end of their first year." This latter type of interpretation can be supported; the former cannot.

### DOUBLE-ENTRY EXPECTANCY TABLES

As Wesman has pointed out, the same general principle can be extended to two (or even more) predictor variables.

An illustration of the usefulness of double-entry expectancy tables has been drawn from an industrial study. A large electronics firm administered a series of tests to a group of eighty-two computer service representatives. Among the tests used were the *Mechanical Comprehension Test*, Form CC (*MCT*), and the *Wesman Personnel Classification Test* (*PCT*). The immediate supervisors of these representatives assigned ratings of Highly Successful and Less Successful to these men. To observe the relationship between scores on the tests and the performance rating, a double-entry expectancy table was prepared. The company decided on cutoff scores for each of these tests on the basis of this study and of their local personnel needs. The chosen cutoff scores were 41 for the *Mechanical Comprehension Test* and 38 for the *Wesman Personnel Classification Test*. The table [4.4] shows the results of these procedures.

The table shows that among the currently employed computer service men, fourteen had scored 41 or above on *MCT* and 37 or below on *PCT*. Of these fourteen, ten were rated Highly Successful, and four were rated Less Successful. The other three cells show the placement of the remaining men according to their scores and ratings.

The basis for the selection of the particular cutoff scores is revealed by the table. Of the eighty-two men studied, fifty-one were rated in the high group, thirty-one in the low. Applying the cutoff score on *MCT* alone, twenty-six high-success men and five low-success are included in the upper group. Applying only the *PCT* cutoff score, twenty-two high men and two of the low are included in the upper group. When both cutoff scores are employed, only one of the less successful men remains as compared with sixteen of the highly rated.

**Table 4.4***

*Relationship between* PCT *Total Score,*
MCT *Score, and Success Ratings for*
*Computer Service Representatives* (N = 82)

| MCT SCORE | PCT SCORE | | | |
|---|---|---|---|---|
| | 37 AND BELOW | | 38 AND ABOVE | |
| 41 and above | High | 10 | High | 16 |
| | Low | 4 | Low | 1 |
| 40 and below | High | 19 | High | 6 |
| | Low | 25 | Low | 1 |

*\*Reprinted from The Psychological Corporation's Test Service Bulletin No. 56, "Double-Entry Expectancy Tables" (1966).*

The decision of the company in this case was apparently to minimize the number of less successful men, at the cost of excluding many of the potentially highly successful men. It is conceivable, certainly, that in another situation the decision reached might be to exclude only those who were below *both* cutting scores; this would accept thirty-two (10 + 16 + 6) of the high group while rejecting twenty-five (lower left cell) of the total of thirty-one rated less successful. The point is, of course, that the expectancy table does not prescribe the decision; it merely displays the information in a form which makes the consequences of a decision readily visible.[2]

When interpreting the results of an expectancy table, we should keep these points in mind:

1. We need to be certain that we are using the same test (including same form, level, edition, etc.).

2. The table is based on results that have been found in the past; it may or may not be relevant to the present group (or individual).

3. If the table is based on the performance of people from another office (company, school, or college), it may or may not apply to ours.

4. We can have more confidence in expectancy tables which are based on large numbers of scores. (Percentages are sometimes used to disguise small numbers.)

5. Even with no special training in testing or statistics, we can make expectancy tables of our own very easily. (Several issues of The Psychological Corporation's *Test Service Bulletin* contain excellent suggestions written by Alexander G. Wesman; see especially *Bulletins Nos. 38* and *56*.)

6. An expectancy table may be used to spot individuals (or subgroups) that do not perform as we would expect; by noting instances in which predictions miss, we may check back to discover possible reasons for the failure.

[2] The Psychological Corporation, *Test Service Bulletin No. 56* (1966).

7. In a sense we may think of an expectancy table as a set of norms in which one's test score is compared with the criterion performance of others who have made that same score.

8. The double-entry expectancy table permits the simultaneous display of relationships among two predictor variables and a criterion.

## An Omission and an Explanation

Some readers will be surprised that I chose to terminate the discussion of inferential statistics without mentioning many of the most important such statistics. There are many more inferential statistics that a well-trained test user should know if he is to read the testing literature or conduct research with tests. He should know that there are standard errors of differences, for example, and he should know that there are statistical tests of significance, etc. But these topics are not essential to an understanding of psychological and educational test scores, and I have chosen to omit them for that reason.

Other readers (or perhaps the same ones) will be surprised that I included expectancy tables in this chapter on statistics. Do these not belong in the chapter on norms or, perhaps, the one on types of derived scores? Certainly the topic might have been located in either of those chapters; perhaps it should have a chapter all its own. I added the topic to this chapter because I felt that the logical basis for expectancy tables was developed naturally from the discussion of the standard error of estimate. I hope that my readers agree that the transition was easily accomplished.

# THE TEST MANUAL

The American Automobile Association issues *Triptiks* to its members on request. The *Triptik* is an individualized map showing the recommended route to travel to get from Heretown to Theresville, together with a summary of the principal attractions offered in route.

In some senses the test manual is analogous to the Triptik. It shows what the particular test is like and how it may be used; however, each of us must do his own individualizing. The information is there—if the manual is a good one—but we ourselves need to plan the most helpful application. Thus, *unlike* the Triptik, which allows almost-automatic piloting of one's car through thousands of miles and dozens of cities, we need to use considerable thought and care in extracting the manual material that is pertinent to our own situations.

## The Test Catalog and Other Sources

Many people new to testing confuse the test *catalog* and the test *manual*. The catalog is a listing of the tests and test-related items which are sold by a company. The amount of detail varies considerably with the publisher. Several companies issue fancy, large-page catalogs. Others publish modest little leaflets. Whatever its appearance, the catalog should contain the following information for each test listed:

1. Title of test, including form designation.
2. Name(s) of author(s).
3. Level of persons for which the test is appropriate.
4. Different scores available from the test (at least the titles of the subtests or subareas for which different scores are obtained—as, for example, on

the *Wechsler Adult Intelligence Scale:* Verbal IQ, Performance IQ, and Full-Scale IQ).

5. Eligibility for purchase and use. [The American Psychological Association suggests a classification of *A, B,* or *C.* Level *A* tests are those having no specific requirements beyond an ability to read and follow directions (e.g., simple paper-and-pencil tests of proficiency and achievement); Level *B* tests require some training in testing (e.g., simple adjustment or interest inventories, paper-and-pencil intelligence and aptitude tests, etc.); and Level *C* tests require extensive relevant training (e.g., individual tests of intelligence or personality).]

6. Length of time required for administration and (if appropriate) scoring.

7. Availability of (or necessity for) using a special scoring service. Some tests can be scored only by a special service (e.g., the *Kuder Occupational Interest Survey*).

8. The formats in which the test, answer sheets, and other test-related materials are available. For example: the *Minnesota Multiphasic Personality Inventory* is used sometimes in a card form, but more commonly in one or another of several booklet forms; the *Henmon–Nelson Tests of Mental Ability* may be purchased in either consumable or reusable test booklets, and may be used with MRC (Measurement Research Center) Answer Cards, IBM 805 Answer Sheets, IBM 1230 Answer Sheets, and Digitek Answer Sheets; and any of these particular answer sheets may be hand-scored if one has the appropriate scoring keys.

9. Need for special equipment. Individual intelligence tests almost always require a special kit of equipment. Some instruments, such as the Rorschach inkblots or the *Twitchell–Allen Three-Dimensional Personality Test*, may require separate books for efficient interpretation.

10. Prices, instructions for ordering, etc.

In short, the catalog is the publication on which a publisher relies to make people aware of the products and services he has for sale. The test publisher has an obligation to describe them briefly and accurately. The publisher has no obligation to give an extended and detailed description of the test and how it can be used, for this material belongs in the manual.

## Test Publishers

Test publishers, as I have noted in other writings, are unique people: they must adhere to professional ethics while competing actively in the world of business. With more than one million tests being used each school day in American schools alone, testing is big business! The desirability of test publishing as a commercial investment is shown by the eagerness with which industrial giants have been getting involved during recent years.

Houghton Mifflin Company, which publishes the *Stanford–Binet*, has been engaged in test publishing since 1916, but is best known, of course, as a major book publishing house. Of the largest test publishers, only two (The Psychological Corporation* and the Educational Testing Service) retain independent indentities as test publishers. The World Book Company has become the Test Division of Harcourt, Brace & World, a major book publishing firm. McGraw-Hill Book Company, another large book publisher, now has the California Test Bureau as its wholly owned subsidiary. Science Research Associates is now a subsidiary of IBM. Several smaller publishers have followed the trend.

But, as competitive as test publishing is, the publishers are expected to adhere to a code of professional ethics. And most publishers do. They are expected, for example, to accept orders only from qualified purchasers. No law restricts the sale of the *Thematic Apperception Test* or the *Welsh Figure Preference Test*, but the publishers will sell them only to qualified professionals. The integrity of all tests depends on the integrity of the men who publish and sell them. And most publishers prove worthy of the trust.

Not only does the reputable publisher sell only to qualified persons, but he will even recommend the products of another publisher when appropriate. One publisher, the Educational Testing Service, has even listed the names and addresses of its chief competitors in some of its catalogs.

Several of the test publishers issue service publications free of charge. The *Test Service Bulletins* of The Psychological Corporation are certainly the best known, and they are of excellent quality. Similar publications are issued periodically by both Houghton Mifflin and Harcourt, Brace & World. The Educational Testing Service produces several serial publications (e.g., *ETS Developments*) and has a number of excellent pamphlets on testing which are available free of charge. The California Test Bureau publications tend to be oriented somewhat more to the use of their own tests than are the free service publications of other houses; however, they do have an excellent glossary of measurements terms. To the best of my knowledge, Science Research Associates has no free publications of a service nature.

## Manuals and the Like

Once upon a time . . . there was a day when the test publisher issued a manual—and that was that! The manual was a tiny leaflet which included some directions for administering and scoring the test, together with a set of norms. And that single set of norms might be based on just one or two hundred people—with no real clue given as to whom they might be.

But those days are gone forever. Test publishers are sophisticated enough

---

*In 1970, the number was reduced to one, as The Psychological Corporation became a wholly owned subsidiary of Harcourt, Brace & World, Inc.

to know that a good test manual should contain a great deal more information. Further—and more important—test *users* realize that more information is needed.

Progress certainly has been made, but not without bringing problems of its own. There are complete manuals (ETS now calls theirs *handbooks*), manuals for administration and scoring, manuals for interpretation, technical manuals and supplements, and so on.

Years ago, the leaflet-manual was included free of charge with each package of twenty-five test booklets. The complete manuals of today may run to more than one hundred pages—and are no longer giveaway items.

The good manual is likely to be an impressive booklet full of tables, statistical formulas, and technical data. It's so imposing, in fact, that it can alarm the casual user. Thus, the paradox: the better a publisher succeeds in preparing a manual that is reasonably complete, the more overwhelming some testers will find it.

The good manual should include at least the following in addition to full identification of the test and its authors:

1. rationale: what the test is all about
2. description of the test
3. purposes for which the test seems appropriate
4. development of test, including items
5. directions for administration
6. directions for scoring
7. reliability data
8. validity data
9. norms tables
10. interpretation of the test
11. profiles
12. bibliography.

In some tests, there is need for additional sorts of information. The achievement test may require an explanation of the items, and perhaps item analysis data. The aptitude battery may require information about the intercorrelation of the several tests in the battery. The test which is available in alternate forms requires evidence that the forms yield similar results. *Et cetera.*

With so much information needed about any test that is published for widespread use, there are always many people involved in the development and standardization of the test from its original planning and item-writing to the eventual establishment of norms and suggestions for interpretation; however, most tests still are identified with the individual(s) most responsible. I like to see test authors clearly identified, but there have been several recent tests for which it has not been possible to tell who is responsible.

## 1. RATIONALE

Most good test manuals contain a statement of the orientation of the test author. What is the author trying to accomplish? What does he have in mind?

Some tests have little need for any detailed statement. One sentence may be enough: "The *Wesman Personnel Classification Test* (*PCT*) measures the two most generally useful aspects of mental ability—verbal reasoning and numerical ability," according to The Psychological Corporation's 1965 manual for the *PCT*. On the other hand, the same publisher devotes seven pages to "The Rationale of the Children's Scale" in its manual for the *Wechsler Intelligence Scale for Children* (1949 and later); even then, it is noted that further details on David Wechsler's views on the nature of intelligence are found in Wechsler's *The Measurement and Appraisal of Adult Intelligence* (Baltimore: Williams and Wilkins, 4th ed., 1958).

Another example: Science Research Associates, in 1968, introduced the *Vocational Planning Inventory*. Because it has several features that differentiate it from other tests, the publishers devote three pages to explaining what it is all about:

> While much attention has been focused on the guidance needs of students headed for college and professional careers, considerably less in the way of guidance services has been afforded students enrolled in vocation curricula. Yet the guidance needs of vocationally oriented students may be even more pressing.... The *Vocational Planning Inventory* (*VPI*) has been developed expressly to meet this need for expanded and more effective guidance services for vocationally oriented high school and post-high school students and for young adults seeking to continue their training in vocational areas.... The *Vocational Planning Inventory* is a comprehensive testing program that yields individual predictions of success in the major vocational curriculum areas....
>
> There are two *VPI* programs, each predicting future performance in course work over a different period of time.... Answer sheets for both programs are scored at the Measurement Research Center in Iowa City, Iowa.

> \*         \*         \*

> [The *VPI* includes not only aptitude and achievement variables, but] the measurement of values as well ... and ... the report results in the form of predicted grades for various areas of study. Thus the complex and involved step of weaving separate test scores into an overall pattern that tells about the

[3] *Program Manual, Vocational Planning Inventory* (Chicago: Science Research Associates, A Subsidiary of IBM, 1968.)

individual's future performance has already been accomplished in the reports that are provided . . . .

If the test differs in major ways from other tests, the author and publisher need to explain what is new and different. If the test is for a familiar and common use (such as in the selection of clerical employees), there may be less need for an extensive statement.

### 2. DESCRIPTION OF TESTS

Here, too, the amount of detail needed depends on a variety of factors such as familiarity or novelty of the variables, number of variables reported, etc. For example, Allen L. Edwards, in the introductory edition of the manual for his *Edwards Personality Inventory* (Science Research Associates, 1967) needs four full pages to describe the fifty-three personality variables for which the full *EPI* is scored.

On typical-performance tests, the descriptions usually are brief paragraphs explaining what each particular variable means. With maximum-performance tests there usually is less likelihood of misunderstanding the nature of the test variables.

Obviously there is less need for detailed descriptions of the test variables if there has been an extensive treatment of the rationale, or, perhaps, the interpretation of scores.

In the description of an achievement battery, the test publisher should include a content analysis—i.e., a detailed statement of the number of items which get at each subtopic. We have reproduced here one part of such a table.

**Table 5.1***

*Part Two: Classification of Punctuation–Capitalization Items*

| PUNCTUATION–CAPITALIZATION TOPIC | FORM 23A | FORM 23B | NO. OF ITEMS | |
|---|---|---|---|---|
| | | | 23A | 23B |
| 1.  CAPITAL LETTER | | | 13 | 10 |
| A.  First word of sentence | 1, 2 | 1 | | |
| B.  Proper name | 2, 3, 5, 8 | 2, 3, 5, 6 | | |
| C.  First person "I" | 3, 4 | 4 | | |
| D.  In letters | 10, 11 | 9, 10 | | |
| E.  Title of publication | 14 | 14 | | |
| F.  In verse | 15 | 15 | | |
| G.  In quotations | 17 | | | |

*Adapted from Table 13, HANDBOOK, COOPERATIVE PRIMARY TESTS. (Princeton, N.J.: Educational Testing Service, 1967), p. 24.

Sometimes publishers include even more detailed information about the items. Consider, for example, the following extract adapted from a table describing the *Comprehensive Tests of Basic Skills*.

**Table 5.2**

*Process/Content Chart*
*Test 1 · Reading Vocabulary*
*Test 2 · Reading Comprehension*
*CTBS, Level 4, Form Q\**

| CONTENT<br><br>PROCESS | WORDS IN CONTEXT | WORDS AND SEN-TENCES | ARTICLES (RULES, ADS) | STORIES | LETTERS | POEMS | TOTAL | LINGUISTIC |
|---|---|---|---|---|---|---|---|---|
| A-1<br>Vocabulary<br>(Test 1 only) | 1–40 | | | | | | 40 | |
| B-5<br>Paraphrasing | | 21–23 | 7, 11, 12, 37 | | 19 | 30, 31, 33 | 11 | 12, 21–23, 30, 31, 33, 37 |
| C-6<br>Main Idea | | | 8, 9, 14, 34, 40 | 45 | 15 | 28 | 8 | |

\*TEST COORDINATOR'S HANDBOOK, COMPREHENSIVE TESTS OF BASIC SKILLS, *Preliminary Ed., (Monterey, Calif.: California Test Bureau, A Division of McGraw-Hill Book Company, 1968).*

### 3. PURPOSES OF THE TEST

Here again, how much needs to be said about the purposes for which the test may be used depends on the test, and on how much of the information has been stated elsewhere in the manual. Regardless of how the information is labeled, the manual should contain somewhere a clear statement of the purposes the publisher believes that the test will serve.

### 4. DEVELOPMENT OF THE TEST

Test publishers vary widely in the attention they give to explaining the research underlying the test. Some are most admirable; some, very deficient.

The manual may show why the author has selected the particular variables he has for the test, e.g.:

> Identification of skills necessary for the reading process was accomplished by a survey of over 200 factorial, experimental, and survey-type studies published in various professional journals and related types of communications.

The list of subtests in *SDRT* represents the authors' judgments as to what these studies reveal about reading in Grades 2–8.[4]

The authors continue by explaining how they developed and tried out items on their own students. The HBW editorial staff refined the items further. About 15,000 pupils took one of three preliminary forms of the test, and item analysis data were obtained. The authors state the exact procedures followed, so that it is possible for the informed reader to decide whether the developmental procedure is reasonable. Most of the better-known achievement batteries have manuals containing comprehensive and detailed statements of development. Usually their publishers are extremely careful in describing the research evidence that makes the current edition comparable to previous editions. Also, they usually give full details about the comparability of any available alternate forms.

Regardless of the type of test, the user has a right to expect some details of the research involved in its development. This is especially true whenever there is little evidence of criterion-related validity.

### 5. DIRECTIONS FOR ADMINISTRATION

Some publishers are careless about the directions for administration. They've been in testing for so long that they forget that there are always newcomers to testing. You and the test publisher and I may know that we need to plan ahead of time whenever we're giving a test—plan to make certain that we have all of the necessary materials, that we have reserved the right room for the right time, that all clearances have been made with school or plant officials, that all examinees know where they are to be, and when, and for what purpose, etc.

*We* may know, but there are newcomers who need to be told. The thoughtful publisher remembers them and includes a section which may be labeled "Preparing for the Test" or "General Directions." The following points are adapted from the *Manual for Administering and Interpreting the Stanford Diagnostic Reading Test*:

1. See that desks are cleared and that there's a sufficient supply of sharpened pencils.
2. Have an extra copy of the test booklet available during the testing.
3. Maintain a natural classroom situation—insofar as this is possible.
4. Keep testing room free from disturbances. Perhaps use a "Testing—Do Not Disturb" sign.
5. Make sure that all examinees understand what they have to do, but do not give help on specific items.

[4] *Manual for Administering and Interpreting the Stanford Diagnostic Reading Test* (New York: Harcourt, Brace & World, Inc., 1966).

6. After a test has been started, the examiner should move quietly around the room—assuring himself that everyone is following the directions.

7. The examiner must adhere rigidly to all time limits.

8. The examiner must see that examinees work on the test they're supposed to, not on some previous or subsequent part.

9. Examinees must be prevented from helping each other, knowingly or not.

Similar general instructions for test administration will also be found in manuals for individual tests; but the emphasis there characteristically is on the need for establishing and maintaining *rapport* (a good testing relationship with the examinee), details of test administration, and the like. For example, more than twenty pages of *The Stanford–Binet Intelligence Scale*[5] (the official title of the *Stanford–Binet* manual) contain general directions for administering the test; and many more, of course, are needed for the *specific* directions. Such topics as these are covered: importance of adhering to the standard procedure, general principles, importance of rapport, testing pre-school children, appraisal of responses, testing environment, manipulating the testing material, maintaining standard conditions, the use of abbreviated tests, the use of alternative items, computing the mental age, and finding the IQ.

Most publishers today realize the importance of giving very detailed *specific* directions for administering a test. Of course, there is still need for the examiner to read the directions carefully in advance of the testing sessions. I think that a new examiner (i.e., one who has seldom given tests in the past and who has never given this particular test) should read the directions at least twice beforehand: (1) to see whether he completely understands the directions; and (2) to familiarize himself with the directions.

There are now so many different ways of scoring tests that there may be (as we noted earlier) several different types of answer sheet on which the test may be taken. When options exist, the examiner needs to note carefully whether there are different directions to be followed for each type of answer sheet. There should be—and the differences may be more important than mere differences in how to make marks on the answer sheets.

If, for example, any parts of a test are timed, it may make a considerable difference which answer sheet is used; this is most true whenever the test is genuinely speeded (i.e., long enough so that a substantial number of the examinees will not finish) or whenever the examinees are not accustomed to taking tests. If there are truly no differences in results, the manual should cite the experimental results to justify the inter-changeable answer sheets.

Gladys Gorne is tested with the *Differential Aptitude Tests* in the fall semester of the eighth grade. Her raw score on the *Clerical Speed and Accuracy Test* is 50.

[5] (Boston: Houghton Mifflin Company, 1960.)

The Psychological Corporation, publisher of the *DAT*, has realized how much more quickly examinees can respond on some types of answer sheets, and has thoughtfully provided us with different norms for this test. Gladys's percentile rank? See below:

| Type of answer sheet: | IBM 805 | DIGITEK | IBM 1230 | MRC |
|---|---|---|---|---|
| Her percentile rank is: | 50 | 70 | 80 | 85 |

(*Source of information:* MANUAL FOR THE DIFFERENTIAL APTITUDE TESTS, *4th ed. The Psychological Corporation, 1966. See also Table 5.7*)

Although it is difficult to generalize about the most desirable indication of the statement of directions for administration, they must be sufficiently clear for both examiner and examinees to understand without difficulty.

## 6. DIRECTIONS FOR SCORING

If there are different types of answer sheet which may be used, the manual must explain the procedure for handling each one. As noted above, it is sometimes possible to hand-score tests even when machine-scorable answer sheets have been used. The manual should explain this, too.

Because of the increasing usage of commercial scoring services, the manual should indicate the availability of such scoring services—and should indicate, whenever applicable, the procedures to follow in preparing and shipping answer sheets to such service centers.

There are now several tests that can be scored only by the publisher because of the empirically developed computer programs involved.

## 7. RELIABILITY DATA

As I noted in Chapter Three, reliability is a complex topic. No manual can dismiss the topic (as some have tried to do in the past) by some such statement as: "The reliability of the test is 0.89." The good manual considers the following questions (and many others): What type of reliability? What sort of group? Why are these estimates of reliability appropriate?

The current edition of the manual for the *Differential Aptitude Tests* spends a full chapter of eight pages on the discussion of reliability. The authors have computed reliability coefficients separately by sex and by grade for each form and for each of the tests in the battery. There are split-half coefficients, test-retest coefficients, and alternate-form coefficients. In addition, there are standard errors of measurement for each sex and each grade for each of the tests. Even though their treatment of reliability is not completely exhaustive, it stands as one of the best that I have ever seen in any manual.

## 8. VALIDITY DATA

When the test is a simple, job-oriented aptitude test, the statement of validity can be fairly straightforward. The manual can state criterion-related validity coefficients, both predictive and concurrent, for various groups. These, when well and appropriately accomplished, may be sufficient for such tests.

With other tests, there is greater need for more consideration of validity data. Let's take a look at the common achievement battery. There is no good criterion; the standardized tests should do a better job than the informal, teacher-made tests; and there is little likelihood that the standardized tests will be designed to parallel exactly the teacher-made tests, anyway. Part of the validity data may be correlation coefficients between the achievement tests and corresponding course achievement, but more is needed.

With achievement tests, publishers tend to lean heavily on evidence of content validity, i.e., evidence of agreement between content of test items and content of courses and textbooks. We saw an example of such evidence of content validity in Tables 5.1 and 5.2. In the *Cooperative Primary Tests*, the Educational Testing Service includes information about the percentage of children in the norms groups selecting each alternative of each item. In this way, we may study the percentage of pupils at each grade placement which answered the item correctly. For example, the manual shows the following percentages for Item 24 (an approximation item) on the Mathematics test, Form 23A: Spring of Grade 2, 48 percent; Fall of Grade 3, 54 percent; Spring of Grade 3, 70 percent. Similar evidence is sometimes cited for intelligence tests. Items for the *Stanford–Binet Scales of Intelligence* have been selected partly on the basis of their ability to discriminate among children of different ages although the 1960 *Stanford–Binet* manual presents such data for only a small sampling of items.

Another evidence of validity that is found in many manuals takes the form of correlations with other tests. This sort of evidence, although rarely sufficient, often is valuable supplementary evidence. After all, if the *only* evidence of validity is that the test relates to some other test, what are we to infer? Is the other test sufficiently valid that we may accept it immediately? Then, why not use that other test?

Correlations with other tests, as used with the *Differential Aptitude Tests*, can be of great help in deciding whether another test is sufficiently different to justify our using both of them, or whether it would be sufficient, perhaps, to use just one. Such correlations are also helpful in determining the exact nature of the test variable. The fourth edition of the manual for the *DAT* contains eight pages of correlations with other tests.

> To be maximally informative, of course, these other-test correlation coefficients must include the tests of various publishers, not just one's own. Despite this fact, one major publisher avoids mention of any tests of other publishers with the same vigor once employed by oleomargarine manufacturers in avoiding the use of the word *butter* in their commercials!

Construct validity data, of course, may take almost any form. Inasmuch as personality and intelligence tests do not adapt well to criterion-related validity, evidence must usually be sought through construct validity. What group differences should be obtained if the test has good validity? What other variables can give evidence of the test's validity?

The manual for the seventh edition of the *Kuhlmann–Anderson Test* shows how evidence accumulated from previous editions is made applicable to the current edition:

> Evidence has been presented for the Sixth Edition *Kuhlmann-Anderson* Tests to show the performance of groups of pupils differing by small, successive increments of chronological age (*Kuhlmann-Anderson Intelligence Tests*, Sixth Edition, *Master Manual*, 1952, pp. 24–25). It has also been shown that the Sixth Edition tests discriminate significantly between average and retarded or accelerated pupil groups, not only over a wide grade range, but also within each grade from the first to the twelfth (pp. 15–16, same reference).
>
> Among the other validity evidence reported for the Sixth Edition in the *Master Manual* were results of one comprehensive study . . . (omission of 6 lines and three studies) . . .
>
> The validity of the Sixth Edition tests was built in the Seventh Edition tests. As explained in another section of this manual, the contents of the trial form of the Seventh Edition K, A, B, and CD booklets (different grade levels of the test) were subjected to item analyses, using the pupils' MA on the Sixth Edition as the criterion. Each item was rejected or retained on the basis of how well it discriminated between the top and bottom 27 percents of the item-analysis group . . . [6]

Differences between age groups, grade groups, and the like are commonly used as evidence of validity of tests for school use. Similar reasoning can be used with occupational groups, as has been done by The Psychological Corporation with the *Wesman Personnel Classification Test*. The logic is that if the test possesses high validity, there should be reasonable order

---

[6] TECHNICAL MANUAL, KUHLMANN-ANDERSON TEST, *7th ed.* (*Princeton, New Jersey: Personnel Press, Inc., A Division of Ginn and Company, 1963*), *p. 15.*

to the means for the various occupations. The following data suggest that the *PCT* may have validity for use in personnel selection:

**Table 5.3\***

| OCCUPATIONAL GROUP | MEAN SCORE | | |
|---|---|---|---|
| | VERBAL | NUMERICAL | TOTAL |
| Chain-store clerks | 12.0 | 6.4 | 18.4 |
| Production workers | 17.1 | 8.2 | 25.3 |
| Female clerical employees | 23.0 | 8.9 | 31.9 |
| U.S. Air Force Captains | 23.9 | 11.2 | 35.2 |
| Executive trainee applicants | 27.1 | 14.5 | 41.6 |
| Technical sales applicants | 29.4 | 14.7 | 44.1 |

*Data extracted from Table 3, WESMAN PERSONNEL CLASSIFICATION TEST MANUAL. The Psychological Corporation (1965). The original table lists twenty-four different occupational groups, together with the number of cases involved in each and the standard deviation for each.*

Validity is the most important attribute of a test. The manual must cite appropriate evidence that the test possesses some sort of validity. It is the test user's responsibility to evaluate the evidence that is presented—and to evaluate it in view of the use which he wishes to make of the test. Remember: a test may have high validity for one purpose, but have little or no validity for some other purpose.

## 9. NORMS AND NORMS TABLES

Norms are vital to an understanding of test results, for they provide us with the standards against which to compare test performance. Most test manuals contain several sets of norms, and it is important for the reader to select the set that is most appropriate for his use. As we shall see, an individual's score may show him either as doing well or as doing poorly—depending on the group with which he is compared. Mitzi may have made the lowest score of all the fifth graders in her Executive Heights School, but the same score might have placed her in the highest quarter of her class if she had been attending the Bottoms District School or the Podunk Junction School. Still, it is a sad—but inescapable—fact that about one-half of any group is below average. The very definition of *average* demands it. The average for any group demands that there be values below as well as above it.

**The Norm**

The simplest statement of norms is given by *the norm*. This is nothing more than the average (either mean or median) score for some specified group. Norm, in fact, is used occasionally as a synonym for average.

A norm is also used sometimes in place of more complete norms if the available scores are inadequate, inappropriate, or suspect for some reason. On a new test, for example, scores may be available on very few people. In such instances, it may be better to describe a person's performance merely as being above or below the norm for those tested to date.

A third general use for the norm is found in situations where the test publisher wishes to report averages for a number of groups (as we did, above, for the *Wesman PCT*) or the averages of a single group on several tests. Research workers make similar use of the norm in summarizing results and in showing trends for several groups.

A *set of norms* for a test consists of a table giving corresponding values of raw scores and derived scores. Derived scores are intended to make test interpretation easier and more meaningful than is possible with raw scores alone.

Norms are frequently designated according to the type of score involved; we may, for example, read of percentile norms, grade-equivalent norms, etc. Because of the large number of different types of derived score in common use, we are devoting one entire chapter (Chapter Six) to discussing them.

### Norms Tables

A good norms table should include a derived-score equivalent for each raw score that can be made. It should include a full description of the group on which it is based. It may present one or several types of derived score for one or several groups for one or more tests.

When a norms table is incomplete, it may be confusing to the test user.

> I once gave a wide variety of tests to a coed of unusually high ability. One of many tests on which she excelled was a test, still in its experimental form, which I had never given before. I scored it carefully and found a raw score of 34. The maximum possible score seemed to be 36, but the single norms table went up only to 27. I spent several frustrating hours in reviewing the scoring instructions and all related information. Finally, months later, I questioned the test's author. His reply? "I thought that 27 was high enough. Almost no one gets a score as high as that."

*Simple Norms Tables.* The simplest norms tables consist of two columns, one containing raw-score values and the other containing corresponding derived-score values. Table 5.4 illustrates such a table with hypothetical results presumed to be based on a national sample of laboratory technicians. Note that the group is described in some detail. The test manual should list the laboratories which contributed data (or should note that the list is available on request). In this example, we might still ask questions about the educational background and work experience of the examinees, for these factors could influence our interpretation. Of course, if we wanted to use the *TAPT* for any individual decisions, we would need to have a much longer test.

**Table 5.4**

*Example of Simple Norms Table (Percentile Norms for the Hypothetical Technician's Aptitude and Proficiency Test)\**

| RAW SCORE | PERCENTILE | RAW SCORE | PERCENTILE | RAW SCORE | PERCENTILE | RAW SCORE | PERCENTILE |
|---|---|---|---|---|---|---|---|
| 11 | 98 | 8 | 75 | 5 | 34 | 2 | 10 |
| 10 | 96 | 7 | 62 | 4 | 23 | 1 | 4 |
| 9 | 85 | 6 | 48 | 3 | 18 | 0 | 1 |

*\*Hypothetical data. Presumably based on 6245 laboratory technicians tested during a given year at 450 hospital laboratories and 785 industrial and commercial laboratories in 39 states. (The complete list of participating laboratories should be included in the manual or made available upon request.)*

*Multiple-Group Norms Tables.* Very often a single norms table is constructed to show results from several different groups. Besides the obvious economy in printing, this practice permits the comparison of a person's raw score with as many of these groups as we wish. Table 5.5 illustrates such a table with data drawn from Project TALENT, and is based on a 4 percent random sample of approximately 440,000 high school students tested in 1960 as part of that research study. The test we are concerned with is the *Information Test—Aeronautics and Space*. Here again there are so few items that we must be cautious in interpreting individual scores. The chance passing of one more item or chance failing of one more item would make a great apparent difference in performance.

> Pauline, a ninth-grade girl, had a score of 3; this gives her a percentile rank of 65 when compared with other ninth-grade girls. Pauline knows very little about aeronautics and space, and she might easily have missed one more item; that would have placed her at the fortieth percentile. On the other hand, if she had happened to guess correctly on one or two more items than she did, she would have had a percentile rank of 83 or 93.

With very short tests such as this, reliability is likely to be extremely low especially when the items are so difficult that lucky guesses become important in determining one's score. We should be very careful in making any interpretations of individual test scores here except for students clearly at one extreme or the other.

We can rely on group differences to a far greater extent. Note that there is no level at which girls have done better than boys, nor is there any level at which youngsters in one grade have done better than those in any higher grade. As we have noted before, we often can have confidence in group

**Table 5.5**

Example of Multiple-Group Norms Table (Percentile Norms for the Information Test—Aeronautics and Space, of the Project TALENT Test Battery)*

PERCENTILE SCORE

| RAW SCORE | GRADE 9 | | GRADE 10 | | GRADE 11 | | GRADE 12 | |
|---|---|---|---|---|---|---|---|---|
| | BOY | GIRL | BOY | GIRL | BOY | GIRL | BOY | GIRL |
| 10 | 99+ | 99+ | 99 | 99+ | 99 | 99+ | 98 | 99+ |
| 9 | 97 | 99+ | 96 | 99+ | 96 | 99+ | 92 | 99 |
| 8 | 92 | 99+ | 91 | 99+ | 89 | 99+ | 84 | 99 |
| 7 | 86 | 99 | 83 | 99 | 80 | 99 | 75 | 98 |
| 6 | 78 | 97 | 73 | 96 | 69 | 96 | 63 | 95 |
| 5 | 66 | 93 | 62 | 92 | 55 | 91 | 51 | 89 |
| 4 | 52 | 83 | 47 | 81 | 41 | 79 | 36 | 77 |
| 3 | 36 | 65 | 31 | 62 | 26 | 61 | 22 | 59 |
| 2 | 20 | 40 | 16 | 40 | 14 | 38 | 11 | 38 |
| 1 | 8 | 18 | 6 | 18 | 5 | 16 | 4 | 16 |
| 0 | 2 | 4 | 1 | 4 | 1 | 4 | 1 | 3 |

*Based on a 4 percent random sample of the approximately 440,000 high school students in 50 states tested in 1960 as part of the Project TALENT study directed by John C. Flanagan. Reprinted from PROJECT TALENT COUNSELORS' TECHNICAL MANUAL FOR INTERPRETING TEST SCORES, University of Pittsburgh (1961). (Used with permission.)

differences in test performance even when test reliability is too low to permit much confidence in individual scores.

> Note that a raw score of 4, having a percentile rank of 83 on ninth-grade girls' norms, ranks only 36 on twelfth-grade boys' norms. A twelfth-grade boy would have to answer twice as many items correctly in order to have a percentile rank as high as that given to a ninth-grade girl for a score of 4.

*Multiple-Score Norms Tables.* Sometimes a norms table includes derived scores for each of several tests (or subtests). For obvious reasons this should never be done unless the same norms group is used for each test. Sometimes scaled scores (*see* Chapter Six) are used instead of raw scores, especially when some of the subtests have many more items than do others. An example is Table 5.6, showing stanines for beginning first graders on the *Clymer–Barrett Prereading Battery*. To make full use of this table in a practical situation, we would need to know and understand the nature of stanines, the norms group, etc.

*Abbreviated Norms Tables.* An occasional norms table includes only alternate raw-score values (or, perhaps, every fifth raw-score value), thereby forcing the test user to interpolate whenever he has a non-tabled raw score. Such a table saves money in printing, but it encourages mistakes and costs the test user additional time and trouble. Abbreviated tables used to be common, but are becoming increasingly rare.

*Condensed Norms Tables.* Very similar to the abbreviated table is the condensed table, where selected percentile (or other) values are given, and the corresponding raw scores shown. This style of table is still used, especial-

**Table 5.6**

*Example of a Multiple-Score Norms Table*
*(Stanine Equivalents of Part Scores*
Clymer–Barrett Prereading Battery, *Form A)\**

| STANINE | VISUAL DISCRIMINATION | AUDITORY DISCRIMINATION | VISUAL MOTOR |
|---|---|---|---|
| 9 | 54–55 | 39–40 | 25–27 |
| 8 | 52–53 | 37–38 | 23–24 |
| 7 | 47–51 | 35–36 | 20–22 |
| 6 | 39–46 | 32–34 | 17–19 |
| 5 | 32–38 | 28–31 | 14–16 |
| 4 | 25–31 | 23–27 | 11–13 |
| 3 | 17–24 | 18–22 | 8–10 |
| 2 | 10–16 | 12–17 | 4–7 |
| 1 | 0–9 | 0–11 | 0–3 |

*\*Based on 5565 public school pupils, all tested in approximately the third week of their first-grade attendance. (Data from Table 10, CLYMER–BARRETT PREREADING BATTERY DIRECTIONS MANUAL. Princeton, N.J.: Personnel Press, Inc., A Division of Ginn and Company, 1968), p. 32.*

ly when the publisher wishes to present a large amount of data in a single table for comparison purposes. Table 5.7 shows a condensed multiple-score norms table illustrating the effect of using different styles of responding to a highly speeded test.

**Table 5.7**

*Example of a Condensed Multiple-Score Norms Table*
National Norms for the Differential Aptitude Test of Clerical Speed
and Accuracy *According to Type of Answer Sheet Used in Fall
and Spring Testing of Eighth-Grade Boys*\*

| PERCENTILE RANK | MRC | | IBM 1230 | | DIGITEK | | PERCENTILE RANK |
|---|---|---|---|---|---|---|---|
| | FALL | SPRING | FALL | SPRING | FALL | SPRING | |
| 99 | 58–100 | 60–100 | 60–100 | 62–100 | 67–100 | 69–100 | 99 |
| 97 | 54–57 | 55–59 | 54–59 | 55–61 | 61–66 | 62–68 | 97 |
| 95 | 49–53 | 50–54 | 50–53 | 52–54 | 55–60 | 57–61 | 95 |
| 90 | 46–48 | 47–49 | 48–49 | 49–51 | 52–54 | 54–56 | 90 |
| 85 | 44–45 | 45–46 | 46–47 | 47–48 | 50–51 | 51–53 | 85 |
| 80 | 43 | 44 | 44–45 | 45–46 | 48–49 | 49–50 | 80 |
| 75 | 42 | 43 | 43 | 44 | 47 | 48 | 75 |
| 70 | 40–41 | 41–42 | 41–42 | 42–43 | 45–46 | 46–47 | 70 |
| 65 | 39 | 40 | 40 | 41 | 43–44 | 45 | 65 |
| 60 | 38 | 39 | 39 | 40 | 42 | 43–44 | 60 |
| 55 | 37 | 38 | 38 | 39 | 41 | 42 | 55 |
| 50 | 36 | 37 | 37 | 38 | 40 | 41 | 50 |
| 45 | 35 | 36 | 36 | 37 | 39 | 40 | 45 |
| 40 | 34 | 35 | 35 | 36 | 38 | 39 | 40 |
| 35 | 32–33 | 33–34 | 34 | 35 | 36–37 | 37–38 | 35 |
| 30 | 31 | 32 | 33 | 34 | 34–35 | 35–36 | 30 |
| 25 | 29–30 | 30–31 | 31–32 | 32–33 | 32–33 | 33–34 | 25 |
| 20 | 28 | 29 | 30 | 31 | 31 | 32 | 20 |
| 15 | 26–27 | 27–28 | 28–29 | 29–30 | 29–30 | 30–31 | 15 |
| 10 | 23–25 | 24–26 | 24–27 | 25–28 | 25–28 | 26–29 | 10 |
| 5 | 19–22 | 20–23 | 19–23 | 20–24 | 20–24 | 21–25 | 5 |
| 3 | 13–18 | 13–19 | 10–18 | 12–19 | 12–19 | 13–20 | 3 |
| 1 | 0–12 | 0–12 | 0–9 | 0–11 | 0–11 | 0–12 | 1 |

\**Adapted from* FOURTH EDITION MANUAL FOR THE DIFFERENTIAL APTITUDE TESTS, *The Psychological Corporation (1966). (Used with permission.)*

### Expectancy Tables and Charts

At this point we need to mention expectancy tables and charts once again (*see* pages 57–62 for a more complete discussion). They differ from norms tables in one important characteristic: whereas norms tables state derived-score values corresponding to each raw score, expectancy tables show criterion performance for each interval of raw scores. In all other respects, expectancy tables are the same as norms tables. We might re-emphasize here that expectancy tables, like norms tables, state the results found for some specified group. When interpreting anyone's score through the use of either an expectancy table or a norms table, we must consider whether the group and the situation are comparable.

### Articulation of Norms

A specified test may vary in edition, form, level, or any combination of these. *Edition* refers usually to date of publication (1970 edition, etc.). Different editions may be needed to keep test content up to date. *Form* refers usually to an equivalent version; that is, different forms will contain different items, but will be similar in content and difficulty. Different forms may be needed to insure test security; i.e., to minimize the likelihood of test items leaking out to examinees. Different form designations may also be given when item content is identical, but scoring method is different; for example, Form AH may be designed for hand-scoring and Form AM for machine-scoring.

*Level* refers usually to the age or grade placement of those for whom a specified version of the test is intended. Different levels may be needed to make subject content and item difficulty appropriate for the examinees; from three to eight levels sometimes are used to cover the range of school grades.

Some excellent tests exist in only a single edition, form, and level. The need for multiple versions of a test becomes greater as the test is used more widely. Thus, the need is greatest, especially for different levels, with tests designed for wide-scale administration throughout whole school systems.

New editions are intended, with few exceptions, to replace and to improve upon earlier editions. There may or may not be a desire to make results from two editions *directly* comparable. Nearly always, however, it is important to make different forms and levels yield somewhat comparable results; the aim is to achieve articulated (neatly jointed) norms. All major publishers of tests for schools are aware of this need for articulation and all take steps toward insuring comparability. The exact procedures followed differ, and some publishers are more successful than others.

Those who use tests should check the manual carefully for evidence of articulation studies to see how comparable are the test scores from different forms and levels. This information may be found under such headings as Articulation, Interlocking Studies, Overlapping Norms, and the like. It is more difficult to obtain reliable information about the comparability of scores from the tests of different publishers, and this will continue to be true until publishers can agree upon a single large nationally representative sample which may be used as a common reference group. Eventually this need for anchoring norms may be supplied by data from Project TALENT (directed by John C. Flanagan, of the American Institutes for Research).

I cannot emphasize too much the tremendous importance of the norms group. Regardless of the type of norms, we are dealing with results that are based on some group of people. But it makes a great deal of difference *which* group of people. Consider the hypothetical example of Alan Alfred.

> Alan Alfred, a graduate assistant in philosophy at Athol University, answered 210 words correctly on the hypothetical *Valentine Vocabulary Test* of 300 items. His raw score of 210 on the *VVT* means that he did as well as or better than:
>
> 99 percent of the seventh-grade pupils in Athol
> 92 percent of the Athol High School seniors
> 91 percent of the high school graduates in Marshall, Ohio
> 85 percent of the entering freshmen at Beverly Junior College
> 70 percent of the philosophy majors at Athol University
> 55 percent of the graduating seniors at Athol University
> 40 percent of the graduate assistants at Athol University
> 15 percent of the English professors at Athol University
>
> Although Alan's absolute performance (210 words defined correctly) remains unchanged, our impression of how well he has done may differ markedly as we change norms groups.

This illustration is extreme. Under no normal circumstances would we compare a graduate assistant's score with those of seventh-grade pupils; however, results every bit as far-fetched as these can be obtained in real-life situations—and results nearly as far-fetched often do occur.

Even professional measurements people occasionally are fooled by differences in norms groups, as in the following situation:

> Two tests (scholastic aptitude and reading comprehension) put out by the same highly reputable publisher often were used together in college admissions batteries. At most colleges students tended to stand relatively higher on the scholastic aptitude test than on the reading comprehension test. The norms most commonly used were the national norms prepared by the publisher and based on thousands of cases from colleges in all sections of the country. The norms could be trusted. Or could they?
>
> The norms should not have been accepted so readily as they were, because more select colleges [i.e., colleges with higher admissions standards] unintentionally had been used in establishing the reading test norms. The net result was that most students who took both tests seemed to do more poorly in reading comprehension than in scholastic aptitude.
>
> Before this difference in norms groups was generally recognized, interoffice memoranda were exchanged at many colleges—asking why their students were so deficient in reading ability!

The same sort of difficulty is encountered frequently in school testing, especially when we use tests from different publishers, as in the following hypothetical example:

> Acme Test Company has used a sample of 5000 students from forty schools in twenty-four states in standardizing its *Acme Achievement Battery* (*AAB*) for the fourth, fifth, and sixth grades. Several select schools were included, but no below-average ones. Better Tests, Inc., used about 4500 students from thirty-five schools in twenty states in standardizing its *Better Achievement Battery* (*BAB*) for the same grades; however, their researchers were more careful in the selection of schools and obtained a more representative national sample of these grades.
>
> Let us assume that both batteries were very carefully developed and that they are very similar in content and in item difficulty. Pupils still will tend to receive lower scores on the *AAB* than on the *BAB*.

The following situation shows what may happen in real-life school settings where different achievement batteries are used at different grade levels.

> Wally Winchester's pupils are tested on the *AAB* at the end of the fifth grade; their mean grade-placement score is 5.4 (which is about one-half grade below the expected norm for his class). The same pupils had taken the *BAB* at the end of the fourth grade and had earned a mean grade-placement score of 5.0 (very slightly above the norm at that time). It looks as if Mr. Winchester has not taught much to his class, especially when these pupils take the *BAB* again at the end of their sixth grade and obtain a mean grade-placement score of 7.1 (once again slightly above the norm for their actual grade placement).
>
> Mr. Winchester is a victim of circumstances. If his pupils had taken the *AAB* at the end of the fourth grade and the *BAB* at the end of the fifth grade, they would have shown great apparent improvement during their year with him.

This same sort of situation occurs in industrial settings where test-naïve personnel workers fail to consider the differences in norms groups from test to test. "After all," they may reason, "Test *Y* and Test *Z* were both standardized on 'mechanical employees'." And such personnel workers may ignore the fact that the "mechanical employees" used for the Test *Y* norms were engineering technicians, whereas those used for Test *Z* were machine wipers and machine-shop porters.

The list of possible mistaken inferences could be extended almost indefinitely. The point we must remember is: be sure to understand the nature of the norms groups. And understand it in as much detail as the publisher will permit through his descriptions.

### Which Norms to Use

Most test manuals include several norms tables. Which should we use? The obvious general answer is that we should use whichever norms are most appropriate for the individual examinee and the situation involved.

We seldom have much difficulty in selecting an appropriate set of norms to use when the test is a maximum-performance test designed for routine school use. With tests not commonly given to all pupils in a school (for example, specific aptitude tests) or tests designed primarily for out-of-school use, our selection is likely to be much more difficult. For a clerical aptitude test, we may have to decide whether an examinee should be compared with 225 female clerk-typists employed by a large insurance company, 456 female applicants for clerical positions with four midwestern companies, or 839 female eleventh-grade students in a secretarial sequence. The same problem exists with many (if not most) tests.

In guidance situations we often decide to use several different norms groups:

> Dottie Divenger has taken an art aptitude test. Her score would place her very high among non-art students and adults, high average among first-year students at an art academy, and low average among employed fashion designers. All of this information may be helpful to Dottie in deciding whether to enter a career in art, whether to attend an art academy, etc.

There are even occasions when we may deliberately employ norms which appear to be unsuitable. In counseling a young lady interested in an occupation in which men predominate, I might compare her scores with male norms as well as female norms. She is, after all, contemplating a career in direct competition with men and she should be compared with them.

### Local Norms

Local norms are sometimes better than national norms. Developing our own norms is not too difficult. We keep a careful record of the test scores made by a defined group (all applicants for some sort of position; all bookkeepers currently employed by our company; all fourth-grade pupils in our school district, etc.) until a satisfactory number has been acquired. We arrange the scores in a frequency distribution and assign appropriate derived scores (*see* Chapter Six).

Circumstances help us to decide whether we should be satisfied with available national norms or whether we should develop our own. In the first place, we have no choice unless we are using the same test on a large number of people. If we use a particular test on only an occasional individual, we will have to depend on national norms because we will not have enough of our own scores to do much good.

If national norms are suitable, we have no problem. We can use them without difficulty if we want to. Yet even when the national norms are not especially appropriate, we may prefer to use them rather than to develop our own—as when it seems that nothing is to be gained by developing our own. On an interest test used for guidance purposes, for example, we may have very little to gain by comparing an individual's score with other local scores.

On the other hand, even though there are adequate national norms, there may be situations in which we would like to be able to compare individuals with other local people. We may be much more interested in knowing how well an applicant compares with other local applicants than in knowing how well he has done when compared with some national normative group.

### Assorted Tests and Integrated Batteries

Tremendous strides have been made in psychological and educational testing during recent years. After all, standardized testing is not very old. Binet and Simon gave us the first acceptable intelligence test as recently as 1905. The first group intelligence test and the first personality inventory appeared during World War I. With the exception of a few standardized achievement test batteries that emerged during the late 1920s and 1930s, almost all tests published prior to World War II were separate tests. By this I mean that each new test was developed independently of every other, and very little effort was made to equate norms groups. Inevitably the test user would find himself with results that looked like these (hypothetical, of course) for Meg Morner:

Percentitle rank of 96 on reading speed; compared with high school students
Percentile rank of 77 on reading comprehension; compared with college freshmen
IQ of 109 on an intelligence test
IQ of 131 on another intelligence test
Standard score of 59 on clerical aptitude; compared with clerks
Score of B+ on mechanical aptitude; female norms.

Under such conditions, even skilled counselors had difficulty making much sense from the results. Because each test had been developed independently by a different author, usually to meet some important need, no one could safely compare the score on one test with the score on another.

The situation has been improving rapidly since World War II. Most major publishers now have at least one multiple-aptitude test battery in which all of the tests have been standardized on the same group, with norms all based on the same group. With integrated batteries such as these, we can now begin to make comparaisons of various scores made by the same person. Has Meg done better on clerical aptitude than on reading comprehension, better on reading speed than on mechanical aptitude? The use of tests in guidance demands answers to such questions, and with integrated test batteries we can begin to find these answers.

There are still many assorted tests that are not part of any integrated test battery. There probably always will be. If we are concerned with selecting people (whether for employment or for training), we want to use the test (or tests) which will do the best job for us; there is no reason for us to consider whether or not a test is part of an integrated battery. An integrated battery of tests is most important in guidance and in differential placement, where the use of the common norms group is valuable in making comparisons of a person's relative ability within the various test areas.

It is impossible to exaggerate the value of a good norms table; the skillful test user must develop competence in studying the data in the manual.

### 10. INTERPRETATION OF THE TEST

Although significant technical improvements have been made in tests, I believe that the increased attention being paid to test interpretation is probably the most important single change in test manuals in the past decade or so. More and more the publishers are recognizing the importance of suggesting how test users can get the most meaning out of their test results.

The Psychological Corporation has an excellent casebook for its *DAT*, *Counseling from Profiles* (published in 1951, however, it is becoming somewhat dated). Not only is the book excellent in showing how that battery may be used in counseling, it is also good in demonstrating how other information (including scores from other tests) fits in. The interpretive folder, part of which is shown in Figure 7.2, is excellent.

The California Test Bureau has some excellent interpretative material, including a separate guide for its *California Test of Mental Maturity*. Science Research Associates has interpretative folders for several of its tests, most notably for the *Kuder* inventories. ETS publishes an interpretive folder for its *School and College Ability Tests* and the *Sequential Tests of Educational Progress.*

Most manuals today have at least a few paragraphs illustrating how meaning can be made from the results of the test; however, it's important to remember that illustrative examples do not establish the validity of a test. Even very poor tests can be right occasionally! The proper role and function of the interpretive material is to suggest ways for using the test— *not* to establish the test's validity.

### 11. PROFILES

The good manual contains a complete description of any profile that may be generated for a multi-score test or test battery. Chapter Seven is devoted to a more complete discussion of profiles than is possible before we have considered the various types of score (the topic of the next chapter).

### 12. BIBLIOGRAPHY

Practices differ in the amount of bibliographic material included in the manuals. In some instances, the list of references is inflated with the inclusion of statistical articles and books consulted in the preparation of validity and reliability studies. There is usually no need for any statistical or general measurements references unless new or unusual procedures have been followed. And yet, only 25 percent of the references in one manual I've recently studied relate in any way to the test itself.

In my opinion, there should be a list of references describing research that has been done with a test. Once again, The Psychological Corporation's *Differential Aptitude Tests* is a good example: 121 references, nearly all of them specific to research with that battery. On the other hand, the same publisher's manual for the *Wechsler Intelligence Scale for Children* has no list of reference (although Buros' *Sixth Mental Measurements Yearbook* shows 288 references that might have been cited by 1965).

### A NOTE OF THANKS

*I am indebted to Dr. Robert Walker, of the Personnel Press, Inc. (a division of Ginn and Company) for the idea of including a chapter on* READING A TEST MANUAL *in this revision of* TEST SCORES AND WHAT THEY MEAN.

*The wealth of illustrative material in this chapter was possible only because of the full cooperation of the following publishers: California Test Bureau (a subsidiary of McGraw-Hill Book Company, Inc.); Consulting Psychologists Press; Educational Testing Service; Harcourt, Brace & World, Inc.; Houghton Mifflin Company; Personnel Press, Inc. (a division of Ginn and Company); The Psychological Corporation; and the Science Research Associates (a subsidiary of IBM).*

*In fairness to these (and other) publishers, I should note that other equally good examples might have been chosen. I had to be highly selective, for they supplied me (gratis) with much excellent material. Many thanks!*

H.B.L.

# DERIVED SCORES

## Chapter Six

We need accurate raw scores so that we can have accurate derived scores. No amount of statistical manipulation can compensate for using a poor test or for mistakes in giving or scoring any test. Nor can the use of derived scores reduce measurement error or increase precision in prediction.

There are two main purposes for using derived scores: (1) to make scores from different tests comparable by expressing them on the same scale, and/or (2) to make possible more meaningful interpretations of scores. We will find that there are many derived scores, each having its own advantages and limitations.

### A Classification Scheme

The following outline is intended for classifying types of derived score used in reporting maximum-performance tests. With minor modifications the outline would be suitable for typical-performance tests as well, but they are not our concern.

The score a person receives on any maximum-performance test depends in part upon his knowledge and skill and upon his motivation while taking the test. These elements play their part in determining a person's score, regardless of how the score is expressed; they are, in fact, the kinds of things we are trying to measure when we give the tests. Beyond these common elements, we shall find three principal bases for expressing test scores: (1) comparison with an "absolute standard," or content difficulty; (2) interindividual comparison, and (3) intra-individual comparison. My classification scheme centers about these three bases and a fourth (assorted) category:

### I. Comparison with "Absolute Standard"; Content Difficulty
   A. Percentage correct scores
   B. Letter grades (sometimes)

In a normal distribution (*see* page 50), Type II A and B scores are inter-related. As shown in Figure 6.1 of Chart 6.1 we can make transformations from one kind of score to another very easily if we assume a normal distri-bution based on the same group of individuals. Under these two assumptions, *normality* and *same group*, the relationships shown in Figure 6.1 will always exist. When different groups are involved, we cannot make direct compari-sons; when the set of scores cannot be assumed to be distributed normally, we find that some of the relationships are changed while others still hold.

> A certain test has been given locally and is found to have a mean of 300 and a standard deviation of 40. When we notice that the distribution of scores seems to resemble closely the normal probability distribution, and we are willing to treat our set of scores as being normal, what can we say about the scores? Let us take a couple of cases and see.
>
> Bob has a raw score of 300. This would give him a $z$-score of 0.00, a $T$-score of 50, a stanine of 5, a percentile rank of 50, etc.
>
> Patricia has a raw score of 320. This would give her a $z$-score of 0.5, a $T$-score of 55, a stanine of 6, a percentile rank of 69, etc.

Figure 6.1 has been drawn with a number of additional baselines. Each of these can be used equally well as the graph's abscissa. To change from one type of score to another, we merely move vertically to another line.

Figure 6.2 of Chart 6.1 shows some of these same types of score in a badly skewed distribution. The sole purpose of this figure is to indicate those scores which change in their relationship to others. Somewhat less detail has been shown here, for this distribution is not subject to generalization as was the distribution in Figure 6.1. Note that $z$- and $T$-scores do not change in their relationship to each other, nor would their relationship to raw scores change. Normalized standard scores and percentiles maintain a constant relationship —but they do not relate to $z$- and $T$-scores (nor to raw scores) in the same manner as in the normal distribution.

### DISCUSSION OF THE CLASSIFICATION SCHEME

*Type I* scores are probably the most familiar, for they are commonly used in reporting the results of classroom tests. These scores are unique in that they consider only the specified individual's performance; the performance of all other examinees is ignored in assigning the score. In a sense Type I scores compare each examinee individually with an absolute standard of perfec-tion (as represented by a perfect score on the test). This absolute-standard reasoning has an attractive appeal at first glance; however, thoughtful testers soon realize that the individual's score may depend more on the difficulty of the tasks presented by the test items than on the individual's ability. Type I scores are not suited for use with standardized tests (although letter grades based on interindividual comparison are sometimes used with such tests).

## II. Interindividual Comparison
  A. Considering mean and standard deviation (linear standard scores)
   1. *z*-scores
   2. *T*-scores
   3. *AGCT*-scores
   4. *CEEB*-scores
   5. Deviation IQs (sometimes)
     (a) Wechsler IQs
     (b) Stanford–Binet IQs
  B. Considering rank within groups
   1. Ranks
   2. Percentile ranks and percentile bands
   3. Letter grades (sometimes)
   4. Normalized standard scores (area transformations)
     (a) *T*-scaled scores
     (b) Stanine scores —▷ Flanagan's Extended Stanine Scores
     (c) *C*-scaled scores
     (d) Sten scores
     (e) Deviation IQs (sometimes)
       (1) Wechsler subtests
     (f) ITED-scores
   5. Decile ranks
  C. Considering the range of scores in a group
   1. Percent placement
  D. Considering status of those obtaining same score
   1. Age scores
     (a) Mental ages
     (b) Educational ages, etc.
   2. Grade-placement scores
     (a) Full-population grade-placement
     (b) Modal-age grade-placement
     (c) Modal-age and modal-intelligence grade-placement
     (d) Anticipated-achievement grade-placement
     (e) Mental-age grade-placement

## III. Intra-Individual Comparison
  A. Ratio IQs
  B. Intellectual Status Index
  C. Educational Quotients
  D. Accomplishment Quotients

## IV. Assorted Arbitrary Bases
  A. Nonmeaningful scaled scores
  B. Long-range equi-unit scales
  C. Deviation IQs (Otis-style)

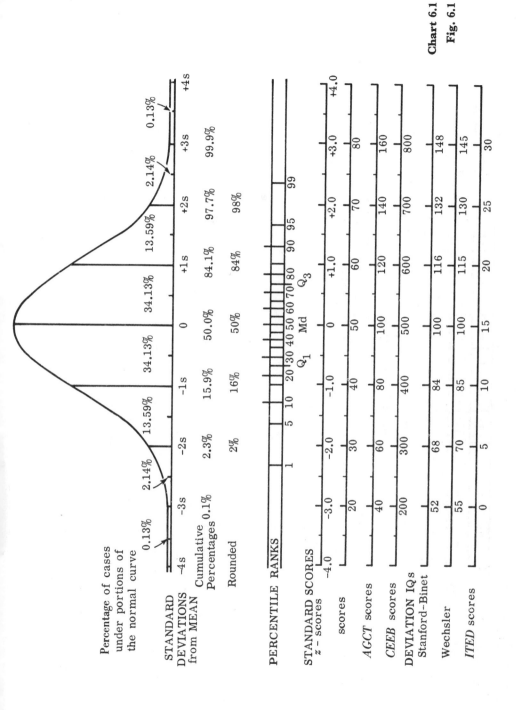

Percentage of cases
under portions of
the normal curve

| | 0.13% | 2.14% | 13.59% | 34.13% | 34.13% | 13.59% | 2.14% | 0.13% |

STANDARD
DEVIATIONS
from MEAN

| -4s | -3s | -2s | -1s | 0 | +1s | +2s | +3s | +4s |

Cumulative
Percentages

| 0.1% | 2.3% | 15.9% | 50.0% | 84.1% | 97.7% | 99.9% |

Rounded

| 2% | 16% | 50% | 84% | 98% |

PERCENTILE RANKS

| 1 | 5 | 10 | 20 30 40 50 60 70 80 | 90 | 95 | 99 |
| | | | Q₁ Md Q₃ | | | |

STANDARD SCORES
z – scores

| -4.0 | -3.0 | -2.0 | -1.0 | 0 | +1.0 | +2.0 | +3.0 | +4.0 |

scores

AGCT scores

| 20 | 30 | 40 | 50 | 60 | 70 | 80 |

| 40 | 60 | 80 | 100 | 120 | 140 | 160 |

CEEB scores

| 200 | 300 | 400 | 500 | 600 | 700 | 800 |

DEVIATION IQs
Stanford–Binet

| 52 | 68 | 84 | 100 | 116 | 132 | 148 |

Wechsler

| 55 | 70 | 85 | 100 | 115 | 130 | 145 |

ITED scores

| 0 | 5 | 10 | 15 | 20 | 25 | 30 |

Chart 6.1

Fig. 6.1

| STANINES | 1 | 2 | 3 | 4 | 5 | 6 | 7 | 8 | 9 | |
|---|---|---|---|---|---|---|---|---|---|---|
| Percent in stanine | 4% | 7% | 12% | 17% | 20% | 17% | 12% | 7% | 4% | |

| C-SCORES | 0 | 1 | 2 | 3 | 4 | 5 | 6 | 7 | 8 | 9 | 10 |
|---|---|---|---|---|---|---|---|---|---|---|---|
| Percent in C-score | 1% | 3% | 7% | 12% | 17% | 20% | 17% | 12% | 7% | 3% | 1% |

| STEN | 1 | 2 | 3 | 4 | 5 | 6 | 7 | 8 | 9 | 10 |
|---|---|---|---|---|---|---|---|---|---|---|
| Percent in sten | 2% | 5% | 9% | 15% | 19% | 19% | 15% | 9% | 5% | 2% |

Adapted from The Psychological Corporation's *Test Service Bulletin*
No. 48 1964 (Used with permission.)

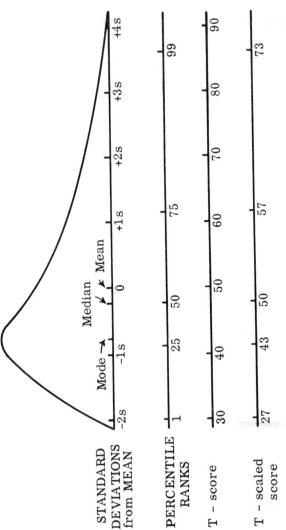

**Fig. 6.2**

Relationships of Selected Scores in a Normal Distribution
(Fig. 6.1) and in a Positively Skewed Distribution (Fig. 6.2).

When test scores are based on each person's own absolute level of performance we have no way of illustrating the scores in a generalized fashion. (In other words, the mean and standard deviation are likely to differ for each test and we have no typical distribution to illustrate.)

With *Type II A* scores, we can show how scores are likely to be distributed for any group. Type II A scores are known as linear standard scores and they will always reflect the original distribution of raw scores; that is, if we were to draw separate graphs of the distributions of raw scores and of their standard-score equivalents, the two graphs would have identical shapes—and it would be possible to change with accuracy from raw scores to standard scores and back again.

With *Type II B* scores, we lose information about the shape of the distribution of raw scores unless the original distribution was normal (and of course it can never be perfectly normal). With nonnormal distributions we lose information that would be necessary to recreate the shape of the raw–score distribution; for example, when we use ranks, we lose all information as to how far apart the scores of any two examinees are. Even with Type II B scores, however, we can generalize the score systems to show what relationships always exist within a normal distribution.

*Type II C* scores, dependent on the two most extreme scores earned by members of a group, are more suited for use with informal than with standardized tests. The scores cannot reasonably be generalized.

With *Type II D* scores, the values expressed are averages of groups differing in age or in grade placement. It would be impossible to generalize these scores, for they are specific to each test and group.

*Type III* scores are based on intra-individual comparisons and there is no reason to expect that such scores could be generalized; therefore, we cannot show how such scores would be distributed except for a specified test and group.

*Type IV* scores do not fit readily into this classification scheme. They are an assortment of primarily scaled scores with more or less arbitrary values, and are not intended for interpretation in themselves.

### COMPARISON OF TYPE II A AND TYPE II B SCORES

As we noted in the previous section, it is possible to generalize Type II A and (to some extent) Type II B scores. In other words, we can show graphically how these scores relate to each other. If the original distribution of raw scores were perfectly normal, we would find the scores related as shown in Figure 6.1 and we could translate freely from one type of score to the next.

Whenever we interpret scores of either Type II A or Type II B, we may find it convenient to assume that the scores for the norm group were normally distributed. In fact, normalized standard scores (Type II B 4) are designed specifically to yield a distribution that is essentially normal even if the distribution of raw scores is far from normal.

Paired with Figure 6.1 in Chart 6.1 is Figure 6.2, a badly skewed distribution. Figure 6.2 is a specific departure from the normal probability model and is not generalizable. Other distributions might be more (or less) skewed in the same direction, skewed in the other direction, truncated, bimodal, multimodal, etc. The sole purpose of including Figure 6.2 is to show which relationships remain the same and which change when the distribution of original scores differs from normal.

Another aid to understanding the similarities and differences among these scores is to be found in the Conversion Table for Derived Scores starting on page 176. This table shows comparable values of several commonly used derived-score systems which exist within a nomal distribution.

### The Scores

In discussing these scores, we are assuming at least a basic understanding of: the mean, the median, standard deviation, range, and the normal probability curve. These concepts, developed in Chapter Four, should be reviewed by the reader who feels uncertain of them at this point.

We shall use the same order here as was used in the outline on pages 88 and 89. After a brief introductory section stating the general characteristics of scores of a given type, we shall consider for each specific score: the use, characteristics, and rationale; an illustrative example; and the advantages and limitations. A brief summary will also be given for a few of the more important scores.

### Type I: Comparison With an Absolute Standard, or Content Difficulty

These scores are suited only for maximum-performance tests and are rarely used except as scores on classroom achievement tests. As noted earlier in the chapter, one's performance on any maximum-performance test is determined in part by his knowledge and skill and by his motivation; these elements are common in determining any person's level of performance. The only other important determinant of a person's Type I score is the difficulty of the test content, for the person's performance is being compared with perfection (that is, with the maximum-possible score on the test). The scores of other examinees play no part in determining the score of any specified examinee.

#### TYPE I A: PERCENTAGE CORRECT

The *percentage correct* score is used in reporting the results of classroom achievement tests, but is almost never used with any other type of test. As noted above, it compares an examinee's score with the maximum-possible score. Viewed differently, it may be thought of as one's score per 100 items. In either case, the resulting percentage correct score is the same.

FORMULA:

$$X_{\%c} = 100R/T, \text{ where}$$
$$X_{\%c} = \text{percentage correct score}$$
$$R = \text{number of right answers (items answered correctly)}$$
$$T = \text{total number of items on test.}$$

EXAMPLE:

Horace Head answers correctly forty-four items on a fifty-item test. His percentage correct score is 88. $[(100 \times 44)/50 = 88]$.

Percentage correct scores are the only derived scores (except for Type I letter grades) that tell us anything about an examinee's knowledge of test content *per se*. We can understand their natural appeal to the school teacher who wants to consider what students achieve according to predetermined standards of quality. On the other hand, many teachers come to realize that these predetermined levels of quality are not so objective and unchanging as might be desired, for the apparent achievement level of students can be altered tremendously by writing either easier or harder test questions over the same subject-matter unit. Many experienced teachers use a *J*-factor to "jack up" scores (by adding a few points to everyone's score) when scores have been very low. Over the years many teachers have come to believe that it is more meaningful to base test scores on a system in which the performance of a student is considered in comparison with others.

*Do not confuse percentage-correct scores with percentile ranks.*

### TYPE I B: LETTER GRADES (SOMETIMES)

The basis for the assignment of *letter grades* at most schools and colleges is stated in terms of percentage-correct scores. Thus letter grades are one of our most common types of score. Although they may be determined on some comparative basis (Type II B 3), letter grades are more commonly Type I. Often the grading system of a school or college will state something like the following: *A* for 90 to 100; *B* for 80 to 90, etc., where the numbers refer to average percentage correct on classroom tests. Some teachers have absolute faith in such a system. I have even known a teacher to refuse an *A* to a student whose semester average was "only 89.9," even though two or three slightly easier (or even clearer) questions on the final examination would have put the student above 90.0.

The basic rationale, advantages, and limitations of letter grades are the same as for percentage-correct scores. The only important difference between these scores is that letter grades are expressed in coarser units. Because of this, letter grades cannot reflect small differences in ability; but, by the same token, they are not likely to differ greatly from hypothetical true scores. Note, however, that even a single unit of change is relatively large.

Type I letter grades are found by either of two methods: (1) direct grading

according to judged quality (as is often done in grading essay examinations);
or (2) conversion from percentage-correct scores to letter grades, following a
predetermined schedule as in the school and college grading system mentioned above.

When letter grades are assigned with strict adherence to quality standards
(without any consideration to relative performance within the group), they
are determined more by test difficulty than by anything else.

> "Don't take 'Introductory' from Jones," I heard a student say the other
> day. "He doesn't know that the letter *A* exists." I have known such teachers;
> haven't you? Two teachers of the same subject may differ greatly in the
> number of *A*s, *F*s, etc., given to students of similar ability.

No type of score is perfect. But Type I letter grades are worse than most
others because they really depend more on test difficulty than on true quality
of performance (their apparent basis).

Compare with Type II B 3 letter grades.

### Type II: Interindividual Comparisons

Type II scores are much more commonly used with standardized tests than
with classroom tests. Almost all standardized tests use some version of Type
II A, B, or D scores in their norms tables. Types II A and B may be used
with typical-performance tests as well as with maximum-performance tests;
however, we shall be concerned largely with their use in the latter instance.

Type II scores are relatively independent of content difficulty, for they
base an examinee's score on the performance of others in a comparative (or
normative) group. If the test content is inherently difficult, any specified
person's score is likely to be lower than on an easier test; however, this difficulty of content will also affect the scores of the other examinees. This makes
it possible to use the same test for individuals (and for groups) ranging widely
in level of ability. It also permits the test constructor to aim for test items of
about 50 per cent difficulty, the best difficulty level from a measurement
point of view because it permits the largest number of interindividual discriminations. On the other hand, all Type II scores are influenced by the
*level* of the comparison group; e.g., I will score higher when compared with
college freshmen than when compared with college professors.

#### TYPE II A: INTERINDIVIDUAL COMPARISON CONSIDERING MEAN AND STANDARD DEVIATION

In Type II A scores, we find that interindividual comparison is expressed
as the number of standard deviations between any specified score and the
mean. As with all Type II scores, a change in comparison group will influence
the level of score.

Type II A scores are all linear standard scores. They are called *standard* because they are based on the standard deviation; we shall see shortly why they are *linear*. They may be viewed as statements of standard-deviation distance from the mean; or they may be seen as scores that have been given a substitute mean and standard deviation. All Type II A scores have properties which make them more valuable in research than most other derived scores: (1) for every test and every group, each Type II A score gives the same mean and standard deviation; (2) these scores retain the shape of the raw-score distribution, changing only the calibration numbers; (3) they permit intergroup or intertest comparisons that are not possible with most other types of score; (4) they can be treated mathematically in ways that some other scores cannot be.

**1. z-Score**

The basic standard score is *z*. All other linear standard scores may be established directly from it. It tells in simple terms the difference (or distance) between a stated group's mean and any specified raw-score value.

FORMULA:

$$z = \frac{X - \bar{X}}{s}, \text{ where}$$

$X =$ a specified raw score
$\bar{X} =$ mean raw score for some group
$s\ =$ standard deviation of that same group.

(Thus, if *z*-scores are found for each examinee in the comparison group, the mean will be 0.00 and the standard deviation will be 1.00.)

EXAMPLE:

Gail Gilber had a score of 49. She is to be compared with other local examinees; the mean and standard deviation of this group are 40 and 6, respectively. Gail's *z*-score = (49 − 40)/6 = 9/6 = 1.5. In other words, Gail's score is 1.5 standard deviations above the mean of this comparison group. (Assuming a normal distribution, we find that she did as well as or better than about 93 percent of this group.)

Although *z*-scores have many advantages for the research worker, they are not too handy for the test user, except as a step in computing other types of linear standard score. By their very nature, about one-half of all *z*-scores are negative and all *z*-scores need to be expressed to one or two decimal positions. All other linear standard scores have been designed to eliminate the decimal point and obtain smaller units (by multiplying each *z*-score by a constant) and to eliminate the negative values (by adding a constant value to each *z*-score).

The $T$-score is one of the most common linear standard scores. Its rationale is the same as for the $z$-score, except that it is made to have a mean of 50 and a standard deviation of 10.

FORMULA:

$T = 10z + 50$, where

$z = \dfrac{X - \bar{X}}{s}$, as shown above

$10 = $ a multiplying constant (i.e., each $z$-score is multiplied by 10)

$50 = $ an additive constant (i.e., 50 is added to each value of $10z$).

EXAMPLE:

Gail Gilber's $z$-score was 1.5; therefore, her $T$-score $= 10(1.5) + 50 = 15 + 50 = 65$. [Assuming a normal distribution, we find that she did as well as or better than about 93 percent of her comparison group. In any event (normal distribution or not), her $T$-score of 65 is directly under her $z$-score of 1.5 (*see* Chart 6.1).]

The $T$-score has much the same advantages and limitations as does the $z$-score. It is somewhat less useful than $z$ for certain research purposes, but it is more convenient to interpret since there are no negative values. (The probability of obtaining a value which is more than five standard deviations below the mean in a normal distribution is less than one three-millionth.) Nor do we typically use decimals with $T$-scores.

Unfortunately, $T$-scores are easily confused with certain other types of score, especially the $T$-scaled score (considered shortly as a Type II B score). These two $T$s are identical in a normal distribution, but may differ considerably in a badly skewed distribution. $T$-scores are often confused with percentile ranks, too, for they use similar numbers. The reader may wish to check these similarities and differences in Chart 6.1.

This score gets its name from the *Army General Classification Test.* It is similar to $z$ and to $T$, except that it has a mean of 100 and a standard deviation of 20.

FORMULA:

$AGCT = 20z + 100$, where

$z$    $= $ a $z$-score, as defined above; and 20 and 100 are multiplying and additive constants, respectively.

EXAMPLE:

Gail Gilber's $z$-score was 1.5; therefore, her $AGCT$ score $= 20(1.5) + 100 = 30 + 100 = 130$. [Assuming a normal distribution, we find that she did as well as or better than about 93 percent of her comparison group. In any event (normal distribution or not), her *AGCT* score of 130 is directly under her *z*-score of 1.5 and her *T*-score of 65 (*see* Chart 6.1).]

As originally used, the *AGCT* score was based on a large sample of soldiers who took the first military edition of the test; their mean was set at 100 and their standard deviation at 20. Subsequent editions of the test have been made to give comparable results. These scores are very similar to the deviation IQs, which will be considered shortly. It should be noted, however, that *AGCT*s have a standard deviation somewhat larger than commonly used with IQs. Although a convenient scale, *AGCT* scores are not in general use except in connection with the military and civilian editions of the *Army General Classification Test*. Possibility of confusion with I.Q.

### 4. CEEB Score

This score was developed for the purpose of reporting the results of the *College Entrance Examination Board* tests and is used by the Educational Testing Service as the basis for reported scores on many of its other special-program tests. It is similar to other linear standard scores, but has a mean of 500 and a standard deviation of 100.

FORMULA:

$$CEEB = 100z + 500, \text{ where}$$
$$z = \text{a } z\text{-score, as defined above.}$$

EXAMPLE:

Gail Gilber's *z*-score of 1.5 would be expressed on this *CEEB* scale as 650. (Her percentile rank would be 93, assuming a normal distribution. In any distribution, her *CEEB* score of 650 lies directly under a *z* of 1.5, a *T* of 65, etc.)

As originally used, the *CEEB* scores were set up differently each year according to the mean and standard deviation of that year's examinees. They now are keyed to the mean and standard deviation of 1941s examinees, so that it is possible to compare results from one year to the next. Note, however, that because *CEEB* scores are not based on the present set of examinees, the Educational Testing Service also reports percentile ranks based on current examinees.

### 5. Deviation IQs (Sometimes)

The *IQ* (*Intelligence Quotient*) suggested about sixty years ago by the German psychologist Stern sounded very reasonable; Terman used it with the *Stanford–Binet* in 1916, and soon other test constructors began using it. Very few tests still use the ratio IQ (a Type III score) where IQ is based on the ratio of mental age to chronological age. One big advantage of a deviation IQ is that it has a common standard deviation for all ages covered by the test on which it is determined.

The term *deviation IQ* is used to describe three different types of score. We shall deal here with the first meaning, a linear standard score [*but see also* Type II B 4(e) and Type IV C]. The deviation IQ has the same advantages and limitations as other linear standard scores except that it has a mean of 100 and a standard deviation as fixed by the test's author. We shall mention briefly the deviation IQ on the *Wechsler* intelligence tests and on the 1960 edition of the *Stanford–Binet;* earlier editions of the *Stanford–Binet* used a ratio IQ (Type III A).

(*a*) *Wechsler IQs.* Three popular individual tests of intelligence are the *Wechsler Preschool and Primary Scale of Intelligence* (*WPPSI*), the *Wechsler Intelligence Scale for Children* (*WISC*), and the *Wechsler Adult Intelligence Scale* (*WAIS*). Although they differ in some respects, their IQs are determined in somewhat similar fashion, and we will illustrate with the *WAIS*. There are six verbal subtests and five performance subtests, which combine to yield a Verbal IQ, a Performance IQ, and a Total IQ. Seven different norms groups are used to cover the age range from sixteen to sixty-four years.

A raw score is found for each of the eleven subtests. Each subtest score is converted to a normalized standard score [*see* Type II B 4(e), page 110] with a mean of 10 and a standard deviation of 3. The sum of these eleven normalized standard scores is found. This sum of scores is converted to a deviation IQ with the aid of a table (a separate table for each of the seven different age groups).

In constructing the test, the mean and standard deviation of subtest sums were found for each of the seven age groups. The author had decided in advance that he wanted his test to have a mean of 100 and a standard deviation of 15. Therefore he used the formula: $IQ = 15z + 100$, computed separately for each age group. The *WAIS* user now need only consult the appropriate table to find the IQ value corresponding to the sum of the subtest scores. Verbal and Performance IQs are found in the same manner, but are based on only six and five subtests, respectively.

(*b*) 1960 *Stanford–Binet IQs.* Until the 1960 revision, *Stanford-Binet* (*S-B*) *IQ*s were ratio *IQ*s; in fact, it was the first test on which IQs were ever used. The authors of the 1960 revision decided to adopt the deviation IQ so that the standard deviation would be constant from age to age; in spite of careful and extensive effort in preparing the previous revision (1937), standard deviations for different ages had differed by as much as eight IQ points!

The *Stanford–Binet* has tasks arranged by age levels from two years to superior adult. Following carefully described procedures, the examiner finds a mental age from the test. This MA is entered into a table opposite the examinee's chronological age (an adjusted age, of course, for adults) and the IQ is found.

For each chronological age group of examinees, the authors found the mean and standard deviation of MAs. The mean MA was set equal to an

IQ of 100 for people of that specified CA. The authors then found the MA that was one standard deviation below the mean; that was set equal to an IQ of 84. One standard deviation above the mean was set equal to 116, etc.

In the case of the *S-B*, then, we have a linear standard score with a mean of 100 and a standard deviation of 16. Separately for each chronological age group, the authors have used the formula $IQ = 16z + 100$. The scale employed is thus very similar to that used on the *Wechsler* tests, as may be seen in Figure 6.1. (Note, however, that IQs found for the same examinee on the two tests might still differ; in addition to error in measurement, the tests also differ in content and in their norms groups.) and in the $\sigma$ of the I.Q.

SUMMARY: LINEAR STANDARD SCORES   All linear standard scores tell us the location of an examinee's raw score in relation to the mean of some specified group and in terms of the group's standard deviation. In any distribution, normal or not, we can convert freely from raw-score values to linear standard-score equivalents without in any way changing the shape of the original distribution. Because of these properties, we can average these scores exactly as we can raw scores; we cannot average other Type II scores.

### TYPE II B: INTERINDIVIDUAL COMPARISON CONSIDERING RANK

Like Type II A scores, these are very commonly used in reporting standardized test results. Unlike Type II A scores, they are based on the number of people with scores higher (or lower) than a specified score value. We lose all information about distance away from the mean, etc. On the other hand, some of these scores (especially Type II B 4) have the effect of creating a distribution which is more nearly normal than the distribution of raw scores on which they are based. As with all other scores (except Type I), values will change for different comparison groups.

#### 1. Rank

The simplest possible statement of relative position is rank: first for highest or best, second for next, third for next, etc. It has the unique disadvantage of being so completely bound by the number of cases that it is never used formally in reporting test results.

#### 2. Percentile Rank and Percentile Band

The percentile rank (sometimes called centile rank) is probably the score used most frequently in reporting the results of standardized tests. All things considered, it is probably the best type for general use in test interpretation; however, it does have limitations as we shall see presently.

A percentile is any one of the ninety-nine points dividing a frequency distribution into one hundred groups of equal size. A percentile rank is a person's relative position within a specified group.

We find the percentile rank of an examinee or of a given raw-score value. We find a specified percentile value by finding its equivalent raw-score value. Thus a raw score of 162 may have a percentile rank of 44; the forty-fourth percentile will be a raw score of 162.

Because of the importance of percentiles and percentile ranks, Chart 6.2 has been included to describe and illustrate their computation. The raw-score values used were selected deliberately not to conflict with the numbers used to express any of the more common derived scores. The range in raw scores is certainly less than we would expect to find for most groups; this, too, was done deliberately in order to simplify the presentation.

---

### CHART 6.2

*Computation of Percentiles and Percentile Ranks*

| 1<br>$X$ | 2<br>$f$ | 3<br>$cf$ | 4<br>$cf_{mp}$ | 5<br>$cP_{mp}$ | 6<br>$PR$ |
|---|---|---|---|---|---|
| 226 | 0 | 50 | 50.5 | 100.0 | 99+ |
| 225 | 1 | 50 | 49.5 | 99.0 | 99 |
| 224 | 1 | 49 | 48.5 | 97.0 | 97 |
| 223 | 2 | 48 | 47.0 | 94.0 | 94 |
| 222 | 4 | 46 | 44.0 | 88.0 | 88 |
| 221 | 2 | 42 | 41.0 | 82.0 | 82 |
| 220 | 5 | 40 | 37.5 | 75.0 | 75 |
| 219 | 6 | 35 | 32.0 | 64.0 | 64 |
| 218 | 8 | 29 | 25.0 | 50.0 | 50 |
| 217 | 5 | 21 | 18.5 | 37.0 | 37 |
| 216 | 4 | 16 | 14.0 | 28.0 | 28 |
| 215 | 4 | 12 | 10.0 | 20.0 | 20 |
| 214 | 4 | 8 | 6.0 | 12.0 | 12 |
| 213 | 3 | 4 | 2.5 | 5.0 | 5 |
| 212 | 0 | 1 | 1.0 | 2.0 | 2 |
| 211 | 1 | 1 | 0.5 | 1.0 | 1 |
| 210 | 0 | 0 | 0 | 0.0 | 1- |

Symbols:

$X$ = value of raw score

$f$ = frequency (number of examinees making this score)

$cf$ = cumulative frequency

$cf_{mp}$ = $cf$ to midpoint of score

$cP_{mp}$ = cumulative percentage to midpoint of score

$PR$ = percentile rank for the specified raw-score value

---

*To Find PRs for Stated Raw-Score Values*

1. List every possible *raw-score value*.
2. Find the *frequency* with which each score occurs.
3. Find the *cumulative frequency* up through each score by adding that score's frequency to the frequencies of all lower scores; e.g., *cf* through score of 214 (i.e., through its upper limit, 214.5): 4 + 3 + 0 + 1 = 8.

4. Find the *cumulative frequency to midpoint* of each score by adding one-half of frequency at the score to cumulative frequency up through next lower score; e.g., $cf_{mp}$ for 212.0: $(^1/_2 \times 0) + 1 = 1.0$; $cf_{mp}$ for 216.0: $(^1/_2 \times 4) + 12 = 14.0$. For 211.0 : $(^1/_2 \times 1) + 0 = 0.5$

5. Convert to *cumulative percentage* by the formula: $cP_{mp} = 100(cf_{mp})/N$, where $cP_{mp}$ and $cf_{mp}$ are defined as above, and $N$ = number of cases; or, use $100/N$ as a constant to multiply by successive $cf_{mp}$ values, as here: $100/N = 100/50 = 2.0$.

6. Find *percentile ranks* by rounding these $cP_{mp}$ values to nearest whole numbers (except use *1−* for *0* and *99+* for *100*).

*To Find Raw-Score Equivalents of Stated Percentile Values*

1. Prepare Columns 1–3, as above.

2. Change from *percentile* to *number of cases* by multiplying it by $N/100$; e.g., in finding $P_{20}$: $20 \times 50/100 = 10$.

3. Count up through the *number of cases* found in step 2, assuming that cases are distributed evenly across each score; i.e., one third of the cases at a score lie one third of the way between real lower limit and real upper limit of score, one quarter of the cases lie one quarter of the way through score, etc. See examples below.

4. Corresponding *raw-score* value is the desired *percentile*.

*Examples:*

**Find $P_{30}$, the raw-score value at or below which fall 30% of the cases:**

A. 30% of fifty cases = $30 \times 50/100 = 15$; we must count up through 15 cases.

B. Find the biggest number in the *cf* column that is *not greater than* 15—i.e., 12.

C. Subtract number found in step B from number of cases needed: $15 − 12 = 3$.

D. We need to get these cases from those cases at next higher score; in other words, we need three of the four cases at score of 216.

E. We go that fractional way through the score: $^3/_4$, or $0.75 + 215.5$ (real lower limit of score) = 216.25. $P_{30} = 216.25$.

**Find $P_{50}$ (the median):**

A. 50% of fifty cases is 25.

B. We note 25 in the $cf_{mp}$ column; $P_{50}$ = midpoint of the score, 218, or 218.0.

**Find $P_{80}$, the eightieth percentile:**

A. 80% of fifty cases is 40.

B. We note 40 in the *cf* column; $P_{80}$ = upper limit of the score, 220, or 220.5.

We should note that in Chart 6.2 we have found cumulative frequencies up to the midpoint of each raw-score value, and have translated these $cf_{mp}$ values into percentages which, rounded to whole numbers, are the percentile ranks.

I hope that this paragraph is not confusing. I wish that it could be omitted. Some test publishers base percentile norms not on cumulative frequencies to the midpoint as we have, but on cumulative frequencies to the upper limits of each score. Still others who work with tests base their percentile norms on cumulative frequencies up to the lower limits of each score. I dislike the latter two methods for three reasons: (1) they are confusing and ambiguous; (2) they produce percentile ranks that are incompatible with percentile values; and (3) they more logically are percentile ranks for limits of scores, rather than for midpoints of scores (e.g., a percentile rank for a score of 213.5 or 214.5, rather than 214.0). We find that some test manuals state which procedure has been followed. More often, though, manuals say nothing about which procedure was followed, and the reader is left wondering. Please note, however, that only when the range is small (say, less than twenty to thirty score units) do the differences in procedure make much practical difference.

*Advantages and Limitations of Percentile Ranks.* The principal advantage of *PR*s lies in their ease of interpretation. Even a person who thinks of percentiles as being equally spaced (which they could not be unless the same number of persons obtained each raw score) can understand something about these scores if he knows only that a *PR* is a statement of the percentage of cases in a specified group who fall at or below a given score value.

On the other hand, we find it very easy to overemphasize differences near the median and to underemphasize differences near the extremes; in Figure 6.1 we should note the slight difference between *PR*s of 40 and 50 as compared with *PR*s of 90 and 99. And even these varying differences are altered when a distribution departs markedly from the normal probability model, as may be seen in Figure 6.2.

*Averaging Percentile Ranks.* Because interpercentile distances are not equal, we cannot average them directly (as we could Type II A scores). This point applies equally against averaging the performance of one person on two or more tests and against averaging the performance of a group of people on one test.

To find the average *PR* of one person on several tests: convert each *PR* to a *z*-score, using the Conversion Table on page 176; average the *z*-scores; convert the average *z* to a *PR*. Note: this method assumes a normal distribution for each test and the same normative group for each test; only slight errors will be introduced if the distributions are nearly normal, but the averaging cannot be done if the *PR*s are based on different groups.

To find the average *PR* for a group of persons on one test: average the raw scores, and find the *PR* corresponding to this average raw score. Note: this method is one we might follow to determine how our local group compares with a national normative group; there would be no point in doing this with the same group on which the norms were based. Note further that this procedure gives the *PR* corresponding to the average raw score. Since group averages vary less than do individual raw scores, the value found should never be thought of as the *PR* of the group (in comparison to other groups).

*More Advantages and Limitations.* With percentiles, we are using a common scale of values for all distributions on all tests. Regardless of the range of raw scores, the range of *PR*s will be the same: 0 or 1— to 100 or 99+ (unless more than 0.5 percent of the examinees make either the lowest possible score or the highest possible score). On every short tests, a difference of twenty or thirty *PR*s may represent a difference of only one or two raw-score values as we may note in Chart 6.2.

Some publishers use *PR*s of 0 and 100; some do not. This reflects a philosophical issue:

> Lazilu Lucas has a score lower than anyone in the normative group. A *PR* of 0 would certainly describe her performance. On the other hand, we like to think of a normative group as being a sample representative of a large population. If Lazilu is being compared with an appropriate group, she presumably belongs to the population from which the normative group was taken. It is not logical to say that she did less well than everyone in the population of which she is part. Following this line of reasoning, I prefer to use 1— instead of 0 and 99+ instead of 100.

By now some readers will wonder how this issue can exist if a percentile rank is one of the ninety-nine points which divide a frequency distribution into one hundred groups of equal size as defined a few pages ago.

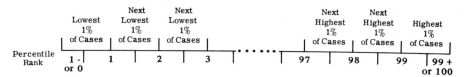

**Fig. 6.3**
Graphic Explanation of Percentile Ranks at Upper and Lower Extremes of a Distribution. (See further explanation in the text.)

Figure 6.3 gives us the answer. If we divide the ranked distribution of scores into one hundred subgroups of equal size, as shown across the top of the line, there are ninety-nine percentile points setting off the one hundred subgroups. In expressing a percentile rank, however, we round to the nearest whole percentile value—as shown by lines drawn across the bottom of the line to indicate the real limits of each percentile rank. Ninety-nine of these units leave 0.5 percent at each extreme of the distribution: it is these extremes that we call 1— and 99+.

One final disadvantage of percentile ranks is that they use a scale of numbers that is shared with several other types of score: percentage-correct scores, $T$-scores, and IQs. There is the possibility of confusion, especially with percentage-correct scores; we must remember that percentage-correct scores are based on percentage of content, whereas PRs are based on percentage of cases in a specified group.

SUMMARY OF PERCENTILE RANKS  Although PRs have many limitations, they are very commonly used in expressing the results of standardized tests. They are reasonably easy to understand and to explain to others. Considering all advantages and limitations, PRs are probably the best single derived score for general use in expressing test results. Consider, too, the following application.

### An Application of Percentile Ranks: The Percentile Band

An interesting application of percentile ranks is to be found in the percentile band now being used by the Educational Testing Service with some of its newer tests. As the name suggests, the percentile band is a band or range of percentile ranks. The upper limit of the band corresponds to the percentile rank for a score one standard error of measurement above the obtained score, and the lower limit of the band corresponds to the percentile rank for a score one standard error of measurement below the obtained score.

ETS provides the full information on percentile bands with its tests. The test user may make his own percentile bands for any test for which he has percentile norms and the standard error of measurement by following the directions above.

The purpose of this application of course is to emphasize to every user of the test that measurement error is present in each score. The percentile band is useful, too, in interpreting differences between different tests within the same test battery.

I believe that this approach has considerable merit and hope that it may come into widespread use. It seems to combine the stated advantages of the percentile rank with an emphasis that the score should not be treated as a precise value. In addition, it seems to have the advantages of other coarse-unit scores while avoiding their principal limitation (i.e., that a single unit of change is relatively large) by centering the band on the obtained score—thereby changing the limits of the band only slightly for slight differences in score. This may prove to be the most valuable single type of score for general test interpretation purposes.

The band approach, of course, can be used with other types of score; however, this is the only present use of which I'm aware.

### 3. Letter Grades (Sometimes)

As suggested earlier, *letter grades* may be based on comparative performance; when so used, they are a Type II B score. A few standardized tests use such scores, each clearly indicating those values to be assigned *A*s, those to be assigned *B*s, etc. Far more commonly, a teacher will use some inter-individual comparison in assigning course grades.

Note that it is not necessary to decide in advance how many students will receive each letter grade. "Grading on the curve" is rather old fashioned anyway. The practice of basing letter grades on a normal curve (perhaps by giving 10 percent *A*, 20 percent *B*, 40 percent *C*, 20 percent *D*, and 10 percent *F*) is indefensible unless one has very large numbers of unselected students. One way of assigning grades on the basis of comparative performance that I like is as follows:

I make no assumption about the number of students who will fail or who will get any particular grade. I do assume that I will give at least a single *A* (and actually give more, usually). During the semester, I give several quizzes and make certain that the standard deviation of each is about the same (for tests "weight" themselves according to size of standard deviation). I make the standard deviation of the final examination about twice those of the quizzes. I add these raw scores and arrange the students in order of summed scores. I may even draw a histogram similar to Figure 4.1 so that I may see how each student compares with every other student. Oftentimes the results will show several clusters of students—suggesting that they be given the same grade. If there are several students whose summed scores seem almost "to drop out" of the distribution, these may receive *F*s. I will, however, consider carefully whether any of these students has shown a little promise—perhaps by great improvement on the final examination—that might justify some grade other than *F*. I try to be a little more generous with higher grades when my class has been a bit better than average (as the year when three of my thirty students made Phi Beta Kappa); some years my students seem less promising, and I am more cautious about assigning many high grades.

I think that every teacher recognizes that grades are somewhat arbitrary and subjective. I try to make the grades I assign as fair as possible, reflecting comparative performance for the most part, but with just a dash of consideration for the sort of class I have.

This grading scheme works fairly well for me. I am not proposing that it is ideal—but let me know if you ever do find the *perfect* grading system, won't you?

### 4. Normalized Standard Scores (Area Transformations)

*Normalized standard scores* are derived scores that are assigned standard-score-like values, but are computed more like percentile ranks. With linear standard scores, the shape of the distribution of raw scores is reproduced faithfully; if additional baselines were drawn for a frequency polygon, we would find that values of any of those standard scores would lie in a straight line below the corresponding raw-score values regardless of the shape of the raw-score distribution. With normalized standard scores this is true only when the raw-score distribution is normal—as shown in Figure 6.1.

As suggested by their name, normalized standard scores have the property of making a distribution a closer approximation of the normal probability distribution. This is accomplished in similar fashion for all normalized standard scores, so we shall consider the general procedure here rather than treating it separately for each score.

*Computing normalized standard scores.* The following procedure is used in computing normalized standard scores:

1. List every possible raw-score value.
2. Find the frequency with which each score occurs.
3. Find the cumulative frequency up through each score.
4. Find the cumulative frequency up to the midpoint of each score.
5. Convert the cumulative frequencies to cumulative percentages.
(Note: Steps 1–5 are identical with the first five steps in finding *PR*s; this procedure is shown in Chart 6.2.)
6. Substitute the normalized standard score value that is appropriate for this cumulative percentage in a normal probability distribution. **These values, different for each normalized standard score, may be found from the Conversion Table in the Appendix.**

*Area transformations.* As we can see from the computation procedures above, these scores are known as *area transformations* because they are based on standard-score values that would correspond to specified cumulative percentages in a normal distribution (and area, we recall from Chapter Four, indicates frequency or percentage of cases).

> To say that 23 percent of the cases lie below a specified score is the same as saying that the 23 percent of the area of a graph showing that distribution lies below that same score value. In finding a normalized standard score, we are merely substituting for that score value a standard-score-like value that would be at a point where 23 percent of the normal curve's area falls below it.

(*a*) *T-Scaled Score.* In a normal distribution, this has exactly the same properties as the *T*-score (including its mean of 50 and standard deviation of 10). In fact, this score is called *T-score* more commonly than *T-scaled score*. It has all the advantages and limitations of the normalized standard scores mentioned above. It has the aditional limitation of being confused with the *T*-score, which is of practical significance only when the distribution of raw scores deviates appreciably from the normal probability model.

(*b*) *Stanine Score.* Developed by World War II psychologists for use with the U.S. Air Force, *stanine scores* were intended to maximize the information about test performance that could be entered into a single column of an IBM punched card. Obviously one card could hold more one-digit scores than two- or three-digit scores. Whereas earlier standard scores had indicated specific values, stanines (from **sta**ndard score of **nine** units) were intended to represent bands of values; except for the open-ended extreme stanines of 1 and 9, each stanine was to equal one-half standard deviation in width and the mean was to be the midpoint of the middle stanine, 5.

Apparently some Air Force psychologists used the stanine as a linear standard score at first, thereby giving it exactly the properties mentioned above; however, others treated it as a normalized standard score, and it is so used today. When distributed normally, stanines will have a mean of 5 and a standard deviation of about 2; in addition, all stanines except 1 and 9 will be exactly one-half standard deviation in width. With distributions which are not normal, of course, these values will only be approximated.

As a normalized standard score, values may be found by: (1) arranging test papers in order of score; and (2) assigning stanine values, following these percentages as closely as possible:

| LOWEST 4% | NEXT 7% | NEXT 12% | NEXT 17% | MIDDLE 20% | NEXT 17% | NEXT 12% | NEXT 7% | HIGHEST 4% |
|---|---|---|---|---|---|---|---|---|
| Stanine 1 | Stanine 2 | Stanine 3 | Stanine 4 | Stanine 5 | Stanine 6 | Stanine 7 | Stanine 8 | Stanine 9 |

At least one publisher (Harcourt, Brace & World, Inc.) is promoting the general use of stanines in test interpretation. In addition to using these scores in some of its own norms tables, the publisher points out the relative ease of using them in preparing local norms for both standardized and classroom tests. When finding stanines for our own distributions, we may have to approximate the above figures; we must assign the same stanine value to everyone obtaining the same raw score, and it is unlikely that our cumulative percentages will allow us to follow the table precisely.

In general, stanines have the advantages and limitations of other coarse-unit scores. It is unlikely that a person's obtained score is many units away from his true score, but a test interpreter is perhaps more likely to put undue confidence in the accuracy of the obtained score.

The Conversion Table on pages 176-181 shows stanine values and equivalent values in a normal distribution (*see also* Chart 6.1).

*Flanagan's Extended Stanine Score.* For use in reporting scores on his *Flanagan Aptitude Classification Tests*, Flanagan splits each stanine value into three units by using plus and minus signs; stanine 1 is made into three stanine values: 1−, 1, and 1+, and every other stanine is treated similarly. In this way Flanagan achieves a twenty-seven-unit normalized standard score scale. His scale has certain obvious advantages over the usual stanine scale, but it is not in general use. The percentile equivalents of these extended stanine values differ slightly for each test in the *FACT* battery; they may be found in the *FACT Examiner's Manual*.

(c) *C-Scaled Score.* Guilford has proposed the use of a *C*-scale that provides one additional unit at each end of the stanine scale. The *C*-scale has eleven units assigned values of 0–10. This scale is used in the norms tables of tests published by the Sheridan Psychological Services. *C*-scores are computed exactly as are stanines, except that the values given are as shown in this table:

| LOWEST 1% | NEXT 3% | NEXT 7% | NEXT 12% | NEXT 17% | MIDDLE 20% | NEXT 17% | NEXT 12% | NEXT 7% | NEXT 3% | HIGHEST 1% |
|---|---|---|---|---|---|---|---|---|---|---|
| $C = 0$ | $C = 1$ | $C = 2$ | $C = 3$ | $C = 4$ | $C = 5$ | $C = 6$ | $C = 7$ | $C = 8$ | $C = 9$ | $C = 10$ |

(d) *Sten Score.* Similar in rationale to the two preceding scores is the *sten* (a normalized standard score with **ten** units). This system provides for five normalized standard-score units on each side of the mean, each being one-half standard deviation in width except for the sten values of 1 and 10, which are open-ended. Since it is a normalized standard score, these interval sizes apply exactly only in a normal distribution. This scale is used for norms of some of Cattell's tests (Institute of Personality and Ability Testing). Stens may be computed in the same way as stanines, except that the values given are as shown in this table:

| LOWEST 2% | NEXT 5% | NEXT 9% | NEXT 15% | LOW MIDDLE 19% | HIGH MIDDLE 19% | NEXT 15% | NEXT 9% | NEXT 5% | HIGHEST 2% |
|---|---|---|---|---|---|---|---|---|---|
| Sten 1 | Sten 2 | Sten 3 | Sten 4 | Sten 5 | Sten 6 | Sten 7 | Sten 8 | Sten 9 | Sten 10 |

(e) *Deviation IQs (Sometimes).* Although to the best of my knowledge no intelligence test presently uses deviation IQ in this normalized standard-score sense, such a use will probably come before long. Such deviation IQs would have the same general advantages and limitations as the *T*-scaled scores, except that their mean would be 100 and their standard deviation would be as determined by the author and publisher. In all other characteristics, they would resemble the deviation IQ (Type II A 5).

*Wechsler subtests.* Something similar to deviation IQs of the sort mentioned in the previous paragraph is already found in the subtests (or scales) of the *Wechsler* Intelligence Tests. Each of the separate scales on these three tests uses a normalized standard score with a mean of 10 and a standard deviation of 3; however, these scale scores are used principally to find total scores on which the Wechsler IQs [Type II A 5(a)] are based, and are rarely interpreted in themselves.

(f) *ITED-score.* One final type of normalized standard score will be mentioned. The *ITED* score was developed for use with the *Iowa Tests of Educational Development,* but is now also used with the *National Merit Scholarship*

*Qualifying Examination* and other tests. This score is given a mean of 15 and
a standard deviation of 5 and is based on a nationally representative sample
of tenth- and eleventh-grade students.

### 5. Decile Rank

Cattell uses what he calls *decile scores* in some of his norms tables. In common usage, a *decile* is defined as any one of nine points separating the frequency distribution into ten groups of equal size. Thus the first decile $(D_1)$
equals the tenth percentile, $D_2$ equals the twentieth percentile, etc. Cattell modifies this meaning of decile to include a band (or range) of 10 percent of the cases—5 percent on each side of the actual decile point; for example, Cattell's decile score of 1 includes values from the fifth to fifteenth percentiles. (Values below $P_5$ are given a decile score of 0; values above $P_{95}$, a score of 10.) Cattell believes that these scores should be used in preference to percentile ranks when the range in raw scores is very small. In order to prevent confusion between decile and decile score (and to point out their similarity to percentile ranks), I prefer to use the term decile ranks.

### TYPE II C: INTERINDIVIDUAL COMPARISON CONSIDERING RANGE

Only one derived score, the percent placement score, is based on interindividual comparisons considering the range of raw scores. So far as I know, it is used in rare instances to express scores on classroom tests of achievement —and nowhere else.

### Percent Placement Score

The *percent placement* score indicates a person's position on a 101-point scale where the highest score made is set at 100 and the lowest at 0.

FORMULA:

$$X_{\%pl} = 100\frac{(X - L)}{(H - L)}, \text{ where}$$

$X$ = any specified raw score
$L$ = lowest raw score made
$H$ = highest raw score made.

EXAMPLE:

On a 300-item test, there is a range from 260 to 60; range $= H - L$
$= 260 - 60 = 200$. Barry's raw score was 60; his percent placement score
is 0. Harry's raw score was 260; his $X_{\%pl} = 100$. Larry's raw score was 140;
his $X_{\%pl} = 40$ [i.e., 100 (140 − 60)/200 = 40].

### TYPE II D: INTERINDIVIDUAL COMPARISON CONSIDERING STATUS OF THOSE MAKING SAME SCORE

Type II D scores include age scores and grade-placement scores. These are set up to express test performance in terms of averages of groups which differ in status (either in chronological age or in grade placement). Thus the examinee's score is not a statement of how well he has done when compared with some single specified group, but rather a statement of which group (among several that differ in level) he is presumably most like.

Type II D scores are used most commonly with standardized tests of achievement and intelligence for children of school age. They are not suited for use with informal, local tests.

Although Type II D scores seem easy to understand, they have many limitations which are not immediately apparent.

### 1. Age Scores

Age scores may be developed for any human characteristic that changes with age; however, they are used most frequently with intelligence and achievement tests for children of school age or below. The most common age score is the *mental age* (MA), a concept developed by Alfred Binet more than sixty years ago for use with the earliest successful intelligence test.

An age score is an expression of an examinee's test performance stated in terms of the developmental level characteristic of the average child of that corresponding chronological age.

> Karl gets an MA of seven years six months (expressed as 7–6) on an intelligence test. This means that Karl's level of performance is equal to the mean score made by children with a chronological age of 7–6. Alternatively, although less frequently, an MA may be defined as the average chronological age of individuals making a given raw score. By this definition, Karl's MA of 7–6 would indicate that the average chronological age of children with the same raw score as his was 7–6.

When used with young children, age scores are reasonably easy to understand. The logic is straightforward and simple. On the other hand, age scores are easily overinterpreted. A five-year-old who obtains an age score of 7 on a test is still only five years of age in most respects. There can be no assumption that all people with the same age score have identical abilities.

Test makers have difficulty in getting good representative samples for age norms, because some children are located a grade or two ahead of (or behind) their age peers. These youngsters must be included if the norms are to be meaningful, but they are especially difficult to locate when they do not attend the same schools as their age peers. For example, some bright youngsters may enter junior high school one or two years ahead of their age peers, while dull ones may be transferred to special classes at other schools.

An age score by itself tells us little about the individual's achievement or potentiality, even though it may be used in combination with chronological age or other measure to form a quotient score that will do so.

(a) *Mental Age.* Although the MA served Binet's need for a score that could be understood easily, it has been extended beyond reason. As originally conceived, MA units were credited to a child for each task he passed. The sum of these units gave him an MA; this MA had the property of being equal *on the average* to chronological age.

On certain intelligence tests, however, MAs are determined by finding first the number of items correct; then an MA is assigned according to the chronological age group for which that score is the average. When used in this manner, MA is merely an extra step in computing an intelligence quotient (IQ).

Still another unwarranted extension of the MA has been its application to adults. Although there is increasing evidence that at least some aspects of intelligence may continue to grow on into middle age, it is also true that the increment between successive ages becomes smaller with increasing age. There are more obvious mental differences between ages of 6 and 7 than between 16 and 17 or between 26 and 27. Even within the age range of 5 to 15, there is no basis for believing that MA units are equal in size. An age-scale approach is not feasible beyond the middle teen years; and, on tests where an age scale is used, all people beyond a given chronological age level are treated (in computing an IQ) as having the same chronological age. Any MAs reported as being above about sixteen or seventeen years are necessarily for the convenience of the test, rather than a reflection of the typical performance of people with those higher chronological ages. Some people, for example, will obtain scores which are higher than the mean for *any* age group. The nature of the mean guarantees this.

We must use considerable caution when interpreting MAs. Within the range of about five to fifteen years, MAs may be reasonably meaningful for children of approximately those same chronological ages; however, it is not correct to think of a mentally defective adult having, let us say, an MA of 6-0 as being equal to the average child of that age. The adult will have habits and motor skills differing greatly from those of the typical child, whereas the child will probably be able to grasp many new ideas much more readily than the retarded adult.

One difficulty with the interpretation of MAs is the fact that the standard deviations differ from test to test and even from age to age within the same test. Therefore there is no way of generalizing age-score values that are any stated distance from the mean; e.g., an MA of 13-3 for a child of 12-3 does not indicate the same degree of superiority as does an MA of 6-3 for a child of 5-3.

Mental age scores are tricky to interpret. It is easy to believe that their apparent meaning is real. In the elementary school, MAs may be useful to the teacher in her thinking about the potentialities of her pupils. Even here, she will want to refer to the school psychologist pupils who are having extreme learning difficulties. The school psychologist will probably use individual, rather than group, tests in helping to understand the children and in check-

ing the validity of inferences made from scores on group tests. Aside from
school and clinical settings, the mental age is a type of score that should not
be used. In my opinion, the mental age should *never* be used in personnel
and industrial settings.

(*b*) *Educational Ages, etc.* Very similar to the mental age is the educational
age. An *educational age* (EA) indicates test performance at a given level—which
level is expressed as the age of individuals for whom this is average performance.

> Susie Silber has an EA of 8–6 on a test. In other words, her achievement
> on this test is equal to the average (mean or median) performance of children
> in the norm group who were eight years six months of age, when tested; or,
> less frequently, this may mean that the average chronological age of children
> earning the same score she did, is 8–6.

Actually, what we are calling simply educational age goes under many
different names: *achievement age, reading age,* or [*any* subject matter] *age.*

All the difficulties and limitations mentioned for the MA hold for the EA
at least equally as well.

> The hypothetical *Arithmetic Acuity Test* was standardized on groups of 500
> children tested at each of the following chronological ages: 7–0, 7–3, 7–6,
> 7–9, 8–0, 8–3, 8–6, 8–9, and 9–0. Mean raw scores were found for each of
> these nine age groups. Test statisticians then interpolated to find probable
> mean scores for each of the omitted in-between ages. (For example: the
> mean raw score for 7–3 was 26, and the mean for 7–0 was 20; the test manual
> shows 24 as equal to an arithmetic age of 7–2 and 22 as equal to an arithmetic
> age of 7–1.)
>
> Obviously some children who are tested with the *Arithmetic Acuity Test* are
> going to earn scores which are lower than the mean for the lowest age group
> tested, and others are going to obtain scores higher than the mean for the
> oldest age group tested. To provide arithmetic ages that may be reported for
> such extreme cases, the test statisticians went to work again—this time extend-
> ing (extrapolating) arithmetic age values at each extreme, basing estimates
> on educated guesses as to probable performance of older and younger groups
> of children. These extrapolated values are shown by the dotted line in Figure
> 6.4.

To some extent these extreme scores may be verified by the publisher
through research with other levels of the test in articulation studies (*see*
Chapter Five). At some point, however, the EA system must break down, for
superior older children will earn scores which are above the average for *any*
chronological age. EA values assigned at the upper limits must be arbitrary.

An assumption basic to the EA seems to be that children acquire knowledge and skill more or less uniformly throughout the calendar year—that is,
that the child learns just as much per month during the long summer vaca-

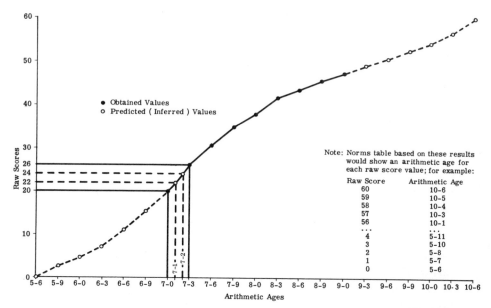

Fig. 6.4
Illustration of Interpolated and Extrapolated Age Scores on the
Hypothetical *Arithmetic Acuity Text.*

tion as during the school year. Another basic assumption of EAs seems to be
that age is more important in determining a child's level of test performance
than is his grade placement, thereby ignoring the fact that certain skills and
facts are taught at designated grades. Both assumptions are probably false.

Perhaps EAs may be of some use in comparing intra-individual variability—in deciding whether Paul has a higher arithmetic age or a higher reading age. Even in such instances, we must have evidence that the same or
similar normative groups were used in developing the age scores. And other
types of scores will do even this job better (for example, percentile ranks and
percentile bands).

### 2. Grade-Placement Scores

Probably the most common score used in reporting performance of standardized achievement tests is the *grade-placement* (or *grade-equivalent*) score.
This is unfortunate! In spite of intrinsic appeal and apparent logic, these
scores are very confusing and lend themselves to all sorts of erroneous interpretations.

The basic rationale of grade-placement scores is similar to that of age
scores, for their values are set to equal the average score of school pupils at
the corresponding grade placement. They are established by: (1) testing

youngsters at several grade placements with the same test; (2) finding the average (mean or median) for each grade-placement group; (3) plotting these averages on a graph and connecting these plots with as straight a line as possible; (4) extending (extrapolating) this line at both extremes to account for scores below and above the averages found; (5) reading off the closest grade-equivalent values for each raw-score value; (6) publishing these equivalents in tabular form.

Grade-placement scores are usually stated in tenths of a school year; e.g., 8.2 refers to second month of grade eight. (This system gives a value of 1.0 to the beginning of the first grade—which presumably is the true zero point in school grade placement.)

Here again, a basic assumption seems to be that children learn more or less uniformly throughout the school year (but that no learning occurs during the summer vacation). Although this is more reasonable than the corresponding assumption for EAs, it is far from true for all subject matters taught in school; for example, it is probably less true of reading than of arithmetic. Especially in the high school, subjects may be taught at different grade placements. Furthermore, children in school systems which are atypical in the content taught at certain grades may be penalized—or given a special advantage—when compared with youngsters from more conformative school systems.

Grade-placement scores are intrinsically appealing. It seems reasonable at first glance to think of children who stand high in comparison with others in their school grade as doing the same quality of work as youngsters slightly more advanced in school. And in a sense they are. But that does not mean that these children should be promoted immediately to a higher grade. (Why not—if they are working at that higher grade level?) Ponder, if you will: these grade-placement scores are based on the average performance of pupils having that actual placement in school. In obtaining that average, we had to have some better and some poorer scores.

Furthermore, regardless of how high a child's grade-placement score is, he has had only a given amount of time in school. And there are probably breadths and depths of understanding and competency that are closely related to the experiences and to the length of his exposure to school. A child's higher score is more likely to mean a more complete mastery of (and therefore fewer errors on) material taught at his grade. When this fact is considered, we see that the direct meaning of grade-placement scores is more apparent than real.

Grade-placement scores resulting from tests produced by different publishers are likely to give conflicting results. Not only is there the always-present likelihood of their selecting different normative samples, but the tests of different publishers are likely to place slightly different emphases on the same subject matter at the same level. For example, among grammar tests, one test may include many more questions on the use of the comma than another test does. Such differences inevitably will alter the grade-placement scores of individual pupils and of entire classes of pupils.

Because of their nature of computation, standard deviations are bound to differ for various subject matters—even when the tests are included in the same standardized achievement test battery and based on the same normative groups. Students are much more likely, for example, to have grade-placement scores several grade equivalents higher than their actual grade placement in reading and English than in arithmetic and science. The latter subjects depend much more on specific, school-taught skills. The result is that standard deviations are almost certain to be larger for English and reading than for arithmetic and science; similar, perhaps less extreme, differences exist for other subjects.

Test manuals of all the major publishers of achievement tests carefully point out these differences in standard deviations. Many test users, though, do not understand the critical importance of these differences in any interpretation of scores. Among many other points, these different standard deviations reflect the greater possible range in grade-placement scores on some tests of an achievement battery than on others. Grade-placement scores on one test may extend up 4.5 grade equivalents, as compared with only 2.5 grade equivalents for another test in the same coordinated achievement battery.

Grade-placement scores are so confusing that a lower score on one test may indicate relatively higher performance than does a higher score on another test. Because of the difference in size of standard deviations, this might easily happen: a grade-placement score of 8.5 on reading may be equal to a percentile rank of 60, but a grade-placement score of 8.2 on arithmetic fundamentals may be equal to a percentile rank of 98. Especially for higher elementary grades and beyond, grade-placement scores cannot meaningfully be compared from test to test—even within the same battery!

The difficulties noted above are accentuated when we consider subtests based on very few items. Here the chance passing or chance failing of a single test item may make the difference of one full grade equivalent. Who can get any meaning out of such a state of affairs?

All of these limitations exist even when the test difficulty level is appropriate for the pupil. If the test is so easy that a pupil answers all questions correctly on any part, we cannot know the score he should have—he might have done much better if there had been more items of appropriate difficulty for him. Thus again the paradox: tests which are too easy for a pupil give him a score that is too low. The same reasoning holds at the other extreme, too, of course.

Test publishers know the limitations of grade-placement scores and point them out carefully in their manuals. But not all test users have PhDs in educational measurement. And the more carefully the publisher documents the limitations of his tests and their scores, the less likely is the typical user to read the manual as carefully as he should. To the best of my knowledge, every major publisher includes at least some information about the equivalence of grade-placement scores to other types of score (percentiles, stanines, *T*-scores, etc.).

Test publishers have also been careful to point out that: (1) grade-placement scores based on all pupils assigned to a given grade differ from those based on only those pupils whose actual grade placement is appropriate for their age (*see* "Modal-Age Grade-Placement Scores"); (2) grade-placement scores are not standards that should be obtained by all pupils as a prerequisite for promotion; and (3) separate tables are needed when comparing average grade-placement scores for different classes or schools (because averages differ less than do individual scores).

Yet these mistaken beliefs persist. Perhaps the time is already overdue for publishers to stop using this type of score!

(*a*) *Full-Population Grade-Placement Scores.* Many sets of grade-placement norms are based on all of the pupils in those classrooms used in developing the norms. This practice has been found to produce rather large standard deviations of grade-placement scores and to make the raw score corresponding to a given grade-placement score seem rather low. When all pupils are included in the normative samples, there is a fair percentage of children included who are overage for their actual grade placement (because of nonpromotion or illness), and a few who are underage for their actual grade placement.

Most publishers have taken steps to make their grade-placement norms produce results that seem to typify school classes better. They offer modal-age grade-placement norms either instead of, or in addition to, full-population norms.

(*b*) *Modal-Age Grade-Placement Scores.* As mentioned above, there are some overage and some underage pupils in most classrooms. The presence of these pupils in classes used for normative purposes is thought to be undesirable. Most publishers now use modal-age grade-placement scores either exclusively or in addition to the full-population norms.

*Modal-age* indicates that only those pupils who are of about average age for their grade placement are used. The practices of publishers differ somewhat, but their aims are similar. One publisher may include all pupils who are not more than one year underage or overage for their grade placement; a second publisher may use only those pupils within three months of the modal chronological age for a specified grade placement.

Modal-age norms are, of course, a little more select. When both full-population and modal-age grade-placement norms are compared, we find that higher raw scores are needed to attain a given grade-placement score on modal-age norms. When we use standardized achievement tests and grade-placement scores, we should be certain to notice whether modal-age norms are being used.

(*c*) *Modal-Age and Modal-Intelligence Grade-Placement Scores.* A further refinement of grade-placement scores is the practice of basing the norms only on pupils who are of near-average intelligence as well as being near-average in chronological age for actual grade placement. This should not have any pronounced effect on grade-placement values, but it is believed by the California Test Bureau to provide a better guarantee of a grade-placement score that is truly representative of average performance. The reasoning seems to be that the use of only those individuals who are near-average on an intelligence measure does away with the necessity for any assumption that low-ability and high-ability individuals will balance out to give a value that is a good average.

In developing these age- and intelligence-controlled score values, the California Test Bureau used only pupils with IQs of 98–102, who were within three months of average age for their actual grade placement (for grades one–eight); progressively higher IQs were used for successively higher grades.

(*d*) *Anticipated-Achievement Grade-Placement (AAGP) Scores.* Another concept used by the California Test Bureau in connection with its *California Achievement Tests* battery is the *anticipated-achievement grade-placement* score. This is a statement, separate for each test in the battery, of the average grade-placement score made by pupils in the norming groups who have a given grade placement and mental age. In this fashion the publishers have developed somewhat more individualized norms.

Unlike the other scores explained in this chapter, these are expected score values. They demand a special explanation for they are not predicted score values based on correlation techniques. Rather they are a statement of expectation based on actual empirical data.

In practice, the *AAGPs* are used in this fashion: (1) the *California Test of Mental Maturity* is administered to pupils and scored; (2) the *California Achievement Tests* are administered and scored; (3) a special table is entered with information about actual grade placement at the time of the two testings and MA obtained on the CTMM; and (4) the table is read for *Intellectual Status Index* (*see* score Type III B) and for *AAGPs* for the six achievement tests.

The *AAGP* scores are to be thought of as expected values considering MA and actual grade placement. Each pupil's six obtained grade-placement scores are then compared with the corresponding six *AAGPs* in deciding whether he is achieving about as should be expected or very much above or below the expected level.

There seems to be considerable logic and careful work behind the development of the *AAGPs* and the modal-age and -intelligence grade-placement norms. The publisher has made grade-placement scores about as meaningful as they can be made. On the other hand, the publisher has also introduced an extremely complicated procedure with many opportunities for mistakes and misunderstandings. Although the work may be commendable, it seems formidable, too.

(e) *Mental Age Grade-Placement Scores.* This score is used occasionally in reporting the intelligence test performance of a school pupil. The mental age found for a pupil is translated into a grade-placement score—the grade placement for which this MA is the average.

The only advantage possible to claim for this score is that it is stated in grade-placement units—and that grade placement may be a more familiar concept than mental age. Like other Type II D scores, it has the disadvantage of telling us nothing directly about the brightness of the examinee. It has the additional limitations of other grade-placement scores. There is a degree of logic to stating achievement test scores in grade-placement units, but I can find none for expressing intelligence test scores in such units.

## Type III: Intra-Individual Comparison

All Type III scores are unique in that they are based on two measurements of the same person; all are found as ratios or fractions. The first two are in current use, but the last two are in general disrepute.

### TYPE III A: RATIO IQ (INTELLIGENCE QUOTIENT)

Although we have considered the IQ twice before and will return to it once again (under Type IV), this is the original IQ—the one first proposed by Stern and first used by Terman more than fifty years ago. The *ratio-type intelligence quotient* is found by the formula: $IQ = 100 \ MA/CA$, where $MA$ is a mental age found from an intelligence test, and $CA$ is the examinee's chronological age at the time of testing (with an adjusted $CA$ used for older adolescents and adults). It is becoming a relatively less common score.

The rationale of the ratio-type IQ is widely understood, but its many limitations are less well known. The score depends on an assumption of equal-sized mental-age units, which may not exist. Ratio-type IQs work reasonably well between the ages of about five to fifteen years, but tend to be of questionable value outside those approximate limits. Adult IQs of necessity are based on artificial mental ages (as explained earlier) as well as "adjusted" chronological ages.

The most telling argument against the ratio IQ, however, is the observable fact that standard deviations are likely to differ from one age level to the next. If standard deviations are permitted to vary (and this cannot be controlled with a ratio IQ), the same IQ indicates different degrees of superiority or inferiority at different ages. The deviation IQ (Type II A or II B) is much better than the ratio IQ—so much better, in fact, that the ratio IQ is rapidly becoming extinct.

### TYPE III B: INTELLECTUAL STATUS INDEX

A concept introduced by the California Test Bureau for use with its *California Test of Mental Maturity* is the *Intellectual Status Index*. This is a sort of IQ substitute with the denominator changed from a child's actual chronological age to the average chronological age of children with his same grade placement in school.

This score is based on the premise that a pupil's score on an intelligence test is determined more by his placement in school than by his chronological age. The logic sounds reasonable, but the user should check carefully the size of standard deviation at different age levels. One must be careful, too, not to confuse *ISI* with IQ, especially for children who are either overage or underage in their respective grades.

### TYPE III C: EDUCATIONAL QUOTIENTS

An *Educational Quotient* is found by dividing an educational age (EA) by chronological age (CA) and multiplying by 100. Just as we may have subject-matter ages of all sorts, so may we have all sorts of subject-matter quotients. EQs have never been very widely used, for grade-placement scores have been preferred.

EQs have much the same advantages and limitations as ratio IQs, except that we can always use the pupil's actual CA. Since EQs are used only with school-level achievement tests, we do not have the problem of working with arbitrary divisors—although of course we still have extrapolated EAs with which to contend.

Because of the limitations of EAs, we cannot make direct comparisons from one subject matter to another even when the tests have been standardized on the same groups. With even less confidence can we make any meaningful comparisons when different norming groups have been used for two or more tests.

### TYPE III D: ACCOMPLISHMENT QUOTIENTS

There is almost unanimous agreement that the *Accomplishment* (or *Achievement*) *Quotient* (AQ) is a poor type of score. Not only is it based on two test scores, each with its own errors of measurement, but it gives illogical results.

It compares a pupil's achievement test score with a measure of his intelligence, and is presumed to indicate how completely he is living up to his capacity.

FORMULA:

$$AQ = 100 \frac{EA}{MA}, \text{ where}$$

$EA$ = educational age, determined by an achievement test
$MA$ = mental age, determined by an intelligence test.

The ideal AQ is 100, indicating that a pupil is realizing his complete potential. How, then, do we explain AQs above 100? Although logically impossible, AQs above 100 are not unusual—suggesting that some pupils are achieving better than they are capable of achieving. A much more reasonable explanation of course is that the two scores entering into the AQ are fallible measures and that errors of measurement have combined to produce this "impossible" result.

All other Type III scores are based on one essentially error-free measure (actually measurement error is so slight that it is negligible), either CA or grade placement. These other scores then are of the same order of accuracy as are the age scores which form their numerators. With the AQ, however, both numerator and denominator values are determined by separate tests—and the AQ is subject to the measurement errors of both. The result is a remarkably poor type of score.

## Type IV: Assorted Arbitrary Bases

Although the three main bases for expressing test scores are sufficient to account for most commonly used scores, there are still a few that are unique. We shall mention several very briefly.

### TYPE IV A: NONMEANINGFUL SCALED SCORES

Several publishers use scaled scores that are nonmeaningful in themselves but which are extremely useful in giving a common basis for equating different forms and/or levels of a test. The previously mentioned *CEEB* score, as used today, has many elements of such a scaled score. *CEEB* scores originally were linear standard scores with a mean of 500 and a standard deviation of 100; however, for about thirty years the results of each year's edition have been keyed statistically to the 1941 results. Thus, these *CEEB* scores are not directly interpretable for today's examinees, and percentile ranks are used for that purpose.

We shall consider only one more example: the *SCAT* scale developed by the Educational Testing Service. This is a nonmeaningful scaled score used with its *School and College Abilities Tests (SCAT)* and its *Sequential Tests of Educational Progress (STEP)*. ETS sought deliberately a scale using numbers that would not be confused with scores from other scales. The scale was constructed so that a scaled score of 300 would equal a percentage-correct score of 60; and a scaled score of 260, a percentage-correct score of 20. These scaled score values are used as a statistical convenience for the publisher, but percentile bands are used for interpreting results.

### TYPE IV B: LONG-RANGE EQUI-UNIT SCALES

None of the scores mentioned has a scale of equal units except within a narrow range or under certain assumptions. For some purposes, it is most desirable to have a single equi-unit scale covering a wide span of ages.

An early attempt at constructing such a scale resulted in the *T*-score and *T*-scaled score, mentioned earlier. As originally conceived by McCall, this scale was to use 50 for the mean of an unselected group of twelve-year-olds. The mean for older groups would be higher, for younger groups lower. The standard deviation would be 10 at all age levels.

Another early attempt was made by Heinis, who developed mental growth units that he believed were more nearly uniform in size than mental age units. These, in turn, were made to yield a Personal Constant, which he felt was more consistent than the IQ over a period of years. Although *Kuhlmann–Anderson* norms have used the PC, they have never been widely accepted.

A present-day example of such a scale is the *K-score* scales developed by Gardner. The average score of tenth-graders is set at 100, and the unit of measurement is set at one-seventh the standard deviation of fifth-graders. The rationale underlying the scale is too complex to go into here, but it has been applied to the *Stanford Achievement Tests* (published by Harcourt, Brace & World, Inc.).

The principal advantage of such long-range equi-unit scales is to be found in various research applications. For the most part, they do not lend themselves well to direct interpretation. Their underlying rationale is usually involved and their development complicated. The reader who is interested in such scores may obtain further information from any of the more technical measurements references.

### TYPE IV C: DEVIATION IQ (OTIS-STYLE)

It is fitting, perhaps, to come to the end of our long succession of scores with another IQ—the fourth one we have mentioned. (Is it any wonder that the IQ is a confusing score?)

The deviation IQ as used on earlier *Otis* intelligence tests and certain others is basically different from the Type II deviation IQs. In the development of the Otis-style deviation IQ, a norm (or average) is found for each of several age groups. We obtain an examinee's IQ by finding his raw score, subtracting his age norm, and adding 100; the result shows an examinee's deviation from his age norm in raw-score units.

FORMULA:

$$(\text{Otis}) \ IQ = 100 + (X - \bar{X}_{\text{age norm}}), \text{ where}$$
$$X = \text{any person's raw score on an Otis intelligence test}$$
$$\bar{X}_{\text{age norm}} = \text{average raw score for those in norm group whose chronological age is same as examinee's.}$$

This deviation IQ has a mean of 100, but the standard deviation is not controlled as were the standard deviations of the Type II deviation IQs. Because of this, the standard deviations of Otis-style IQs may vary from age to age and make interpretations difficult. [Note: the newer *Otis–Lennon Mental Ability Test* (Harcourt, Brace & World, Inc.) uses a Type II A 5(a) score, the Wechsler-type of deviation IQ.]

## A Final Word

We have considered many types of test score in this chapter. With only one or two exceptions, they are all in widespread use. The personnel worker in industry is likely to encounter relatively few of them—probably only Types II A and II B (interindividual comparisons considering mean and standard deviation, and considering rank within group). The school teacher or the guidance worker may very well encounter any of them.

Test scores would be much easier to interpret—for all of us, experts and novices alike—if only we could agree upon a single type of score, or even on just a few.

Considering all factors, I should like to see the day when we would use only percentile ranks or percentile bands in test interpretation. This score has limitations, to be sure, as all scores do. But the score has some inherent meaning and is easy for the layman to grasp. With a single type of score, we could direct our attention to educating everyone to its meaning and to its principal limitation, the difference in distances between various percentile points. We could stress, too, the importance of knowing the composition of the norm group (or groups).

There is little question but that percentile ranks can do everything that the IQ can, regardless of which of the four types we use. And percentile ranks within grade or within age have many advantages over grade-placement and age scores.

We might still have need for special warning about the use of percentile ranks on very short tests where the difference of a single raw-score value may mean a great difference in percentile rank, but the percentile band, of course, is a protection here. And we still have need for other kinds of score for research, because percentile ranks do not lend themselves well to mathematical manipulation; indeed, we cannot even average them.

We must remember that a test score must be understood before it can be interpreted. And it would be easier to learn one score thoroughly than to try to learn something about many assorted scores.

Even more significant than any of these considerations, of course, is the quality of the test itself. I cannot emphasize too strongly that the quality of the test itself is more important than anything else! A poor test is still a poor test even if it has fine printing, elaborate norms tables, and a wealth of statistical work-ups. A good test is one that will do the job we want it to, will do so consistently, and will possess those practical features (such as cost, time required, etc.) which make it usable for our purposes.

Test scores are used to express test performance. If they permit us to understand more about how well a person has done on a test, they are better scores than those which obscure such understanding. But no score can be meaningful if the test is poor in quality, or lacks validity, or has low reliability. And, although derived scores can be more meaningful than raw scores, they cannot be more accurate.

# PROFILES

## Chapter Seven

There is a map-maker, I hear, who deliberately draws some nonexistent feature—perhaps a tiny village, a lake, or a stream—on each of his maps in an effort to trap any would-be copier. The place of course does not exist after it appears on the map any more than it did before appearing there. A good map reflects features that exist in reality, but it does not make their existence any more real or any less real.

In exactly the same way, a test *profile* (sometimes called *psychograph*) portrays the test scores of an individual. The profile is a graphic device enabling us to see the over-all performance of an individual at a glance. An important point to remember, though, is that the profile does not make the scores any more true. Most of us find it surprisingly easy to believe that a score must be accurate if we have seen it on a test profile. And most of us find it especially easy to see apparent differences in score as being real differences. We need to remind ourselves that the differences are not necessarily significant just because they are some distance apart on the profile form.

Profiles are a convenient way of showing test scores. They provide an excellent means for gaining an over-all picture of a person's strengths and weaknesses. Profiles can be very helpful provided we use suitable caution in their interpretation.

In general, a profile is used only when we wish to show two or more scores for the same person. These scores may be based on parts of the same test or of the same test battery—or they may be based on different tests entirely. In the latter instance, we should be especially careful when using the same profile sheet for tests with distinctly different norms groups. Any observed difference in score is likely to be more a function of the different norms groups than of any real difference in aptitude, achievement, etc.

### Specific-Test Profiles

There are two basic types of profile. The first is prepared by the test publisher for a *specific* test or test battery; the second is a *general* profile form which may be used for almost any test.

Figure 7.1 shows a profile for Sam Sweeney who has taken the *Kuder Preference Record: Vocational (Form C)*. This form has been designed so that the examinee may construct his own profile. His raw scores for each of the several interest areas are entered at the top of the respective columns. The examinee locates each score in the half of the column labeled "M" (for his sex), and draws a line across the column. By blackening the entire column beneath that line, he has constructed a bar graph showing his relative preference for activities in these ten vocational areas as defined by Kuder. Sam's percentile rank for each area may be read along the calibration at either side of the graph. Note how the percentiles "bunch up" around 50—just as we would expect from our knowledge of the normal curve.

Sam is a twenty-four-year-old male who, having completed his military service, is now a college junior. He is interested in science and thinks that he might like college teaching. There is nothing in this profile to suggest that this would be an unwise choice; the high score on Scientific supports his stated interest in that area, and high scores on Persuasive are common among people who go into teaching. We might have urged caution if he had shown high measured interest in Artistic or Musical and low in Scientific and Persuasive. We still need additional information, of course, before offering positive encouragement. What sort of ability does he have? What are his grades? *Et cetera*.

A somewhat different use of the bar graph approach to showing test results is found in Figure 7.2, representing Grace Gibbs's performance on the *Differential Aptitude Tests*. Although the vertical axis again shows percentile ranks, the bars here are drawn out from the median; the publisher, The Psychological Corporation, prefers to emphasize deviation from the average in this manner. National norms for eleventh-grade girls were used.

This profile sheet is taken from a six-page interpretive folder, "Your Aptitudes as Measured by the *Differential Aptitude Tests*." Here again the percentile points are closer together near 50, as they should be. An important feature of this profile sheet is the discussion of "important differences" directly below the profile; note, however, that the original page size is larger than that shown here. Other pages in this student folder describe the meaning of aptitude and of the test areas of the *Differential Aptitude Tests*. In addition, one whole page is devoted to "How Much Confidence Can Be Placed in Tests?" and includes an excellent discussion of expectancy tables.

This case, adapted from the *DAT* casebook published by The Psycho-

NAME *Sweeney, Sam S.* AGE *24* SEX *M* GROUP *Men* DATE OF TEST *10-10-70*
Print Last First Initial M or F

First Revision, February 1951

REPRODUCTION BY ANY MEANS STRICTLY PROHIBITED

# PROFILE SHEET

**for the**

**KUDER PREFERENCE RECORD**

**VOCATIONAL**

**Forms CH, CM**

**MEN and WOMEN**

## DIRECTIONS FOR PROFILING

1. Copy the V-Score from the back page of your answer pad in the box at the right. *41*

   *If your V-Score is 37 or less,* there is some reason for doubting the value of your answers, and your other scores may not be very accurate. *If your V-Score is 45 or more,* you may not have understood the directions, since 44 is the highest possible score. *If your score is not between 38 and 44,* inclusive, you should see your adviser. He will probably recommend that you read the directions again, and then that you fill out the blank a second time, being careful to follow the directions exactly and to give sincere replies.

   If your V-Score is between 38 and 44, inclusive, go ahead with the following directions.

2. Copy the scores 0 through 9 in the spaces at the top of the profile chart. Under "OUTDOOR" find the number which is the same as the score at the top. If your score is not shown, draw a line *between* the scores above and below your own. Use the numbers under M if you are a man and the numbers under F if you are a woman. Draw a line through this number from one side to the other of the entire column under OUTDOOR. Do the same thing for the scores at the top of each of the other columns. If a score is larger than any number in the column, draw a line across the top of the column; if it is smaller, draw a line across the bottom.

3. With your pencil blacken the entire space between the lines you have drawn and the bottom of the chart. The result is your profile for the *Kuder Preference Record—Vocational.*

   An interpretation of the scores will be found on the other side.

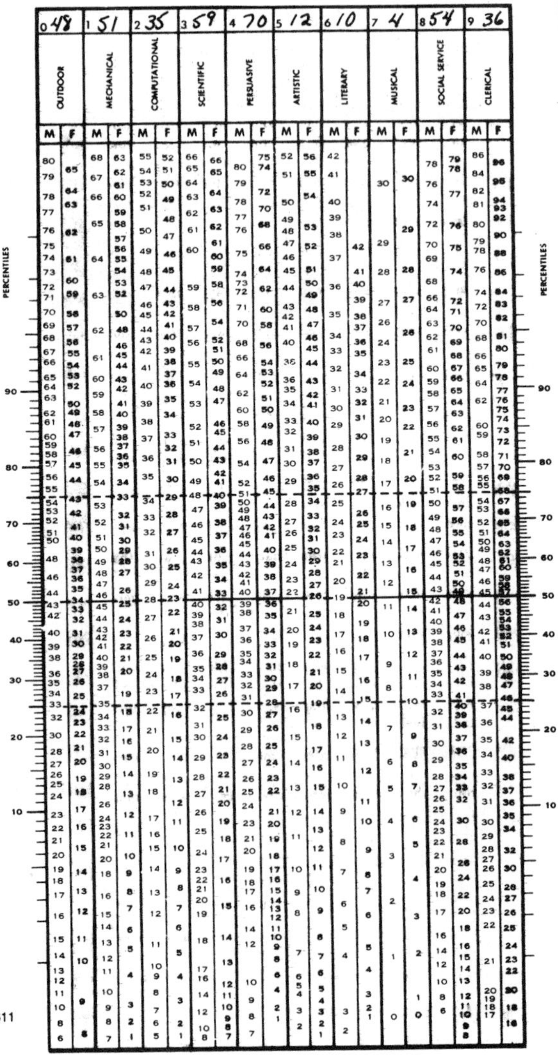


S R A Science Research Associates, Inc.
259 East Erie Street, Chicago, Illinois 60611

A Subsidiary of IBM



Reorder No. 7-299

**Fig. 7.1**

*© 1951, G. Frederic Kuder. Reproduced by permission of the publisher, Science Research Associates, Inc.*

## Profiling Your DAT Scores

The numbers that tell how you did on each test are in the row marked "Percentiles." Your percentile tells where you rank on a test in comparison with boys or girls in your grade. These percentiles are based on test scores earned by thousands of students in numerous schools across the country. If your percentile rank is 50, you are just in the middle — that is, one-half of the students in the national group did better than you and one-half did less well. (If your school uses local norms, your counselor will explain the difference.)

In the columns below each percentile you can draw your aptitude profile. For each test make a *heavy short line* across the column at the level which corresponds to your percentile rank on that test.

Your aptitude profile will be more visible if you black in each column *up to* or *down to* the 50-line from the short lines you have just made. The vertical bars on your profile show the strength of your tested aptitudes, *up* or *down* from the rank of the *middle student* of your grade and sex.

### More about Percentiles

Think of "percentile" as meaning "per cent of people." In your case, the people are boys or girls in your grade in many schools across the country. The percentile shows what per cent of this group scored no higher than you did. If your percentile rank on one test is 80, you are at the top of 80 per cent of the group —only 20 per cent made higher scores than yours. If you scored in the 25th percentile, this would mean about 75 per cent of the group did better than you on the test. Thus, a percentile rank always indicates your relative standing among a theoretical 100 persons representing a large "norm" group — in this case, students of your sex and grade. It does NOT tell how many questions (or what per cent of them) you answered correctly.

### Note

If your teacher gives you a label with your name, raw scores, and percentiles on it, first peel off the backing and expose the sticky surface. Then place it carefully so that the percentile numbers are just above the columns in the chart, and press it down firmly.

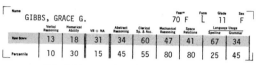

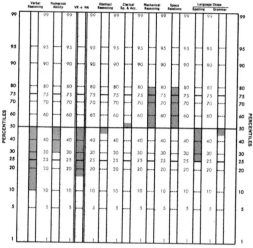

Norms Used_____(If no entry, percentiles are based on national norms)

*F — first (fall) semester testing and percentiles; S — second (spring) semester testing and percentiles.

### How Big a Difference Is Important?

Of course we do not want to over-estimate small differences in ability on tests because a test cannot be perfectly accurate, and your score might not be exactly the same if you could take the same test twice.

To estimate the importance of a difference between your scores on any two tests on this profile, use a ruler to measure how much higher on the chart one mark is than the other. It is the *vertical* distance ↕ that counts, of course, *not* how far *across* the chart ╱ or ╲ .

If the distance is *one inch or greater,* it is probable that you have a real difference in your abilities on the two tests.

If a difference between the two percentile ranks is *between a half inch and one inch,* consider whether other things you know about yourself agree with it; the difference may or may not be important.

If the vertical distance between two tests is *less than a half inch,* the difference between the two scores may be disregarded; so small a difference is probably not meaningful.

**Fig. 7.2**

*Reproduced by permission. Copyright 1947, 1952, © 1959, 1963, 1966 by The Psychological Corporation, New York, N.Y. All rights reserved.*

logical Corporation, concerns an eleventh-grade student of about average ability who was failing in her school's commercial curriculum. After counseling, Grace decided to transfer to a dress-making course, thereby presumably capitalizing on her above-average ability in Space Relations and Mechanical Reasoning. In this new curriculum, Grace's attitude toward school improved, her grades picked up, and she graduated from high school the following year.

There was reason to believe that Grace had fooled herself into thinking that she wanted commercial work. Her highest scores on a vocational interest test were Computational and Clerical. She was sufficiently mature, however, to discuss her problem with her school counselor and to act on sensible advice. Also helpful here was the fact that her parents were cooperative and did not object to Grace's change to a lower-status objective.

Still another approach is shown in Figure 7.3, portraying Nancy Namyl's performance on the *Stanford Achievement Test* (*Advanced Battery*). The top chart gives her scores as grade-placement scores (with the decimal point removed) and as percentile ranks, and calls for the plotting of stanine values. The bottom chart shows grade-placement scores only. In this profile, the shaded bars show the approximate size of the standard errors of measurement for the respective tests; under certain assumptions, we may consider Nancy's *true* scores to be no more than one bar-length away (plus or minus) from the corresponding obtained scores—on the average, this will be true about two-thirds of the time. As noted elsewhere, we can make use of this information in deciding whether there are significant differences between the various test areas. Rather clearly, Nancy's achievement in arithmetic areas is lower than her achievement in other areas.

Nancy's profile illustrates one good use for an achievement battery: to identify areas of possible difficulty. Nancy is just starting junior high school. Her grades during the fifth and sixth grades were uniformly good—all *A*s and *B*s. These results suggest that her teachers have been overlooking her arithmetic work. At least, her seventh-grade teachers will want to consider the possibility that she may need additional assistance in arithmetic. Hopefully, Nancy will keep up her good work in English.

Figure 7.4 shows a different kind of profile—this time, a line graph. The information shown, of course, is similar; however, this approach directs attention to the relationship among some of the subtests. Note that every value plotted on the profile is based on at least twenty-five items; with rare exceptions should separate scores be based on fewer items than this. The figure shows Will Warren's results on the California Test Bureau's *Multiple Aptitude Tests*. Note the statement about the significance of differences between scores.

Will is a fifteen-year-old ninth grader who plans to go to college. At present, he is interested in both the physical and social sciences, and has

# Stanford Achievement Test

**ADVANCED BATTERY**

## INDIVIDUAL STANINE AND GRADE SCORE PROFILE CHARTS

Name _Namyl_ (LAST) _Nancy_ (FIRST) _N_ (INITIAL) Boy ☐ Girl ☒

School _Clifton J.H.S._ City or Town _Whitfield_ Teacher _Mrs. Carlson_

Date of Testing _1970_ (YEAR) _Oct._ (MONTH) _7–16_ (DAY) Date of Birth _1958_ (YEAR) _Aug._ (MONTH) _20_ (DAY)

Form of Test Used _W_ Grade Placement _7–1_ Age _12–1_ (YRS. MOS.)

DIRECTIONS FOR USING EITHER OR BOTH CHARTS MAY BE FOUND ON THE REVERSE SIDE

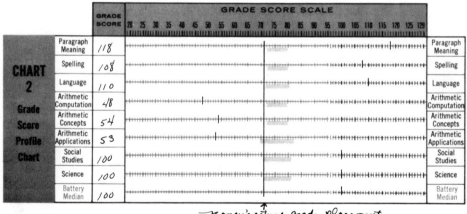

| CHART 1 / Stanine Profile Chart | | GRADE SCORE | PERCENTILE RANK* | STANINE* |
|---|---|---|---|---|
| | Paragraph Meaning | 118 | 98 | 1 2 3 4 5 6 7 8 ⊠9 |
| | Spelling | 108 | 90 | 1 2 3 4 5 6 7 ⊠8 9 |
| | Language | 110 | 94 | 1 2 3 4 5 6 7 ⊠8 9 |
| | Arithmetic Computation | 48 | 8 | 1 ⊠2 3 4 5 6 7 8 9 |
| | Arithmetic Concepts | 54 | 16 | 1 2 ⊠3 4 5 6 7 8 9 |
| | Arithmetic Applications | 53 | 18 | 1 2 ⊠3 4 5 6 7 8 9 |
| | Social Studies | 100 | 82 | 1 2 3 4 5 6 ⊠7 8 9 |
| | Science | 100 | 84 | 1 2 3 4 5 6 ⊠7 8 9 |

*Percentile Ranks and Stanines based on tables for Beginning ☒ Middle ☐ End ☐ of grade (check one)

| CHART 2 / Grade Score Profile Chart | | GRADE SCORE |
|---|---|---|
| | Paragraph Meaning | 118 |
| | Spelling | 108 |
| | Language | 110 |
| | Arithmetic Computation | 48 |
| | Arithmetic Concepts | 54 |
| | Arithmetic Applications | 53 |
| | Social Studies | 100 |
| | Science | 100 |
| | Battery Median | 100 |

GRADE SCORE SCALE: 20 25 30 35 40 45 50 55 60 65 70 75 80 85 90 95 100 105 110 115 120 125 129

_Nancy's actual grade placement_

**Fig. 7.3**

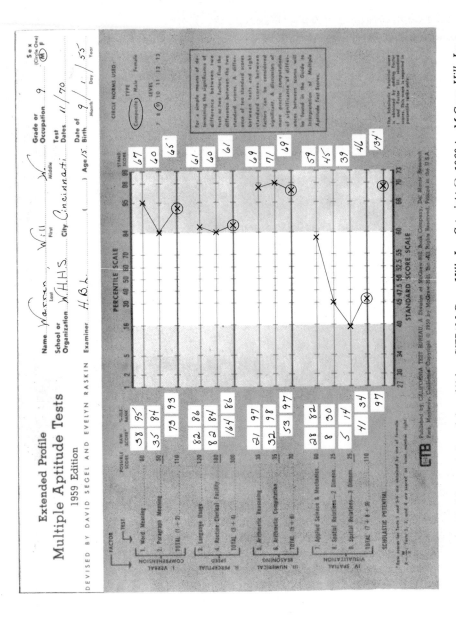

**Fig. 7.4** *Used by permission of the publisher, CTB/McGraw-Hill, Inc. Copyright © 1969 by McGraw-Hill, Inc. From Multiple Aptitude Tests devised by David Segel and Evelyn Raskin. Copyright © 1959 by McGraw-Hill, Inc.*

also considered engineering. On the basis of these results, we could assure Will that he has sufficient potential for college work. We might advise him to continue thinking about college and about different occupations. His relatively low scores in Spatial Visualization suggest that he may be wise to consider occupations other than engineering, but we may decide to wait for another year or two before stressing any negative implication these scores may have for engineering. We might want to stress that good grades are also important for any student who wants to go to a first-class college.

Figure 7.5 is a profile of Dorothy Darley's scores on two different adminstrations of the *Iowa Tests of Basic Skills*. This profile, by the Houghton Mifflin Company, is planned for handy comparison of as many as six different adminsistrations of the battery. It does so at the expense of using small spaces between successive units on the scale of scores, thereby effectively flattening the appearance of the profile. The units used here are grade-placement scores with the decimal points removed; thus, 35 means 3.5, or fifth month of the third grade, etc.

There are obvious advantages to having two or more administrations of a test battery drawn on the same profile form. If the tests are carefully constructed to be comparable (the specific items, of course, differ from grade to grade), we can study the child's progress. Dorothy shows excellent progress, having increased her over-all score by 2.8 grade equivalents in two years. In Reading Comprehension her improvement is 3.2 grade equivalents. Probably the most important point to note is that Dorothy now tends to score somewhat above her actual grade placement whereas only two years ago she tested at or very slightly below her grade placement. It will be interesting to see whether Dorothy retains her increased achievement rate when retested in another two years; there seems to be a promise in the second testing that was not evident in the first. Even now, Dorothy apparently could use some additional study in the area of Work-Study Skills.

Another sort of profile is shown in Figure 7.6, the *Wechsler Adult Intelligence Scale* results for Mona Manley. The *WAIS* is an individual test of intelligence published by The Psychological Corporation. The profile is obtained as a by-product in getting the scaled scores necessary for computing the IQs. Some psychologists, however, have tried to use it as a personality test by noting relative peaks and dips—despite the publisher's warning at the bottom of the profile.

Mrs. Manley is a forty-six-year-old widow who is receiving psychotherapy from a clinical psychologist. Her *WAIS* results indicate high average intelligence and may suggest something about the nature of her present difficulties. Skilled clinicians can obtain additional clues from such individual tests by observing the counselee's behavior, noting unusual responses, etc. Although administration of the individual tests requires more skill and more time, they often are worthwhile because of the greater yield of information.

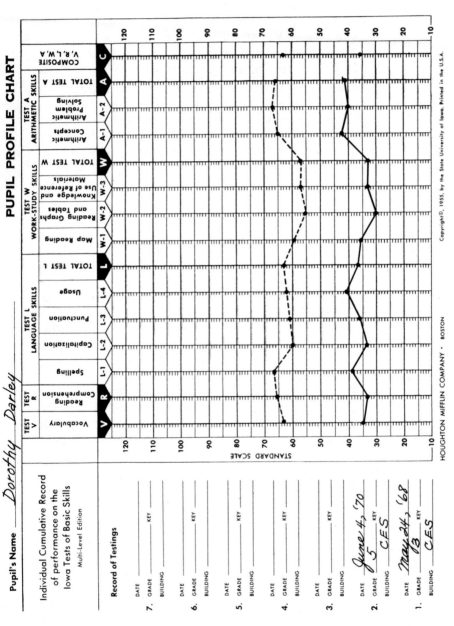

Fig. 7.5

# WAIS RECORD FORM

**Wechsler Adult Intelligence Scale**

Name _Mona Manley_

Birth Date _2/11/24_ Age _46_ Sex _F_ Marital: S M D (W)

Nat. _U.S._ Color _White_ Tested by _H.BL._

Place of Examination _Office – U.C._ Date _3/10/70_

Occupation _News Reporter_ Education _1 yr. Graduate Work_

## TABLE OF SCALED SCORE EQUIVALENTS*

### RAW SCORE

| Scaled Score | Information | Comprehension | Arithmetic | Similarities | Digit Span | Vocabulary | Digit Symbol | Picture Completion | Block Design | Picture Arrangement | Object Assembly | Scaled Score |
|---|---|---|---|---|---|---|---|---|---|---|---|---|
| 19 | 29 | 27-28 | | 26 | 17 | 78-80 | 87-90 | | | 36 | 44 | 19 |
| 18 | 28 | 26 | | 25 | | 76-77 | 83-86 | 21 | | 36 | 44 | 18 |
| 17 | 27 | 25 | 18 | 24 | | 74-75 | 79-82 | | 48 | 35 | 43 | 17 |
| 16 | (26) | 24 | 17 | 23 | 16 | 71-73 | 76-78 | 20 | 47 | 34 | 42 | 16 |
| 15 | 25 | (23) | 16 | 22 | 15 | 67-70 | (72-75) | | 46 | 33 | 41 | 15 |
| 14 | 23-24 | 22 | 15 | 21 | (14) | 63-66 | 69-71 | (19) | 44-45 | 32 | 40 | 14 |
| 13 | 21-22 | 21 | (14) | 19-20 | | 59-62 | 66-68 | 18 | 42-43 | 30-31 | 38-39 | 13 |
| 12 | 19-20 | 20 | 13 | 17-18 | 13 | 54-58 | 62-65 | 17 | 39-41 | 28-29 | 36-37 | 12 |
| 11 | 17-18 | 19 | 12 | 15-16 | 12 | 47-53 | 58-61 | 15-16 | 35-38 | 26-27 | 34-35 | 11 |
| 10 | 15-16 | 17-18 | 11 | 13-14 | 11 | 40-46 | 52-57 | 14 | 31-34 | 23-25 | 31-33 | 10 |
| 9 | 13-14 | 15-16 | 10 | 11-12 | 10 | 32-39 | 47-51 | 12-13 | 28-30 | 20-22 | 28-30 | 9 |
| 8 | 11-12 | 14 | 9 | 9-10 | | 26-31 | 41-46 | 10-11 | 25-27 | 18-19 | 25-27 | 8 |
| 7 | 9-10 | 12-13 | 7-8 | 7-8 | 9 | 22-25 | 35-40 | 8-9 | 21-24 | 15-17 | 22-24 | 7 |
| 6 | 7-8 | 10-11 | 6 | 5-6 | 8 | 18-21 | 29-34 | 6-7 | 17-20 | 12-14 | 19-21 | 6 |
| 5 | 5-6 | 8-9 | 5 | 4 | | 14-17 | 23-28 | 5 | 13-16 | 9-11 | 15-18 | 5 |
| 4 | 4 | 6-7 | 4 | 3 | 7 | 11-13 | 18-22 | 4 | 10-12 | 8 | 11-14 | 4 |
| 3 | 3 | 5 | 3 | 2 | | 10 | 15-17 | 3 | 6-9 | 7 | 8-10 | 3 |
| 2 | 2 | 4 | 2 | 1 | 6 | 9 | 13-14 | 2 | 3-5 | 6 | 5-7 | 2 |
| 1 | 1 | 3 | 1 | | 4-5 | 8 | 12 | 1 | 2 | 5 | 3-4 | 1 |
| 0 | 0 | 0-2 | 0 | 0 | 0-3 | 0-7 | 0-11 | 0 | 0-1 | 0-4 | 0-2 | 0 |

## SUMMARY

| TEST | Raw Score | Scaled Score |
|---|---|---|
| Information | 26 | 16 |
| Comprehension | 23 | 15 |
| Arithmetic | 14 | 13 |
| Similarities | 9 | 8 |
| Digit Span | 14 | 14 |
| Vocabulary | 72 | 16 |
| **Verbal Score** | | 82 |
| Digit Symbol | 74 | 15 |
| Picture Completion | 19 | 14 |
| Block Design | 29 | 9 |
| Picture Arrangement | 18 | 8 |
| Object Assembly | 33 | 10 |
| **Performance Score** | | 56 |
| **Total Score** | | 138 |

VERBAL SCORE _82_ IQ _124_

PERFORMANCE SCORE _56_ IQ _120_

FULL SCALE SCORE _138_ IQ _123_

*Clinicians who wish to draw a "psychograph" on the above table may do so by connecting the subject's raw scores. The interpretation of any such profile, however, should take into account the reliabilities of the subtests and the lower reliabilities of differences between subtest scores.

**Fig. 7.6**

*Reproduced by permission. Copyright 1947, © 1955 by The Psychological Corporation, New York, N.Y. All rights reserved.*

Test profiles that may be shown to examinees (or to parents) should show clearly the titles of the various tests; however, personality tests are an exception to that principle—especially if any of the variables might be construed as threatening by the examinee. Figure 7.7 shows a profile of David Dyman's scores on the *California Psychological Inventory* (published by the Consulting Psychologists Press, Inc.). Note that the titles of the scales are given only in abbreviated form, meaningful to the test user, but not to the examinee. The breaks in the profile call attention to the four classes of measures found with the *CPI*: (1) measures of poise, ascendancy, and self-assurance; (2) measures of socialization, maturity, and responsibility; (3) measures of achievement potential and intellectual efficiency; and

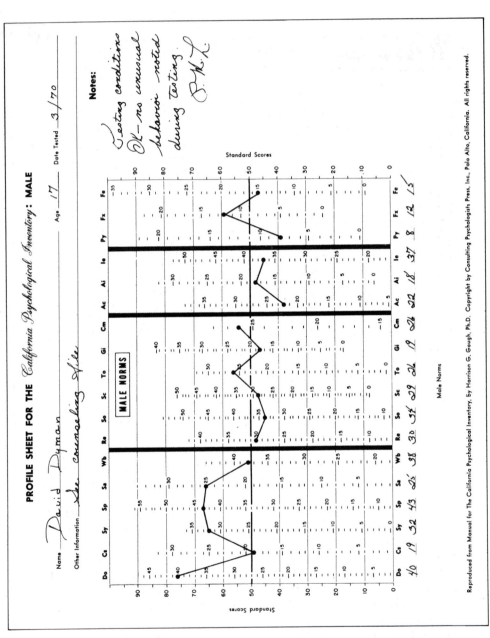

**Fig. 7.7**

(4) measures of intellectual and interest modes. *T*-score values are the derived scores shown at the left and right in the profile.

David Dyman, a case adapted from the *CPI Manual* (with permission of the publisher, the Consulting Psychologists Press, Inc.), is a seventeen-year-old high school student named by his principal as an outstanding student leader. Although he ranks high in scholastic aptitude, his achievement had been only average. The test profile is high for the Class I measures, especially Do (Dominance). Most other scores are near average (50) and would be difficult to interpret meaningfully. Of some interest, though, is the low Ac (Achievement) score, which suggests that the boy's academic achievement may be below what would be expected of him considering his ability, drive, etc.

Profiles are especially useful when it may be desirable to consider relative scores or the interaction of scores on several scales of a test.

We could go on almost endlessly noting additional profiles, each indicating something just a bit different from the others. But let us finish this particular section with just two more profiles (Figures 7.8 and 7.9). These illustrate Helen Hill's performance on the *Sequential Tests of Educational Progress* (*STEP*) and the *School and College Ability Tests* (*SCAT*). The profiles are adapted from cases presented in manuals prepared by the publisher, the Educational Testing Service, and are used here with their permission.

Figure 7.8 shows Helen's profiles on the *STEP* and *SCAT* as they would appear in the guidance file at her school. On the original form, *STEP* and *SCAT* profiles are on different sides of the sheet, and instructions for interpretation are included. (The form is modified here for easier presentation on a single sheet.) Figure 7.9 shows the same scores on a special individual report sheet, which might be given to either Helen or her parents. ETS focuses our attention immediately on the fact that test scores are approximate by creating a percentile band (the shaded portion). This percentile band extends from approximately one standard error below an obtained score to approximately one standard error above the score. This approach is commendable, for it minimizes the likelihood of gross misinterpretation when it directs attention to the error of measurement. If the bands for two scores overlap (as, for example, Social Studies and Writing, and Mathematics and Science), the difference in score is probably inconsequential; however, if the two bands do not overlap, we may have some confidence that the obtained difference is not merely a chance difference.

Helen is a high school junior, sixteen years of age, who hopes to major in theoretical physics in college. Her Mathematics (especially), Science, and Listening scores are high. In her Social Studies and Writing tests, she is only about average when compared with other eleventh-graders nationally. On Reading, she is slightly above average. On the *SCAT*, her

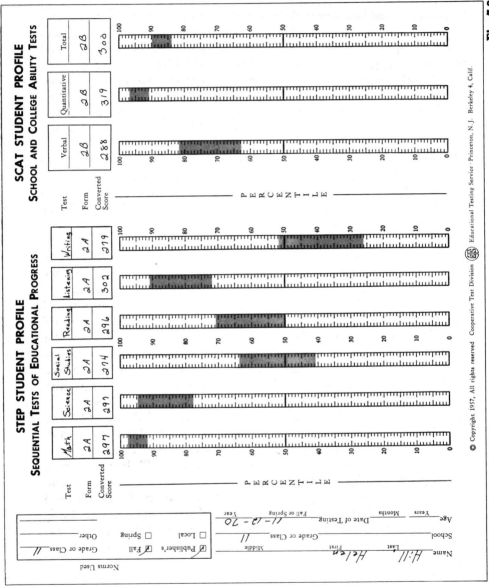

**Fig. 7.8**

1. Your standing on each test is reported as a percentile band. These percentile bands may be pre-printed on a score label, or may be given to you by your teacher. On the label they are identified as "%ile bands."
2. If you have been given a score label, paste it over the box above. If you have not been given a label, fill in the blanks as instructed by your teacher.
3. Enter the percentile bands in the spaces to the left of the graphs below. Take care to place each band in the space that has the same name as the test.
4. Look at the first percentile band. Draw a vertical line on the graph corresponding to the *lower* number of the band, followed by another vertical line corresponding to the higher number. Shade the area between the lines. Continue marking each percentile band in the same way.

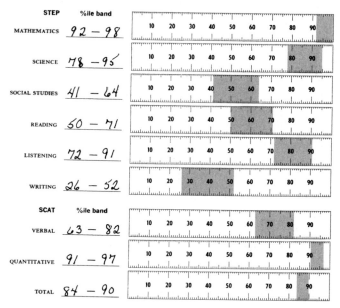

**INTERPRETING YOUR SCORES**

1. You will notice that a 'band' or range of numbers is used to describe your performance, rather than a single number. This is to remind you that if you took several similar tests, you would not get the same score each time. But it is most probable that your standing is within the shaded area for each test.
2. Now look at each band. The *lower* number shows about how many students out of 100 in your comparison group scored lower than you did. If you subtract the *higher* number from 100, you find the number of students who scored higher.
3. To find out whether you really did better on one test than on another, see if the bands overlap. If they do, it is impossible to say with certainty that the difference is not due to chance. However, when two bands do not overlap, you may be reasonably certain that there is more than just a chance difference between your standings on the two tests. In other words, you are really better in, say, mathematics than you are in social studies.

**Fig. 7.9**

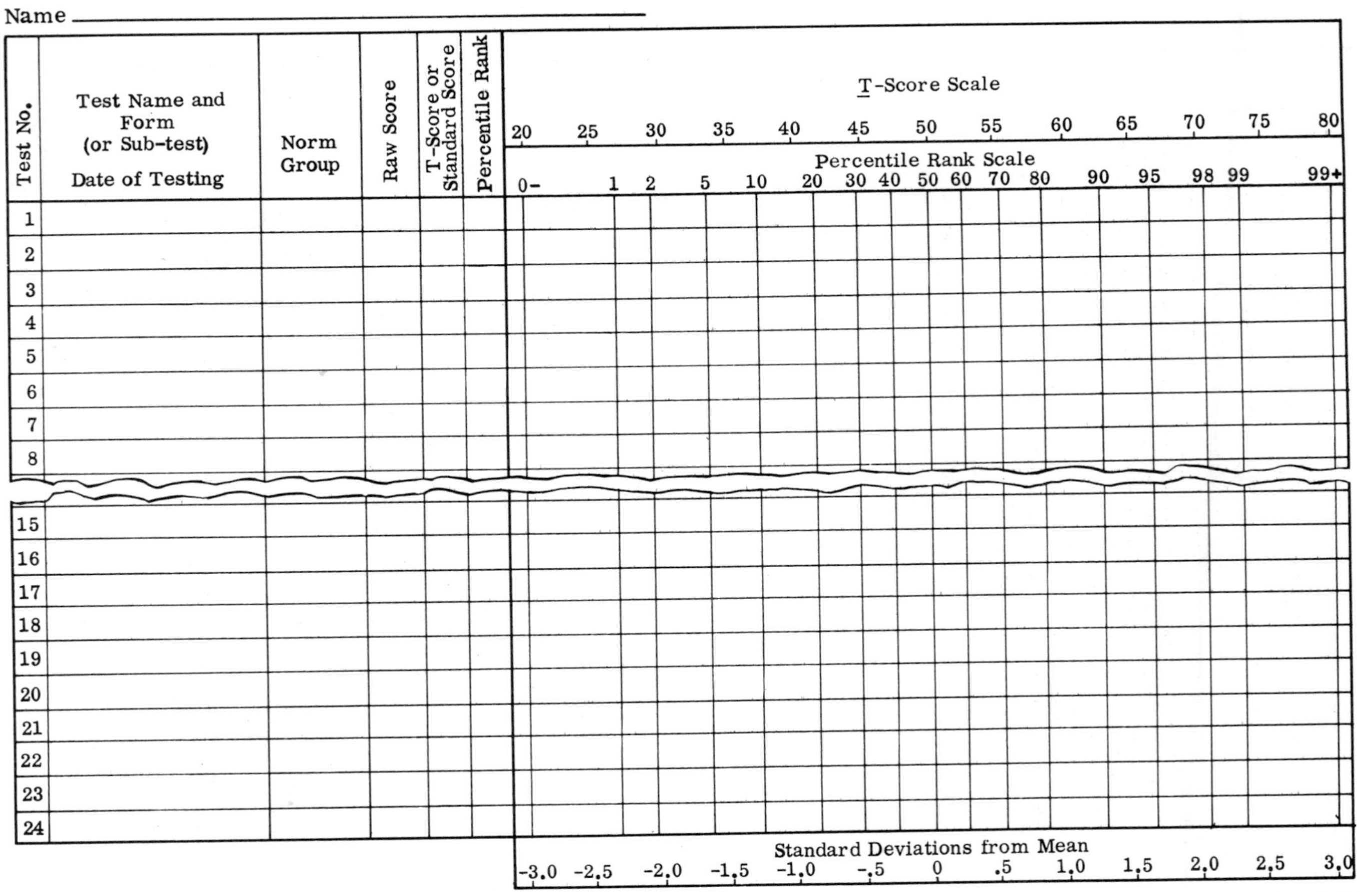

Name _____

| Test No. | Test Name and Form (or Sub-test) Date of Testing | Norm Group | Raw Score | T-Score or Standard Score | Percentile Rank |
|---|---|---|---|---|---|
| 1 | | | | | |
| 2 | | | | | |
| 3 | | | | | |
| 4 | | | | | |
| 5 | | | | | |
| 6 | | | | | |
| 7 | | | | | |
| 8 | | | | | |
| 15 | | | | | |
| 16 | | | | | |
| 17 | | | | | |
| 18 | | | | | |
| 19 | | | | | |
| 20 | | | | | |
| 21 | | | | | |
| 22 | | | | | |
| 23 | | | | | |
| 24 | | | | | |

T-Score Scale

20 25 30 35 40 45 50 55 60 65 70 75 80

Percentile Rank Scale

0― 1 2 5 10 20 30 40 50 60 70 80 90 95 98 99 99+

Standard Deviations from Mean

-3.0 -2.5 -2.0 -1.5 -1.0 -.5 0 .5 1.0 1.5 2.0 2.5 3.0

**Fig. 7.10**

Test Record and Profile Chart.

Quantitative score is very high; her Verbal score, although above average for high school juniors, is significantly lower than the Quantitative. Her high scores support her present vocational goals. If her course grades are in line with her test scores, she should have little difficulty in getting into a good college. If I were Helen's counselor, I would encourage her to devote some effort during her senior year to developing greater competence in social studies and writing, perhaps noting the relevance of such skills to the work of the physicist.

Figure 7.9 shows exactly the same results as Figure 7.8, but is part of a Student Bulletin designed to be given to the student and her parents.

## General Profiles

The greatest advantage of general profile forms is that several different tests may be shown on the same sheet. The greatest limitation of such forms is the ease with which we may put tests with drastically dissimilar norm groups on the same sheet.

Figure 7.10 is an example of a good general profile form, for it has both a percentile scale and a standard-score scale and calls for: title and form of the test, the norms group, the raw score, two different derived scores, and the date of testing. When preparing such a profile we should be careful to give complete information on all tests. What seems self-evident at the moment of recording may not be so obvious months later.

We need to be especially careful to record a complete designation of the norms group. My personal feeling is that it is best not to draw the profile for any test that has norms very much different from those for the other tests shown. In any event, we should never draw lines connecting scores from completely separate tests—unless, of course, the same norms group has been used in standardizing the different tests (as with the *Differential Aptitude Tests*, the *Sequential Tests of Educational Progress*, etc.).

### THE GOOD PROFILE

What then may we say about the characteristics of a good profile form? One way or another, there must be full information about the test: title, form, level, etc. There must be no ambiguity as to the nature of norms group used. The examinee's name should appear, along with other appropriate identifying information. The date or dates of testing must be indicated. The examiner's name may be important, especially if an individual test is involved. If there has been any deviation in testing conditions (as, for example, when the test's time limits are altered, either deliberately or accidentally), this fact should be noted, too.

A good profile form should be designed so that the derived-score scale is appropriate. If it shows percentile ranks, the scale should be drawn so that units near the median are much smaller than units near the extremes. In other words, the scale should be drawn in accordance with the properties of the normal probability curve. (The need for this is not so great when percentile bands are used—as in the case of the *STEP* and the *SCAT* shown in Figures 7.8 and 7.9—for the bands themselves call attention to the standard error of measurement.) The use of several derived scores may be very helpful, as we saw in Figure 7.3.

Clear directions for the preparation of the profile should accompany the form; if feasible, the directions should be printed on the form itself. A clear and precise statement of the types of scores used should also accompany the profile, preferably printed on the form itself. The composition of the norms group should be explained fully in material accompanying the profile. If any of several norms groups can be used, there should be space on the form for indicating which group is being used.

We should be certain to record the raw score (or its equivalent non-meaningful scaled score) for every test variable in the profile. In the first place, it should be there so that we may check the profile plots. Mistakes are more likely to be made in plotting profile points than in copying raw scores from one sheet to another. If the raw scores appear on the profile sheet, we are more likely to check the accuracy of the plots.

Then, too, the presence of the raw scores makes it easier for us to compare the examinee with another norm group.

> Janie's profile showed her scores when compared with a group of applicants. I wanted to compare her with employees, as well. Since the raw score for each test variable was appropriately recorded on the profile, I was able to obtain this additional information with a minimum of work.

The presence of the raw scores also facilitates research, either formal or informal. The counselor who develops a hunch that a certain subgroup is different from some other subgroup can make a quick preliminary check from the raw scores readily available to him. As we have noted before, raw scores are better for research than most derived scores—much better, of course, than percentile ranks.

### DIFFERENCE IN PROFILE POINTS

How far apart must scores be before we can be sure that they are really different? It all depends.

If the norms groups used for the two (or more) test variables are not the same, we probably cannot say; certainly we cannot say unless the groups are truly comparable. Whether we like it or not, this is the case. No amount of rationalization can justify our comparing scores on two tests when the norms groups are markedly different.

If the scores are not reported in the same units, we cannot say—at least not until we convert them to the same type of score unit.

We have noted several times that no score is perfectly accurate. Every test score includes some amount of error. If a person were to take a large number of comparable forms of the same test, his score would vary somewhat from form to form even if the forms were designed to give identical results on the average. As we found in Chapter Four, the standard error of measurement is an estimate of what the standard deviation of an individual's scores would be if he were to take these many forms.

When two tests are involved, both scores are subject to measurement error and we must consider both measurement errors. We can be very certain that a given difference represents a real difference (that is, one caused not just by the unreliability of the scores) if bands extending out two standard errors of measurement from each score do not overlap.

> For example, Pat obtains $T$-scores of 76 and 65 on two different tests of the same aptitude battery. Let us assume that the $SE_{meas}$ for each test is 3.1. We may be about 90 per cent confident that Pat's true score on the first test is between 71 and 81 (i.e., $76 \pm 1.6\,SEs$) and that her true score on the second test is between 60 and 70 (i.e., $65 \pm 5$). Since there is no overlap between 71–81 and 60–70, we may be highly confident that the observed difference is in the true direction; in other words, we may be reasonably certain that Pat has more of the first aptitude than of the second.

This is a more rigorous standard, however, than we need to use. We can estimate the $SE$ of measurement of a difference through the use of the formula

$$SE_{diff\ meas} = \sqrt{SE^2_{meas\ x} + SE^2_{meas\ y}},\ \text{where}$$
$$SE_{meas\ x} = \text{standard error of measurement on Test } X$$
$$SE_{meas\ y} = \text{standard error of measurement on Test } Y.$$

> Using this statistic on Pat's scores, we would find that the $SE_{diff\ meas} = \sqrt{3.1^2 + 3.1^2} = \sqrt{19.22} = 4.4$. If we apply this statistic, we would conclude that any difference between the two aptitude tests that was greater than $1.6\ SE_{diff\ meas}$ (here, $1.6 \times 4.4$, or 7.04) would not be reasonably attributed to chance. Since there is a difference of 11 between Pat's scores, we would conclude that she was really higher on the first test than the second.

But neither of these methods considers the extent of correlation between the two tests. It can be shown that the reliability of a difference in scores is a function of the reliability of the two tests and the correlation between them. If the correlation between two tests is high, both are measuring much the same thing; therefore, more differences will be only chance differences. Several people have used these facts in developing still other approaches to the study of significance of differences between scores.

No completely satisfactory way now exists for deciding definitely how big a difference in score must be before it can be considered a true difference. Therefore it seems best to follow the suggestions contained in the test manual or on the test profile form. We should, however, study the manual carefully to determine what rationale the publisher is using. Where the manual for the multiple-score test or test battery suggests no method for determining significant differences between scores, I use the $SE_{\text{diff meas}}$.

### PROFILE ANALYSIS

When there are several scores reported for an individual (as in a profile), we may be tempted to try a profile analysis—that is, we may try to find additional meaning through the relative peaks and dips. On the *Wechsler Adult Intelligence Scale*, for example, some clinical psychologists believe that relationships between scores on certain of the eleven scales can be used as a basis for personality diagnosis. Research, however, has not resulted in much clear-cut evidence that such diagnoses are meaningful.

Nevertheless research on profile analysis continues with further study of the *WAIS* and other multiple-scale tests. The authors of the California Test Bureau's *Multiple Aptitude Tests* have prepared a number of typical profiles of occupational and other groups, suggesting that an examinee's profile may be compared with these examples. Gough proposes certain interpretations for various combinations of scores on his *California Psychological Inventory* (Consulting Psychologists Press). Much research has also been done with *Minnesota Multiphasic Personality Inventory* profiles.

We should remember that any sort of profile analysis depends upon the reliability of two or more tests, and we need to be very cautious. Some of these approaches may be promising, but we should examine their research basis carefully before using them.

Please note that there are many circumstances in which scores may be used jointly to obtain better prediction of criterion values than can be obtained through the use of any one variable by itself; however, this topic (multiple correlation and multiple regression) is beyond the scope of this book.

# COMMON SENSE

*Chapter Eight*

When test results do not make sense, the test results may be wrong—or our "common sense" may be faulty. Neither is perfect.

Any testing program should call for checking at every stage where mistakes are possible. As test users, we should be prepared to check the scores that are put into our hands. If the test results do not seem reasonable, they may be wrong:

> Several years ago I was looking over a multiple-score test taken by a college student as part of a campus-wide testing program. I was surprised that this good student had no scores above the median. Upon checking, I discovered that one of the scoring clerks had not understood the directions for using the norms table. She had taken raw-score values from the test, entered these in the percentile-ranks column, and read out the corresponding entries in the raw-score column as percentile ranks. Since there had been no systematic checking of results, more than 1000 test sheets and profiles had to be re-examined.

On the other hand, the expectations may have been in error, and the tests may be right:

> A company was testing several people for a junior-level management position. Al Athol had been an employee of the company for several years, had a good work history, and was well-liked by fellow employees and by management. The other candidates were very recent college graduates and new to the firm. Al did as well as the other candidates except on a spatial relations test; on this, he did very poorly. The personnel director decided to select one of the other men because of this one very low score—and it is doubtful whether spatial relations skill is even involved in the management position! This personnel director should have used common sense, for Al was clearly

superior to the other men on the various nontest factors that should have been considered.

When test results and common sense seem to be in conflict, we need to check all possibilities. There are four: (1) tests may be wrong; (2) common sense may be wrong; (3) both may be wrong; and (4) neither may be wrong.

Later in this chapter we shall deal at some length with common mistakes in testing. For the moment, let us see how common sense can be wrong. Are we sure that our preconceptions are correct? Is this really an able man, or has he succeeded by saying the right thing at the right time? Is this student really good or is he an "apple polisher"? Are these tests as valid for this purpose as they should be? What makes these test results seems unreasonable?

Often we may find that questioning the results will help us to find errors in both our reasoning and the results. In such situations, checking really pays off, for it enables us to obtain a better understanding of the entire situation.

What about those situations, though, where test results seem unreasonable, and yet both our reasoning and the test results seem correct even after checking? In such situations we should probably stop to consider whether there is really a discrepancy between the two. Closer scrutiny may prove that the tests are giving us just a slightly different slant than the one we had been considering. Or perhaps the discrepancy is not so great as we had thought at first. If these lines of reasoning fail to resolve the discrepancy, we may want to get further information from tests, interviews, etc., provided that the situation is important enough to justify it.

### DECISION MAKING

As mentioned earlier, Cronbach and Gleser, in their *Psychological Tests and Personnel Decisions*, point out that test scores often are used as one basis for making decisions. Tests are especially helpful, they note, when used in connection with institutional decisions about personnel, for here there is a backlog of information from similar situations in the past, and the expectation is that many similar decisions will have to be made in the future. The institution is not likely to be hurt badly by any single bad decision about the selection or rejection or classification of any individual. And tests, in their place, can provide information that may increase the accuracy of prediction in the long run. Common examples include: selection of students or employees, classification of personnel, etc.

Individual decisions, on the other hand, cannot be evaluated in the long run. Any specified individual is not likely to have to make this same sort of decision again. And the choice that the individual makes right now may very well have a long-lasting effect on his life. Test information, although sometimes helpful, can nowhere be *so* helpful as in institutional decisions. These individual decisions are important to the person and are unique to him. He has no backlog of similar situations—nor the expectation of facing similar situations in the future. Common examples include: deciding which curriculum to study, whether to attend college, which college to attend, which job to take, etc.

We can see why tests are better at helping us to make institutional decisions. Even with the best of tests, we expect to make some mistakes; however, if we have reasonably valid tests we can make better personnel decisions with them than we could without them. The institution expects occasional bad personnel decisions. No particular bad decision is likely to have any lasting effect on the institution.

In contrast are the guidance and counseling situations in which tests may be used. Where the tests are considered in making individual decisions, we must be very cautious. Except in the most extreme cases, no test can tell whether a student should go to college, which type of training one should take, etc. As a general rule tests can be of most help in a negative way; that is, by ruling out certain alternatives.

## SOME COMMON MISTAKES

Besides the measurement error inherent in any test, there are many possibilities of mistakes being made in the administration and scoring of a test and in reporting its results. The test user should make it part of his regular routine to check reported test scores whenever feasible.

Some sort of check should be made at every stage of testing to insure near-perfect accuracy of conditions for administration, scoring, and recording. Most of the mistakes are relatively simple things: failing to start the stopwatch used in timing; failing to stop at the proper time limit; omitting part of the directions; using the wrong answer sheet; using the wrong scoring key; lining up the scoring key incorrectly; making a mistake in counting; using a wrong scoring formula; using the wrong norms tables; reading the norms table incorrectly; misreading a handwritten score; making an error in copying, etc. Over the years I have discovered some classic mistakes. I shall pass a few of them along, partly for comic relief and partly to show that one cannot be too compulsive in checking on tests.

> One national testing program once sent me a set of the wrong tests. The tests were not to be opened until the morning of the examination, and when they were—did we have fun!
> I shall never forget the chaos created when about 500 of 1200 machine-scoring answer sheets proved to have been printed a little off center—not

enough for the eye to notice, but more than enough to throw the scoring machine off. Hand-scoring a sample of answer sheets showed that something was wrong, but it took us several days to find the cause.

I once received three successive orders of a standardized test which was printed just a bit too small; unfortunately, the scoring key was of standard size and did not match.

Nor will I forget the time when a researcher cut off one corner of each answer sheet to keep his promise of anonymity by removing the name. This had the effect of throwing the answer sheet enough out of alignment so that the scoring machine could not get accurate scores. Our resourceful scoring-machine operator solved that one—by balancing her finger on the opposite corner, she aligned each sheet separately for the machine. Once again, the difficulty was located by noting a discrepancy when a sample of tests was prescored by hand.

Errors in the scoring keys of standardized tests are rare today, for they are very carefully checked; however, errors have been known to crop up even here. There is even the story (true, I think) of several people who managed to steal a preliminary scoring key of an important test they were to take; they were caught and found guilty when they turned in perfect papers— except for the three items which had been incorrectly marked on that pre-liminary key.

Have you heard about the university student who turned in a perfect paper —many points better than anyone had ever earned before? A little checking proved that the student had been inadvertently given the check-sheet used in setting up the scoring machine. He had merely printed his name on the sheet and turned it in. (This could not have happened if: (1) the sheet had been properly marked as a check sheet; *or* (2) proper test security had been maintained; *or* (3) the proctors had been performing their job of watching the examinees as they marked their tests.)

Of course, I have made a few mistakes myself. At one time or another, I have: used the wrong answer sheets for a standardized test; missed a time limit while distracted by some other task; mis-scored tests by miscounting and using a wrong scoring formula, etc. I shall never forget the time that I gave a class of students the wrong course exam (I gave them one covering the next unit of study), and no student complained until the period was half over.

It is human to err, we are told. Most of these mistakes, though, could have been prevented. And we cannot blame the tests for mistakes like these.

### *OTHER SOURCES, TOO!*

√ Tests are only one source of information. And test scores are only bits of information. In any important decision, we should make full use of all of the information available to us. As information-collectors, tests do have certain advantages—most especially their objectivity. But tests are fallible instruments, and test scores are fallible bits of information.

√ If tests are to be used, they should contribute something. People managed

to exist and to make decisions without the aid of tests for many years—
and they can today. If tests provide helpful information, we should use
them—if they do not, we should not! And even when we do use tests,
let us not forget to consider nontest factors as well—they, too, can be
important.

# WHAT CAN WE SAY?

*Chapter Nine*

We have been concerned primarily with the task of helping test users to understand the meaning of test scores. This may be sufficient for many test users, but certainly not for all.

School counselors, guidance workers, and many others have the additional problem of trying to communicate test results to all sorts of other persons. This is more involved and requires additional skill. While this task is not our main concern, it is not one that we can ignore.

No amount of reading, of course, is going to help us too much in interpreting test scores. Written admonitions are no substitute for personal experience. Even so, it is possible to learn some general principles and "tricks of the trade." Our primary emphasis in this book is directed at enabling people with limited backgrounds in psychological and educational testing to understand the nature of test scores. There is no suggestion that this book can substitute for a basic course in tests and measurements or for a course in counseling or guidance techniques. These and other courses are needed (along with practice) before a person is prepared to get full meaning from test data.

There are two main topics in this chapter: (1) *Who* is entitled to test information? and (2) *What* do we say?

## Who is Entitled to Test Information?

As a starting point, let us agree that the examinee himself is entitled to receive information about his test results.

### THE EXAMINEE

Information given to the examinee should be as detailed as is warranted by the test and as detailed as he is likely to understand. Specific scores should be given only if the examinee is also given a thorough explanation of what the scores mean and what their limitations are.

Except within the clinical-counseling or court-legal frameworks, the examinee should be told the results of his tests in as much detail as he is likely to understand; however, information should not be forced onto those who cannot assimilate it. This incident, for example, never should have happened:

> Bobby, a third grader, was skipping down the corridor at school and chanting, "I'm a genius! I'm a genius!" Bobby did not know what the word meant, but he did know that it must be something good because his parents had been so pleased when ". . . a lady came to our house and gave me a test. And then she said, 'Why, he's a little genius!'"

### PARENTS OF MINORS

In the case of minors, parents should also be told the test results—especially if they show the slightest interest or curiosity. This principle does not mean that parents should necessarily be given specific IQs. The IQ is not an easy type of score to explain to a layman and is burdened with all sorts of false assumptions; however, percentile ranks can be understood with minimal explanation. Consider, too, some sort of percentile-band approach (see page 106).

### AGENCY POLICY

School and other agencies are likely to have their own policies regarding the interpretation of test results. These policies should be made known to all people within the agency who have access to test scores, including secretaries, file clerks, and receptionists. As a rule, only professional-level workers should interpret scores to examinees, parents, or other laymen; however, in a well-run agency, there may be provision for routine release of scores to specified professional people under stated conditions. (By *professional* in this chapter, I mean to include teachers, personnel workers, and others whose positions involve working with people, but to exclude general office workers.)

### SCHOOLS AND COLLEGES

With schools and colleges, routine test results should be handled in the same way as grades and personnel files. In the event of transfer to another institution or system, these routine test results should be sent along. It is imperative that furnished test information include date of testing, names of tests (with form, level, and edition), and raw scores; if derived scores are included, the norm groups should be identified.

On the other hand, tests given for counseling purposes (especially at the college level) should ordinarily *not* be transferred automatically. This is testing that has been done for the student's personal benefit, and test scores should not be transmitted without the permission of the student or his parents. This limitation may be modified somewhat by the specific policy of the agency and by the nature of the testing. If testing for counseling purposes has included only an interest test or two, there is little point to obtaining permission; however, if extensive testing, especially with personality tests, is involved, the permission clearly should be obtained.

### PROFESSIONAL COLLEAGUES

Within any given agency (including a school system), any professional worker who has need for test data should have access to the scores. If there is reason to believe that the data are being misused, the access should be denied or withdrawn.

> Merry Melody, a music teacher, used to come to the counseling office toward the end of each semester and request intelligence test scores of her pupils. After a semester or two, it was noted that she was using these scores as a basis for assigning her course grades. The director of counseling spoke to her about the inadvisability of this practice. When, after two subsequent sessions, she still used the scores in this fashion, she was refused further access to the test scores.

When professional workers outside the given agency request test data on a person, it should be cleared through channels. These channels should include a release (preferably in writing) from the examinee or his parents. Scores should not be released to nonprofessional workers outside the agency.

### INDUSTRY

Within industry, certain differences in practice may be noted. The testing has usually been done at the request of the company. The company is the client, and there may be a presumption that the company can use the information as it sees fit. If there is any suggestion, however, that the company is securing information under the promise of confidence and then abusing that confidence, the company will suffer at least some loss of public respect. If test data cannot be used to the distinct advantage of the employee, it should not be revealed to anyone outside the company on any pretext—except, of course, at the written request of the employee. Within industry, as elsewhere, no test data obtained as a part of therapeutic counseling (even when this has been a relationship with a psychotherapist employed full-time within the company) should ever be revealed to anyone except at the written request of the employee himself.

### IN CONVERSATION

We do not discuss, either publicly or in casual conversation, the test results of any of our examinees. It is permissible, of course, to identify the individual and his test scores in a case conference in either a school, industrial, or clinical setting. But we cannot ethically continue our discussion of the individual outside the conference room!

## Communicating the Results

The two essential steps in test interpretation are: (1) understanding the test results, and (2) communicating these results orally or in writing to another appropriate individual.

### TO A TRAINED PROFESSIONAL WORKER

When the other person is trained in testing, the task of communicating results is relatively simple. We may start by giving the test name (including form, level, and edition—if pertinent) and the raw scores. We may include derived scores, if desired, along with the norms group(s) used. If both of us know our tests, there is every reason to believe that the information will be communicated accurately. If the information is communicated orally, we may take a few shortcuts; however, if the report is made in writing it should be complete.

When making a written report to another professional worker in whom I have confidence, I find the following method both convenient and economical:

> I include a Xerox copy of test profiles and the like. To this, I add a short letter of transmittal pointing out any unusual aspects of the case (either about the person or his test results); I also note irregularities (if any) in the testing procedures. If the examinee has been in counseling with me, I may include on a separate sheet a brief summary of our contacts to date, together with my observations about probable major problem areas and my expectation of outcome. I address this material to the professional worker personally and mark it "CONFIDENTIAL."

The availability of copying machines is a tremendous boon to those who handle tests, for we can make a copy or two in several seconds at a cost of only a few cents. Furthermore, there is no danger of mistakes when making copies in this fashion.

Whenever there is the slightest doubt about the testing knowledge of the person to whom we send test scores, we should add some further explanation of the tests and the scores.

> "The NEW Test is a new scholastic aptitude test put out by the PDQ Company; we have been trying it out this year to see how well it compares with the OLD Test. The norms groups seem to be reasonably comparable, and we have found that our students tend to do about the same on both

tests; however, the *NEW* is a little more highly speeded, and some of our teachers do not like it as well for that reason. You will note, too, that the publisher's national norms are given in stanines. I do not know whether you have been using stanines at your school, so I have included an approximate percentile value for each one. Please let me know if I can be of further help. . . ."

The aim of test interpretation is, after all, to insure that the other person understands the results of testing. We do not fulfill that purpose unless we take all reasonable steps to state the results meaningfully.

### TO A PROFESSIONAL WORKER UNTRAINED IN TESTING

When test data are being given to a professional worker who is relatively untrained in testing, it is advisable to give both a written report and an oral interpretation. Unquestionably some of the best work of this sort is done by school psychologists in their reports to school principals and teachers. By and large, school psychologists do a remarkably good job of working with individual children and of reporting their findings. They seem much more interested in delivering informative and helpful reports than in showing off their erudition through overuse of technical jargon.

Reports to school teachers, to members of management, to personnel workers, to academic deans, and to others who typically have limited training in testing should be drawn up very carefully. We cannot assume that they know the difference between percentage-correct scores and percentile ranks; they probably do not. We cannot assume that they know what a standard score is—or an IQ—or an age score. Our reports need to be informative, but neither subservient nor patronizing.

"Betty's PR on the *Otis* is 74," is a statement that does not mean much to a person who does not know that PR means *percentile rank*, does not know what percentile rank means, and does not know what the *Otis* is. (And this particular statement would be only a little more meaningful to those of us who do understand these points, for there are several *Otis* tests and many different norms groups.)

This form would be much more helpful:

"On the *Blank Aptitude Test*, Betty did as well as or better than 74 percent of the recent applicants for clerical positions with our company. We find that about 60 percent of the girls with similar scores have maintained at least Satisfactory ratings. . . ."

Or, perhaps, this:

"On the *Blank Aptitude Test*, Betty did as well as or better than 74 percent of the freshmen entering our college this past September. This score suggests that she should be capable of doing the work required in her program."

## *TO A MATURE EXAMINEE*

Although much test interpretation done under this heading would come within the framework of counseling, some is done independently of counseling. The trained and experienced counselor will have developed skills and techniques of his own, and the new counselor should be developing them through his specialized training and in-service supervision. We are concerned with techniques that can be used effectively and safely by relatively untrained test users.

Individuals suspected of severe maladjustment should be referred to specialists wherever possible. Our examinees are presumed to be adolescents or adults who have no disabling problems.

The following list of suggestions is not exhaustive. Although some of these points represent my personal opinion, I think that most of them would be accepted by nearly all experienced test users:

1. Test interpretation usually is done within some greater purposeful interview situation: e.g., counseling, guidance, placement, selection, etc. There are times, however, when the test interpretation itself is sufficient reason for the interview—especially with high school students.

2. Look over the test results before the interpretation interview. Make sure that you understand them and have some idea of what you want to say.

3. Establish a comfortable working relationship with the examinee. Be certain that you have his interest and attention.

4. Be careful of your words. Examinees can be depended upon to remember your careless remarks and to misunderstand what they do not want to hear. Your care can keep distortion to a minimum.

5. Explain something about every test variable you interpret. The examinee may know nothing about the various types of test, and probably knows nothing about the specific tests he took.

6. Explain the nature of the norms groups with which he is being compared, especially when they differ for the various tests.

7. Sometimes, especially in a counseling setting, an opening like this is helpful: "How do you think you did? Do you have any idea which tests you did best on?"

8. If you feel comfortable in doing so, show the examinee the profile sheet(s); use this (them) as your basis for interpretation. Note, however, that some counselors believe that this is not a good practice and that it encourages an examinee to "read ahead" and thus to pay less attention to the explanation.

9. Do not force the interpretation on the examinee. If he does not want to know the results, let him alone. You are wasting time—yours and his. Let him know that you may be available later if he changes his mind, but that you feel it is pointless to continue under these circumstances. (I can think of some exceptions, but not many; the point is that, desirable though it might be for the examinee to know his test results, he is not likely to understand them under stress.)

10. Interpret *all* of the test variables, not just those on which the examinee has done a good job. He has a right to learn his limitations as well as his strengths. (A trained counselor, though, may prefer *not* to interpret some *personality* test variables.)

11. It is more difficult to interpret low scores than high ones. Designations of high and low are somewhat arbitrary, but not entirely so (*see* the suggestions at the end of this chapter).

12. Low scores are more easily accepted if they are stated in objective terms, such as: "Of people with scores like yours, only 10 percent have managed to maintain a passing average and to graduate in that curriculum" [*see* "expectancy tables" pp. 57–62].

13. Sometimes low scores may be made easier to accept when the nature of the test is slightly distorted. I sometimes point out to a student who has done poorly on an intelligence or scholastic aptitude test: "This means that you are very low in book-learning ability when compared with other high school juniors nationally. A few students with scores like yours may succeed in college through very efficient planning and extra-hard studying, but your high school grades suggest that you do not achieve well in the actual class situations, either."

14. Sometimes low scores can be communicated successfully through an analogous statement: "A college director of admissions is like anyone else. He likes to bet on the winners. He knows that students with better high school grades and higher test scores than yours are more likely to do well in college. Like a gambler, he will sometimes play a long shot and will be delighted when one pays off. But, for the most part, he has to select those people who seem most likely to succeed."

15. Never make a direct prediction, such as: "This score means that you will never make it to college," or "This test score proves that you would never succeed on this job," or "With scores like these, you are a cinch to get through college with flying colors." You can be very, very wrong! You are much safer to talk in group terms, such as: "Very few students with such scores . . ." or "Most students with scores such as these are able to do well in college if they study reasonably hard."

16. Do not assume that your examinee will remember everything. Try to help him to remember the important elements by summarizing the

results; perhaps something like this: "In general, then, you show average or better ability to learn, and you show near-average achievement in most areas. But you seem to be lower than we would expect in dealing with abstract or mathematical reasoning."

17. If appropriate, make general suggestions: "Our company will not promote men who have low scores on tests of verbal ability. Have you considered going to night school? You could pick up an English course or two that might be helpful—and our company policy is to pay at least part of the expense." Or, perhaps: "Your scores suggest that you may have difficulty in getting into medical school. On the other hand, you do have good grades here in high school—and this is important. You might be wise to select a small liberal arts college where you can hope for more individual attention and try for good grades in premedical work. Perhaps you will make it. Just to be on the safe side, though, you may want to consider some possible alternatives if you do not make med school. Sometimes people find it very difficult if they have given no thought to other things and then have to change plans at the last minute." Or, perhaps: "You have scored very high on the various English tests. Have you ever thought of working on the school paper? You might find it very rewarding."

18. Do not forget: the examinee decides what he will do. As a test interpreter, you may make suggestions but not decisions. (As an academic dean, placement director, etc., you may make institutional decisions; the examinee makes individual decisions.)

19. Test interpretation often provides a good way of opening a discussion of the examinee's problems, plans for the future, etc. If you are not a trained counselor, decide in advance how far you can go in receiving the examinee's confidences.

20. Never interpret an examinee's scores solely in writing. Supplementary interpretation, especially through interpretive folders such as those mentioned in Chapter Seven, may be very helpful. Most counselors feel strongly, however, that we should not rely exclusively on written interpretations because they offer no opportunity for counselee feedback.

**21. Most important of all: know what you are doing, do what seems natural and effective to you, and try to be genuinely helpful to the examinee.**

*TO A CHILD*

Some teachers try to explain achievement test results to elementary school children, especially when using the results in deciding in what areas the pupils may need to give special attention. Other than this, little effort is made to interpret tests to children who are below high school age.

I think that this is unfortunate. Children have considerable capacity for understanding and have tremendous curiosity. Many will disagree, but I believe that some basic interpretation could be done effectively with children as young as ten years of age. The teacher might discuss the general nature of the tests with the class as a group. This could be followed up by an individual conference with each pupil, perhaps focusing attention mainly on areas of highest and lowest achievement and a statement about his achievement relative to his ability (without saying much about his intelligence level itself). Such interpretations would need to be handled carefully, but could help youngsters in their search for an understanding of themselves.

Even with children of junior and senior high school age, most test interpretation should be couched in general terms. Children like to see things in black-and-white terms and are likely to oversimplify or overgeneralize. They are not likely to remember the test limitations so well as they remember specific facts that are mentioned casually or incidentally.

Superior students can handle somewhat more detailed interpretations. The interpretation can perhaps be used as an opportunity for emphasizing the importance of acquiring good study habits and developing a sound background for future work.

Special care must be used when interpreting results to children of below-average ability in order not to discourage them from trying to do their best. In dealing with this problem, the skilled counselor should be able to help the older child come to an acceptance of his limitations, and to an appreciation of what can reasonably be accomplished through sustained effort. There is little kindness in encouraging unrealistic ambitions in the below-average child, but it is cruel to make the child feel that he is worthless and stupid. There is some evidence, too, that children tend to grow up to our expectations—so it may be advisable to overaccentuate the positive.

Encouragement can be especially helpful to the young child. Perhaps his low scores can be explained, "You may have to study harder and longer than some boys and girls do to get good grades." There is ample evidence that young children can respond positively to encouragement.

> One of my graduate students recently reported the following incident to me. Her son, Tommy, came home and said that he had gotten an *A* on a standardized achievement test battery. Tommy's second-grade teacher, it developed, had announced aloud in class letter-grade equivalents (including *F*s) for the test performance of every pupil. Such letter grades exist only in the teacher's mind—they are not given in the manual!
>
> This incident, of course, is an example of bad interpretation. No second grader is likely to learn much from such a procedure, and with few exceptions (e.g., a scholarship competition) public announcement of test scores is grossly unethical—and most sadistic!

*TO PARENTS*

Very much the same considerations involved when interpreting test scores to mature examinees are involved when interpreting scores to parents. Parents, though, are more likely to be argumentative, and to question the accuracy of the test results. Parents of dull children are likely to be very sensitive, and special caution must be used to make the parents view the results as objectively as possible. They must not be allowed to develop hostility toward the child because "he's so dumb," nor should they be given encouragement that he's "just passing through a phase."

Parents of a child of superior intellect may question why he is not doing better work and getting better grades if he is so intelligent. They may also question whether the school is doing its part in challenging the child to do his best work. (Consider carefully whether some such criticism may not be justified. Is the school doing what it can to meet the needs of the superior youngster?)

Parents differ markedly in their ability to understand and accept test results. I would have no hesitancy in discussing actual scores (IQs, percentile ranks, or whatever) with some mature parents. With others, defensive from the start, I shudder at the thought of giving any sort of interpretation. Be careful! And try to know beforehand how detailed an interpretation you will give.

*HIGH AND LOW*

How high is high? Your answer is probably as good as anyone else's. Except for a few considerations, it is an arbitrary decision.

First, we need to remember that scores are never completely accurate. Therefore, we should never say that any score is high unless it is at least one or two standard errors of measurement above the mean; otherwise, the above-average score probably differs from the mean only by chance. The same line of reasoning, of course, operates in calling scores low.

Second, we must remember the way in which scores tend to cluster about the mean in typical distributions of test scores. The distance between successive percentile values is very small near the middle of the distribution. Thus a given difference in percentile ranks reflects only a slight change in raw scores near the average, but a large change in raw scores near the extremes.

Third, we have to remember that scores used in reporting standardized tests are relative rather than absolute. A given raw score may place an examinee high when compared with one group, but low when compared with another group.

Fourth, because of the greater reliability (and relatively smaller standard errors of measurement) of some tests, we may have more confidence in our use of high and low with such tests than with other, less reliable, tests.

I generally use something like the following descriptive scale:

| Percentile Ranks | Descriptive Terms |
|---|---|
| 95 or above | Very high; superior |
| 85–95 | High; excellent |
| 75–85 | Above average; good |
| 25–75 | About average; satisfactory or fair |
| 15–25 | Below average; fair or slightly weak |
| 5–15 | Low; weak |
| 5 or below | Very low; very weak |

This is not an inflexible standard, but I find it a helpful one. Sometimes we vary these designations, or apply more (or less) rigorous standards.

If a graduate engineer were being compared on company norms with general clerical employees (perhaps the only norms the company has for the test), we might regard a percentile rank of 88 as being only "satisfactory" or "reasonably good."

In the same way, a graduate student who scores near the eightieth percentile on national undergraduate norms is probably only "about average."

### In Summary:

1. The person who interprets test results, however casually, must understand the nature of the tests and of the test scores. If he does not understand them himself, he should not try to explain them to others.
2. As a general rule, examinees and/or parents are entitled to an interpretation of all tests taken, and in as much detail as can be understood.
3. Test interpreters should try to avoid hurting people. Whenever possible, they should aim at giving some sort of realistic encouragment to examinees.

# EXPERTS
# STILL NEEDED

*Chapter Ten*

We have touched on some of the most important topics in psychological and educational testing, but there is a great deal that we have not mentioned. One important consideration is the persistent demand for experts in measurement.

For example, we have barely mentioned tests of typical performance. Such tests have their proper place in the hands of thoroughly trained counseling or clinical psychologists. When properly used by qualified persons, typical performance tests may give clues to the personality dynamics of both normal and disturbed people. Their interpretation demands skills and knowledge beyond those covered in this book (although a reasonable job of interpreting interest tests and some simple inventory-style personality tests should not be much beyond the competence of some readers).

Projective tests, certainly, should be interpreted only by well-trained psychologists. And the diversity of projective techniques is so great that some degree of training is needed in each of the specific techniques that the psychologist uses. Projective techniques are not parlor games or classroom exercises for the personal amusement of the test user.

Even with tests of maximum performance, there are some areas which are best left to the expert. Individual tests of intelligence, for example, require special training of the examiner. The trained examiner should be the one, too, to report the results of individual intelligence tests, for the report should include much more than a mere test score; otherwise, the situation does not require the use of an individual test in the first place.

Throughout this book (and especially in Chapter Nine), we have considered briefly some implications of testing for guidance and counseling. On the other hand, we have recognized that the most effective use of tests in guidance and counseling situations requires much more knowledge than can be acquired solely from this book. There is a need for professional counselors and guidance workers—people who can extract the fullest meaning from test results and employ this meaning in their interviews.

Experts in tests and measurements are needed, too, to construct and validate new tests, to conduct research with tests, to advance measurement theory, etc.

There should be at least one top-flight test specialist within each school system, each college, and each large industrial corporation. This specialist and his staff should have such varied duties as the following:

1. keeping up to date on theoretical measurement; there is some excellent work being done that has not yet trickled down to the test user;
2. maintaining a file of tests, both old and new, which might be consulted by other professional workers; this file would include manuals and catalogs;
3. maintaining a library of books and periodical publications on tests and measurements;
4. directing any major research activity involving tests;
5. serving as adviser or consultant to people in the organization who want to do their own test-related research;
6. evaluating new tests for possible use within the organization;
7. selecting new tests for use within the organization;
8. preparing local norms for tests;
9. discussing test-related problems, issues, and questions with interested personnel both within and outside the organization;
10. conducting in-service training programs for all people in the organization who work with tests.

The need for test specialists is obvious. So many tests are available that experts are needed to evaluate them and to select those which best meet the demands of their local situation. Then, too, there must be someone who can serve as a resource person for all those who use tests within an organization.

# TESTING TODAY AND
# SOCIAL RESPONSIBILITY

*Chapter Eleven*

Testing has changed considerably in recent years. First of all, the use of standardized tests in this country has increased tremendously. There is hardly a person between the ages of six and sixty who has not taken such tests in school or college, for the military, in the employment office, for promotion, etc.

Also, there have been an ever-increasing variety of testing applications in recent years. More and more businesses realize that tests can be helpful in the selection of employees at all levels. Schools and colleges are using not only more tests, but a wider variety of tests at all levels. Graduate and professional schools seem to be using entrance examinations in ever-increasing number. In all sorts of situation, we find that performance on tests is influencing our lives.

In kindergarten, a test may help in deciding whether a child is ready to advance to the first grade and to the study of reading. Even before that, occasional children may have been given individual tests to determine whether they should be allowed to enter school underage or, perhaps, at all. Throughout grade school, achievement tests may be used to divide classes into sections or to check on progress. Intelligence tests may be used at various stages throughout elementary and secondary school. Aptitude batteries may be given in junior and senior high school years as a basis for making curriculum selections, vocational choices, or both.

Vocational interest and preference inventories may be given at one stage or another in secondary school or college to aid the counselor in vocational guidance work with the students.

As students prepare for high school commencement and entry into college, they begin to encounter another sort of test, and *PSAT, SAT, ACT,* and *NMSQT* are added to their working vocabularies. Realistic youth know

Scholastic Aptitude Test
Preliminary Scholastic Aptitude Test

National Merit Scholarship Qualifying Examination

American College Testing Program Examination

163

that these tests (the *Preliminary Scholastic Aptitude Test*, the *Scholastic Aptitude Test*, the *American College Tests*, and the *National Merit Scholarship Qualifying Test*) may determine whether they'll be admitted to the colleges of their respective choices, the amount of scholarship, and similar matters. With the numbers of youth who want to enter college increasing each year, college admissions offices have to rely more and more on test results—the applicants for admission are far too numerous for the more–personal approaches that were common a few decades ago.

Meanwhile, noncollege-bound youth find that their entry into trades (even apprenticeships) or other occupations may be determined at least in part by the scores they obtain on tests. Their promotions to supervisory and administrative positions may involve the taking of additional tests.

College-educated youth find additional tests facing them as they enter the senior-year round of employment interviews. And, of course, the graduate-school applicant will find the *Miller Analogies Test* and the *Graduate Record Examination* as (not-always-welcomed) hurdles. Other test batteries may be used with applicants for admission to medical school, dental school, or law school.

It is no secret, of course, that entry to a profession (e.g., medicine or law) may depend on the passing of yet another examination even after the successful completion of training in the professional school. Psychologists with their doctoral degrees and the requisite years of experience may take an examination to qualify for a diploma from the American Board of Professional Psychology. Physicians may take comparable examinations in one or more of a wide variety of specialties.

Meanwhile, other youth have entered military service, where they took a number of tests that determined (to some extent) their placement within the service. The promotion of enlisted men in the Navy and the Air Force is determined in part by performance on special achievement tests. Of course, those who want to enter the service academies at West Point, Annapolis, Colorado Springs, or New London must qualify on the appropriate examination.

It is well known that those who choose a civilian career with the government (federal or state or county or local) are likely to qualify and may be promoted on the basis of examinations.

In this long account of test use, I have not mentioned once any of the tests that one may take if he enters counseling or psychotherapy. Many Americans do take tests in such settings. Still others (or, perhaps, some of the same ones) take tests under the auspices of a court or a penal institution.

Unless an American is reared in the isolation of a semi-hermit's life, he is going to take standardized tests. There seems to be no other way.

But the value of testing has been under scrutiny throughout the entire decade of the 1960s. Standardized tests have been accused of:

1. not measuring innate (i.e., inborn) intelligence
2. being unfair to Negroes and other minority groups
3. not measuring creativity    *nouvelles*
4. labeling children as *morons, dopes, slow learners*, etc.
5. favoring the glib individual and penalizing the thoughtful person
6. invading privacy    ⟶ *qui a de la féconde*
7. giving inconsistent results
8. being grossly misinterpreted,
   *et cetera, et cetera, et cetera.*

Some critics have shown responsibility in their concern over widespread test usage. Some have seemed to be more concerned with selling a magazine article or a book. Even Senators and Congressmen on federal and state levels have entered the battle over the use of tests in recent years.

> In one state, a bill was written which would have outlawed the use of any type of test (apparently even including classroom tests) in the schools! The bill was modified considerably and, eventually, defeated.

How can both these situations exist side by side: how, on the one hand, can tests continue to be used more and more widely all the time—and yet the critics find so much fresh ammunition for their debunking artillery? How can legislators be interested in test suppression when tests are being used in ever greater numbers?

The answers may be a great deal simpler than it would seem at first glance. The truth is that most of the criticisms are true—but only partly so. Some of the legislative attention has been a sincere effort to insure that tests are used responsibly. I believe that there is a very great need to educate people in the *responsible and intelligent use* of tests. Tests can be helpful in many situations, but they are not the complete and ultimate answer to every problem!

My answers to the series of charges against testing?

### 1. Tests Do Not Measure Innate Ability

Of course they don't. Or, they don't measure *only* innate ability; they measure a great deal more: as noted earlier, an ability test (aptitude, intelligence, or achievement) always measures some combination of innate ability, the influence of environment, and one's motivation at the time of testing (and perhaps other factors, as well).

> A short time ago, I gave a short series of lectures on testing to a class of first-year psychiatric residents. These are people who have an M.D. degree and are now starting their training to become psychiatrists. In this particular group were several foreign-born physicians who had been in this country for only a brief period of time. I was illustrating the administration of one of the

most popular individual tests of intelligence. As I went around the table asking sample questions of each one, I received failures on these (simulated) items: "In what direction would I be going if I traveled from Detroit to Caracas?", "What is a 'civil rights' law?", and "What does the word 'collect' mean?" The questions were asked respectively of an Iraqi, a Greek, and a Brazilian. I had little difficulty in making this class appreciate that tests are necessarily at least partially culture-bound!

Rather obviously, people who have survived the educational system—in the United States or elsewhere—for long enough to obtain a medical degree are clearly above average in intelligence . . . regardless of their performance on specific items of this (or any) intelligence test.

### 2. Tests Are Unfair to Negroes and to Other Minorities

To some extent this is true of all maximum-performance tests. The tests are based on the assumption that all people who take a test will be equally familiar or equally unfamiliar with the content matter. That is, the publisher must assume that all examinees will have had the same background of experience (including training). To the extent that the assumption is not true, the test will tend to favor some groups and to penalize others. Because tests usually are developed by upper-middle-class people who have upper-middle-class criteria in mind, the tests naturally are most likely to favor the upper- and upper-middle-class groups.

Although this unfairness probably cannot be completely avoided, there are some tests on which the items are less "culturally loaded" than others. One difficulty with trying to eliminate items that are too culturally biased is that they are often ones which seem to relate best to job or school success.

In very recent years there has been some research indicating that (in some situations) a given test may predict differentially for different socio-cultural groups. This may sometimes mean that a Negro (or other minority group member) may be expected to do better on the job than the White middle-class individual who has the same test score, or that a lower cutoff score can legitimately be used. Or sometimes it may mean that different tests should be used for predicting the same criterion.

Again, as noted above, a test can hardly be fair to individuals who do not understand a given language well if that language is involved in administering or responding to the test.

### 3. Intelligence Tests Do Not Measure Creativity

Of course, no one has ever claimed that they did. Nevertheless the critics denounce intelligence tests for not measuring creativity. None of our intelligence tests gets at all cognitive functions. One psychologist (J. P. Guilford) contends that there are at least 120 recognizably different intellective factors. Perhaps, indeed, there may be many more such factors that will be revealed by future research.

Intelligence tests from Binet on have tended to be school related. Most present-day intelligence tests have a similar school orientation, although some tests are slanted more toward use in an industrial personnel setting or in a clinical situation. Even for these latter uses, intelligence tests rarely include much that could be considered a measure of creativity.

Viewed differently, we may question whether intelligence tests should measure creativity. What is creativity? There is far from universal agreement on the answer to that question. Furthermore, it can be shown that there is less agreement among various definitions of creativity than there is among the different definitions of intelligence. (And there are certainly different definitions for that concept!)

Although there are now several good efforts at the measurement of creativity, none can be considered to be in such an advanced state of development as are many of the better intelligence tests.

The dimension of creativity is an important one; however, until we have more evidence of the validity of creativity tests, we should not be too dismayed that intelligence tests do not measure the concept. We probably should continue to use separate tests for these variables even then.

### 4. People Use Tests to Label Children as Morons, etc.

Unfortunately some people do sometimes *misuse* tests in this way. It should be clear by now that the author of this book believes strongly that tests are best viewed as sources of information. As such, they are appropriately used in helping with decisions by people and about people (i.e., in making individual and institutional decisions).

It is morally indefensible, except in extreme or emergency situations, to use any single test as *the* basis for making a decision. In the clinical application, it is conceivable that a psychologist might make a recommendation on the basis of a single test if the clinical signs were extreme enough to warrant it. In the school, a teacher or administrator might make a *tentative* placement on the basis of an achievement test. But both the psychologist and the educationist should be equally ready to reverse the decisions if behavior warrants. If the child (or adult) proves that he can do the work, he should not be kept from doing the work because of some test score. Tests may reflect or predict ability; they do not cause ability!

> Harriet Hughes, a teacher in nearby Hume High School, is dismayed with what is happening to one of her students, Holly. Despite the fact that Holly has earned *A*s in almost every course she has ever taken, the school counselor has insisted that she must not take the academic courses that would permit her to qualify for admission to college ". . . because Holly's tests show that she can not do quality work in school."
>
> What can we do about such a situation? In the first place, of course, we must evaluate its credibility—is it true? Are there circumstances that modify its accuracy? Beyond that, a concerned person can try to correct the condition.

In Holly's case, I called an official at the Board of Education; he, in turn, arranged for a counseling supervisor to go to the school and review *proper* test use with all the counselors at the school. Holly's case will be discussed with Holly's counselor to see whether the girl should be permitted to take higher-level work.

Along somewhat similar lines, I have heard people criticize maximum-performance tests because they have helped a person form a low concept of himself. True, but concepts of self and of others will be formed even in the absence of any testing. The emphasis should be placed, I feel, on the correct interpretation of test results. And there is no place for the assertions that tests *prove* that one has little ability, that one has too little ability to go to college, etc. In the first place, the tests do not prove any such thing. In the extreme, they may reflect the fact that a person has limited ability. Even in the extreme cases, however, the skilled test interpreter will allow himself a generous margin for possible error.

Test debunkers seem to forget two things: mistakes in classification are made (and have often been made in the past) without the aid of tests; and tests sometimes reveal ability that nontest sources have denied. For example:

Newspapers and magazines report occasionally an elderly man (or, less often, an elderly lady) being released from years of confinement in an institution for the mentally retarded. Years before, these stories go, a child considered stupid by his parents or his teacher was admitted to the institution. Now, after testing has revealed that he is not markedly deficient, he is being released from confinement.

Even in the school setting, something similar happens from time to time. A test may reveal that the pupil has much more mental ability than his teacher (and parents) had thought.

### 5. Standardized Tests Favor the Glib and Penalize the Thoughtful

This line of reasoning argues that standardized tests (usually multiple-choice tests) give extra advantage to the person who can come up with a quick, superficial response; they penalize the person who is capable of more thoughtful analysis of the questions.

Although some multiple-choice questions deserve this criticism, it is no more generally true than the charge that essay examinations favor the fast writer. There is ample evidence that good multiple-choice items may demand reasoning, interpretation, and other high-level processes. As the late Professor D. G. Paterson, of the University of Minnesota, used to say: "Short-answer questions, such as the multiple-choice, demand that the instructor substitute a skill in writing good items for a skill in grading items."

**6. Tests Invade Privacy**

This criticism has usually been leveled against personality tests which are used in a nonclinical setting. When the individual is in counseling, he should be at least as interested as the tester in revealing whatever can be revealed by the test. And when legal matters are involved, the privacy of the individual may be of less importance than other considerations.

On the other hand, there is real question in the minds of many about whether the required use of personality tests in school, in employment, in civil and military government service, etc., is justifiable. Does the school have a right to invade the privacy of its students? If so, under what conditions? All students or just some? Or is personality testing an invasion of privacy?

In my opinion, the routine personality testing of students is not advisable. I don't believe that it is ordinarily worth the time and the expense. In the school setting, I am less concerned with the issue of whether the school has the right to give such tests, for—as any school teacher knows—students reveal themselves in many ways, from the "show-and-tell" session of the primary pupils to the compositions and themes of the secondary students.

The information that is likely to be obtained from routine personality testing is not, in my opinion, worthwhile. I might feel differently if more schools had sufficient personnel skilled in the handling of personality tests results. But there are too many false positives and false negatives (i.e., misleading results), which require test sophistication to handle. Unless one knows how to deal with personality test results, he is likely to be finding disturbances where there are none and overlooking youngsters who really do have disturbances.

Add to these objections the fact that some parents resent the personality tests, and I believe that we have compelling arguments against their *routine* use. On the other hand, school psychologists and others with adequate test training should be allowed to use such tests in the study of individual children. Such an application, of course, is consistent with clinical usage.

I have less definite feelings about the issue of personality tests in government or private employment. There is at least some freedom of choice on the part of the examinee—although refusal to take the test may mean that the individual must choose not to compete for the position(s) available. The federal government now has serious restrictions on the use of personality tests in civil service, although it has always seemed ironic to me that those legislators who have been most vigorously anti-test tend to be the same ones who sometimes refer to the State Department as a Fairyland!

Should a private employer have the right to require an applicant for work to take a personality test? All applicants, or just ones about which there are "doubts"? After all, the employer is going to invest considerable time and money in training a new worker. Beyond that, the employer has a business to operate. Is he unreasonable in wanting to get the best possible employees—employees who are likely to do good work? May the employer not be concerned also with his future employees' ability to get along with their co-workers?

Or, viewed differently, does the employer have any right to pry into an applicant's feelings and values? Should an employer be allowed to reject an applicant because he gives "different" responses to personality test items? Should he be allowed to reject the nonconformists? We now have laws to protect against certain discriminatory hiring practices (e.g., on the basis of sex or race). Should the employer be permitted to safeguard the image of his company by requiring applicants for work to take personality tests?

Tests are not the only vehicle for getting at *personal* information, of course. There are other means: e.g., the application blank and the interview.

> I once completed an application blank that asked whether I "use tobacco in any form?", "use alcohol in any form?", or would "be willing to teach Sunday School?" I replied honestly that I used tobacco and alcohol in moderation, and that I might be willing to teach a Sunday School class—but not if it were a requirement for getting the job. I think that today I would return the blank form with a simple letter to that college stating that if they were interested in such questions, we would not be compatible!

I believe that employers should have some voice in the selection of their employees and that they may legitimately use personality tests; however, I am certain that many employers use such tests more blindly than wisely. Therefore, I feel that employers and consulting firms should use personality tests sparingly and selectively—and then that they should be used only by psychologists trained in their use. Failure to exercise sensible voluntary controls may prove an open invitation to governmental intervention.

In summary, I believe that personality tests, when used unwisely, do constitute an unfair invasion of privacy; however, I think that they can be helpful in a wide variety of applications when interpreted by psychologists trained to use them correctly. I would be more inclined, therefore, to restrict their use to trained people than to forbid their use entirely.

### 7. Tests Give Changing Results

Naturally—and for many valid reasons. Tests are not perfect. Neither are other evaluative methods: the personal interview, the rating scale, direct observation, etc. One should not evaluate any test against a criterion of perfection—only against other possible techniques. If a test gives useful information that we would not otherwise have and does so without prohibitive cost, the test would seem desirable.

As an added indication that tests should be expected to give somewhat changeable results: the individual himself changes over time. We may reasonably expect that test results will change along lines similar to the ways in which people change. And remember, people change in knowledge, in skills, in personality characteristics, etc. They also change in the motivation they bring to the testing room at different times.

And, under the best of conditions, test results show some variation. It has always seemed strange to me that a person whose bowling score may vary by 40 to 50 points from one string to the next expresses surprise when he hears that someone's IQ has changed by 10 to 15 points over several years when tested with different tests.

Always remember that standard error of measurement!

### 8. Tests Are Misused and Misinterpreted

I could not agree more completely with any statement!

The remedy lies, however, through better education in testing—rather than in the abolition of tests. We have substantial evidence that tests do sometimes help in some situations. Let's concentrate on how tests can be used more intelligently and more efficiently, so that we can get more true meaning (and less nonsense) out of the test results.

How? I have no magical formula, but I do think that a better understanding of tests can be sought at all levels:

1. Test publishers can be encouraged to continue their good work in trying to make test manuals and materials readable and intelligible. They need constantly to remember, too, to remind test users of the practical shortcomings of tests.

2. School and business administrators need to insist that their respective personnel offices use their tests wisely and employ suitable safeguards to keep tests, test equipment, and test results secure. Test results should be available only to the individual tested and to qualified personnel. When appropriate, administrators should encourage or support in-service training on what test scores mean.

3. Counselors, guidance workers, school psychologists, personnel workers, and the like should take a few minutes every now and then to review the manuals of the tests they use, to restudy test statistics (especially validity, reliability, standard error of estimate, standard error of measurement, etc.), and to look at new tests. Such people should plan occasional in-service training efforts to instruct individuals who receive test results about the meaning of test scores. And an attempt should be made to make these endeavors interesting. We all know that required reading and required classes can be most boring.

4. Teachers, foremen, and others who have easy or natural access to test results should be encouraged to learn what they can about the nature

of tests and test results. Beyond that, as soon as it becomes feasible, we should *require* training in test interpretation of all people whose positions involve the use of test results.

5. All interested adults should be encouraged to read about tests, their strengths and their limitations. At the present time, there is a shortage of good material for general reading, but plenty of irresponsible nonsense poured out by usually less-than-fully-informed writers. An occasional PTA meeting might be devoted to explanations of tests and testing.

6. Even school children can be trained to be a little bit sophisticated about the meaning of test results. They have already learned to inquire about time limits, whether tests are "corrected for guessing," etc., whenever they take standardized tests. Why not give them some measurement theory in their mathematics? Or a bit about evaluation and assessment in their social studies? Or something about the fallibility of observation in their sciences? I feel certain that, if an effort were made to do so, we could bring school children to a point of being able to recognize the strengths and weaknesses of standardized tests within a very few days.

There is nothing wrong with most tests that educating the consumer cannot cure.

# CONCLUDING REMARKS

*Chapter Twelve*

Are there some general principles which summarize the message of this book? Probably, and since this is likely to be the most widely read chapter, I shall try to list here some of the most important ones.

### KNOW THE TEST

There is no substitute for knowledge of the test that is being interpreted. Test titles are not always descriptive of the actual test content; furthermore, many terms can be defined differently by different people. The underlying rationale of a test may be very important to our understanding of it. Our interpretation of test results may differ for power and speeded tests, for individual and group tests, etc. We should read the test manual of any test we plan to interpret. Whenever practicable, test selection should be made only by people with sufficient background in measurement to understand the technical data descriptive of the test.

### KNOW THE NORMS

It is especially important for us to know what norms are being used. We cannot interpret adequately without understanding what group our test scores are being compared with. We may want to use several different norms groups when they are available. For example, we may want to compare a high school senior's scores with both high school seniors and college freshmen, or a person's aptitude test results with both applicants and present employees, etc. In many situations, we may want to develop our own local norms.

### KNOW THE SCORE

It is always good to "know the score" in the slang sense of that term; however, here we are being literal. We need to know whether a given number is a standard score (and what kind), a percentile rank, a raw score, or something else. Fantastic misunderstandings can result from confusing different types of score. We have used a new classification scheme in explaining test scores (*see* Chapter Six).

### KNOW THE BACKGROUND

Test results do not tell the entire story, and we should not expect them to. We must consider all available information—whether or not it comes from a test.

### COMMUNICATE EFFECTIVELY

In many settings, we will have to communicate test results to others. To get the interpretation across to an examinee, we must be certain to give the examinee all pertinent information. For example, we should give him some indication of what the norms group is like, how he compares with that group, and what the test is supposed to measure. This, of course, is not sufficient; after all, the examinee may very well resist accepting any interpretation that differs from his own conception of himself. Several techniques that I have found helpful are mentioned in Chapter Nine.

### USE THE TEST

Not too surprisingly, we can come to a better understanding of what a test is like by using it. As we develop more experience in working with tests, we can attempt some simple studies to see how well a particular test works out for our own specific purposes. As we develop competence along research lines, we can have increased confidence in the interpretations.

### USE CAUTION

Test scores *reflect* ability; they *do not determine* ability. Test scores may *suggest*, but never *prove*. We are much safer when we make interpretations based on the actual performance of those who have had similar scores (*see* "expectancy tables" on pages 57–62) than when we try to tell an examinee, "This score means that *you* will . . ."

### CONSULT THE EXPERT

Testing can get very technical, and there are many subtleties not even hinted at in this book. There is still need for a testing specialist wherever tests are widely used. And this specialist should be freely available to those who would like his assistance.

*GO AHEAD AND TRY!*

There are many pitfalls to the use of tests and their proper interpretation. There are all sorts of limitations to tests and to test scores. But tests *can* be helpful. Do not be overly cautious or you will never get any testing done. Go ahead and try!

\*     \*     \*

DIRECTIONS FOR USING CONVERSION TABLE (pages 176–181)

This table may be used to convert from one derived-score system to another, assuming a normal distribution. Enter the table with the score in which you are interested; all entries on the same line are its normal-curve equivalents. *Care must be taken when using the table to compare results from different tests, for different norms groups are likely to be involved.*

*See* last page of table for an explanation of symbols.

To use this Conversion Table for types of score *not* shown here, follow these steps:

*For a linear standard score ( Type II A ):*

1. Find the amount by which an examinee's raw score differs from the mean of the group with which you wish to compare him (either from the manual or from the local testing); i.e., $X - \bar{X}$.
2. Obtain the examinee's z-score by dividing this difference by the standard deviation of the same group; i.e., $(X - \bar{X})/s$.
3. Enter this value of z in the first column; all other entries on the same line are linear standard score equivalents (except for the percentile rank in the final column).

*For a normalized standard score ( Type II B 4 ):*

1. Follow the directions for computing a percentile rank (*see* Chart 6.2 on pages 102–103).
2. Enter this value of percentile rank in the extreme-right-hand column of the table. All other entries on the same line of the table are now *normalized* standard-score equivalents.

Customarily, none of these scores (except z) is expressed with a decimal. As a final step, therefore, you will usually round your score to the nearest whole number (if necessary).

**Do not use this table to find IQ equivalents unless "general population" norms are used.**

*Conversion Table for Derived Scores*\*

| | | | | IQ | |
|---|---|---|---|---|---|
| $\left(\dfrac{X - \bar{X}}{s}\right)$ [TYPE II A 1][a] | T[b] $(10z + 50)$ [TYPE II A2 OR II B 4 a][a] | AGCT $(20z + 100)$ [TYPE II A 3][a] | CEEB $(100z + 500)$ [TYPE II A 4][a] | WECHSLER $(15z + 100)$ [TYPE II A 5 a][a] | STANFORD–BINET $(16z + 100)$ [TYPE II A 5 b][a] |
| 3.00 | 80 | *160* | 800 | *145* | 148 |
| 2.95 | 79.5 | *159* | 795 | *144* | 147 |
| 2.90 | 79 | *158* | 790 | *144* | 146 |
| 2.85 | 78.5 | *157* | 785 | *143* | 146 |
| 2.80 | 78 | *156* | 780 | *142* | 145 |
| 2.75 | 77.5 | *155* | 775 | *141* | 144 |
| 2.70 | 77 | *154* | 770 | *141* | 143 |
| 2.65 | 76.5 | *153* | 765 | *140* | 142 |
| 2.60 | 76 | *152* | 760 | *139* | 142 |
| 2.55 | 75.5 | *151* | 755 | *138* | 141 |
| 2.50 | 75 | *150* | 750 | *138* | 140 |
| 2.45 | 74.5 | *149* | 745 | *137* | 139 |
| 2.40 | 74 | *148* | 740 | *136* | 138 |
| 2.35 | 73.5 | *147* | 735 | *135* | 138 |
| 2.30 | 73 | *146* | 730 | *135* | 137 |
| 2.25 | 72.5 | *145* | 725 | *134* | 136 |
| 2.20 | 72 | *144* | 720 | *133* | 135 |
| 2.15 | 71.5 | *143* | 715 | *132* | 134 |
| 2.10 | 71 | *142* | 710 | *132* | 134 |
| 2.05 | 70.5 | *141* | 705 | *131* | 133 |
| 2.00 | 70 | *140* | 700 | *130* | 132 |
| 1.95 | 69.5 | *139* | 695 | *129* | 131 |
| 1.90 | 69 | *138* | 690 | *129* | 130 |
| 1.85 | 68.5 | *137* | 685 | *128* | 130 |
| 1.80 | 68 | *136* | 680 | *127* | 129 |
| 1.75 | 67.5 | *135* | 675 | *126* | 128 |
| 1.70 | 67 | *134* | 670 | *126* | 127 |
| 1.65 | 66.5 | *133* | 665 | *125* | 126 |
| 1.60 | 66 | *132* | 660 | *124* | 126 |
| 1.55 | 65.5 | *131* | 655 | *123* | 125 |
| 1.50 | 65 | *130* | 650 | *123* | 124 |
| 1.45 | 64.5 | *129* | 645 | *122* | 123 |
| 1.40 | 64 | *128* | 640 | *121* | 122 |
| 1.35 | 63.5 | *127* | 635 | *120* | 122 |
| 1.30 | 63 | *126* | 630 | *120* | 121 |
| 1.25 | 62.5 | *125* | 625 | *119* | 120 |
| 1.20 | 62 | *124* | 620 | *118* | 119 |
| 1.15 | 61.5 | *123* | 615 | *117* | 118 |
| 1.10 | 61 | *122* | 610 | *117* | 118 |
| 1.05 | 60.5 | *121* | 605 | *116* | 117 |

| STANINE[c] [TYPE II B 4 b][a] | C-SCORE[c] [TYPE II B 4 c][a] | STEN[c] [TYPE II B 4 d][a] | PERCENTILE RANK [TYPE II B 2][a] |
|---|---|---|---|
| | | | 99.9 |
| | | | 99.8 |
| | | | 99.8 |
| | | | 99.8 |
| | | | 99.7 |
| | | | 99.7 |
| | | | 99.6 |
| | | | 99.6 |
| | 10 | | 99.5 |
| | | | 99.5 |
| | | | 99.4 |
| | | | 99.3 |
| 9 | | 10 | 99.2 |
| | | | 99.1 |
| | | | 98.9 |
| | | | 98.8 |
| | | | 98.6 |
| | | | 98.4 |
| | | | 98.2 |
| | | | 98.0 |
| | 9 | | 97.7 |
| | | | 97.4 |
| | | | 97.1 |
| | | | 96.8 |
| | | | 96.4 |
| | | 9 | 96.0 |
| | | | 95.5 |
| | | | 95.0 |
| | | | 94.5 |
| | | | 93.9 |
| 8 | 8 | | 93.3 |
| | | | 92.6 |
| | | | 91.9 |
| | | | 91.2 |
| | | | 90.3 |
| | | | 89.4 |
| | | | 88.5 |
| | | 8 | 87.5 |
| 7 | 7 | | 86.4 |
| | | | 85.3 |

*See directions for USE on previous page.

[a]Refers to the classification of scores developed for this book; see Chapter six.

[b]Since this table sssumes a normal distribution, these values of T may be either T-scores (*Type II A 2*) or T-scaled scores (*Type II B 4 a*); if the distribution were not normal, T-scaled score *entries would differ.*

[c]*This score takes only a very limited number of different values; therefore, it will have the same value for a range of values on other scores.*

*Conversion Table for Derived Scores (Continued)*

| $\left(\dfrac{X-\bar{X}}{s}\right)$ z | T[b] (10z + 50) | AGCT (20z + 100) | CEEB (100z + 500) | IQ | |
|---|---|---|---|---|---|
| | | | | WECHSLER (15z + 100) | STANFORD– BINET (16z + 100) |
| 1.00 | 60 | 120 | 600 | 115 | 116 |
| 0.95 | 59.5 | 119 | 595 | 114 | 115 |
| 0.90 | 59 | 118 | 590 | 114 | 114 |
| 0.85 | 58.5 | 117 | 585 | 113 | 114 |
| 0.80 | 58 | 116 | 580 | 112 | 113 |
| 0.75 | 57.5 | 115 | 575 | 111 | 112 |
| 0.70 | 57 | 114 | 570 | 111 | 111 |
| 0.65 | 56.5 | 113 | 565 | 110 | 110 |
| 0.60 | 56 | 112 | 560 | 109 | 110 |
| 0.55 | 55.5 | 111 | 555 | 108 | 109 |
| 0.50 | 55 | 110 | 550 | 108 | 108 |
| 0.45 | 54.5 | 109 | 545 | 107 | 107 |
| 0.40 | 54 | 108 | 540 | 106 | 106 |
| 0.35 | 53.5 | 107 | 535 | 105 | 106 |
| 0.30 | 53 | 106 | 530 | 104 | 105 |
| 0.25 | 52.5 | 105 | 525 | 104 | 104 |
| 0.20 | 52 | 104 | 520 | 103 | 103 |
| 0.15 | 51.5 | 103 | 515 | 102 | 102 |
| 0.10 | 51 | 102 | 510 | 102 | 102 |
| 0.05 | 50.5 | 101 | 505 | 101 | 101 |
| 0.00 | 50 | 100 | 500 | 100 | 100 |
| −0.05 | 49.5 | 99 | 495 | 99 | 99 |
| −0.10 | 49 | 98 | 490 | 98 | 98 |
| −0.15 | 48.5 | 97 | 485 | 98 | 98 |
| −0.20 | 48 | 96 | 480 | 97 | 97 |
| −0.25 | 47.5 | 95 | 475 | 96 | 96 |
| −0.30 | 47 | 94 | 470 | 96 | 95 |
| −0.35 | 46.5 | 93 | 465 | 95 | 94 |
| −0.40 | 46 | 92 | 460 | 94 | 94 |
| −0.45 | 45.5 | 91 | 455 | 93 | 93 |
| −0.50 | 45 | 90 | 450 | 93 | 92 |
| −0.55 | 44.5 | 89 | 445 | 92 | 91 |
| −0.60 | 44 | 88 | 440 | 91 | 90 |
| −0.65 | 43.5 | 87 | 435 | 90 | 90 |
| −0.70 | 43 | 86 | 430 | 90 | 89 |
| −0.75 | 42.5 | 85 | 425 | 89 | 88 |
| −0.80 | 42 | 84 | 420 | 88 | 87 |
| −0.85 | 41.5 | 83 | 415 | 87 | 86 |
| −0.90 | 41 | 82 | 410 | 87 | 86 |
| −0.95 | 40.5 | 81 | 405 | 86 | 85 |

| STANINE[c] | C-SCORE[c] | STEN[c] | PERCENTILE RANK |
|---|---|---|---|
| | | | 84.1 |
| | | | 82.9 |
| 7 | 7 | | 81.6 |
| | | | 80.2 |
| | | 7 | 78.8 |
| | | | 77.3 |
| | | | 75.8 |
| | | | 74.2 |
| | | | 72.6 |
| | | | 70.9 |
| 6 | 6 | | 69.2 |
| | | | 67.4 |
| | | | 65.5 |
| | | | 63.7 |
| | | | 61.8 |
| | | 6 | 59.9 |
| | | | 57.9 |
| | | | 56.0 |
| | | | 54.0 |
| | | | 52.0 |
| 5 | 5 | | 50.0 |
| | | | 48.0 |
| | | | 46.0 |
| | | | 44.0 |
| | | | 42.1 |
| | | 5 | 40.1 |
| | | | 38.2 |
| | | | 36.3 |
| | | | 34.5 |
| | | | 32.6 |
| 4 | 4 | | 30.8 |
| | | | 29.1 |
| | | | 27.4 |
| | | | 25.8 |
| | | | 24.2 |
| | | 4 | 22.7 |
| | | | 21.2 |
| | | | 19.8 |
| | | | 18.4 |
| 3 | 3 | | 17.1 |

*See directions for USE on page 175.

[b]Since this table assumes a normal distribution, these values of T may be either T-scores (Type II A 2) or T-scaled scores (Type II B 4 a); if the distribution were not normal, T-scaled score entries would differ.

[c]This score takes only a very limited number of different values; therefore, it will have the same value for a range of values on other scores.

*Conversion Table for Derived Scores (Continued)*

| $\left(\dfrac{X - \bar{X}}{s}\right)\ \mathbf{z}$ | $\mathbf{T}^{b}$ $(10z + 50)$ | **AGCT** $(20z + 100)$ | **CEEB** $(100z + 500)$ | IQ WECHSLER $(15z + 100)$ | IQ STANFORD– BINET $(16z + 100)$ |
|---|---|---|---|---|---|
| −1.00 | 40 | 80 | 400 | 85 | 84 |
| −1.05 | 39.5 | 79 | 395 | 84 | 83 |
| −1.10 | 39 | 78 | 390 | 84 | 82 |
| −1.15 | 38.5 | 77 | 385 | 83 | 82 |
| −1.20 | 38 | 76 | 380 | 82 | 81 |
| −1.25 | 37.5 | 75 | 375 | 81 | 80 |
| −1.30 | 37 | 74 | 370 | 81 | 79 |
| −1.35 | 36.5 | 73 | 365 | 80 | 78 |
| −1.40 | 36 | 72 | 360 | 79 | 78 |
| −1.45 | 35.5 | 71 | 355 | 78 | 77 |
| −1.50 | 35 | 70 | 350 | 78 | 76 |
| −1.55 | 34.5 | 69 | 345 | 77 | 75 |
| −1.60 | 34 | 68 | 340 | 76 | 74 |
| −1.65 | 33.5 | 67 | 335 | 75 | 74 |
| −1.70 | 33 | 66 | 330 | 75 | 73 |
| −1.75 | 32.5 | 65 | 325 | 74 | 72 |
| −1.80 | 32 | 64 | 320 | 73 | 71 |
| −1.85 | 31.5 | 63 | 315 | 72 | 70 |
| −1.90 | 31 | 62 | 310 | 72 | 70 |
| −1.95 | 30.5 | 61 | 305 | 71 | 69 |
| −2.00 | 30 | 60 | 300 | 70 | 68 |
| −2.05 | 29.5 | 59 | 295 | 69 | 67 |
| −2.10 | 29 | 58 | 290 | 69 | 66 |
| −2.15 | 28.5 | 57 | 285 | 68 | 66 |
| −2.20 | 28 | 56 | 280 | 67 | 65 |
| −2.25 | 27.5 | 55 | 275 | 66 | 64 |
| −2.30 | 27 | 54 | 270 | 66 | 63 |
| −2.35 | 26.5 | 53 | 265 | 65 | 62 |
| −2.40 | 26 | 52 | 260 | 64 | 62 |
| −2.45 | 25.5 | 51 | 255 | 63 | 61 |
| −2.50 | 25 | 50 | 250 | 63 | 60 |
| −2.55 | 24.5 | 49 | 245 | 62 | 59 |
| −2.60 | 24 | 48 | 240 | 61 | 58 |
| −2.65 | 23.5 | 47 | 235 | 60 | 58 |
| −2.70 | 23 | 46 | 230 | 60 | 57 |
| −2.75 | 22.5 | 45 | 225 | 59 | 56 |
| −2.80 | 22 | 44 | 220 | 58 | 55 |
| −2.85 | 21.5 | 43 | 215 | 57 | 54 |
| −2.90 | 21 | 42 | 210 | 57 | 54 |
| −2.95 | 20.5 | 41 | 205 | 56 | 53 |
| −3.00 | 20 | 40 | 200 | 55 | 52 |

| STANINE[c] | C-SCORE[c] | STEN[c] | PERCENTILE RANK |
|:---:|:---:|:---:|:---:|
| | | | 15.9 |
| | | | 14.7 |
| | | 3 | 13.6 |
| | | | 12.5 |
| | | | 11.5 |
| | | 3 | 10.6 |
| | | | 9.7 |
| | | | 8.8 |
| | | | 8.1 |
| | | | 7.4 |
| 2 | 2 | | 6.7 |
| | | | 6.1 |
| | | | 5.5 |
| | | | 5.0 |
| | | | 4.5 |
| | | 2 | 4.0 |
| | | | 3.6 |
| | | | 3.2 |
| | | | 2.9 |
| | | | 2.6 |
| | 1 | | 2.3 |
| | | | 2.0 |
| | | | 1.8 |
| | | | 1.6 |
| | | | 1.4 |
| | | | 1.2 |
| | | | 1.1 |
| | | | 0.9 |
| | | | 0.8 |
| | | | 0.7 |
| 1 | | 1 | 0.6 |
| | | | 0.5 |
| | | | 0.5 |
| | 0 | | 0.4 |
| | | | 0.4 |
| | | | 0.3 |
| | | | 0.3 |
| | | | 0.2 |
| | | | 0.2 |
| | | | 0.2 |
| | | | 0.1 |

*See directions for USE on page 175.

[b]Since this table assumes a normal distribution, these values of T may be either T-scores (Type II A 2) or T-scaled scores (Type II B 4 a); if the distribution were not normal, T-scaled score entries would differ.

[c]This score takes only a very limited number of different values; therefore, it will have the same value for a range of values on other scores.

## Bibliography

*TECHNICAL AND GENERAL*

Anastasi, Anne, ed., *Testing Problems in Perspective*. Washington, D.C.: American Council on Education, 1966. Selected papers from various ETS Invitational Conferences on Testing Problems.

Buros, Oscar K., ed., *The Sixth Mental Measurements Yearbook*. Highland Park, N. J.: Gryphon Press, 1965. All six yearbooks are essential references for those interested in critical reviews of tests or bibliographies of articles dealing with specific tests.

Cronbach, Lee J. and Goldine Gleser, *Psychological Tests and Personnel Decisions* (2nd ed.). Urbana: University of Illinois Press, 1965. Highly technical, but excellent.

Flanagan, John C., *et al.*, *The Talents of American Youth: 1. Design for a Study of American Youth*. Boston: Houghton Mifflin Company, 1962. Includes a description of the tests used in Project TALENT.

Ghiselli, E. E., *Theory of Psychological Measurement*. New York: McGraw-Hill Book Company, Inc., 1964. Easy introduction to test theory.

Goslin, David A., *The Search for Ability: Standardized Testing in Social Perspective*. New York: Russell Sage Foundation, 1963. The influence of testing on society.

Guion, Robert M., *Personnel Testing*. New York: McGraw-Hill Book Company, Inc., 1965. Excellent and thorough on industrial applications of tests.

Gulliksen, Harold, *Theory of Mental Tests*. New York: John Wiley & Sons, Inc., 1950. The classic; dated and difficult, but good.

Horst, Paul, *Psychological Measurement and Prediction*. Belmont, Calif.: Wadsworth Publishing Co., Inc., 1966. Good technical work.

Jackson, Douglas N. and Samuel Messick, eds., *Problems in Human Assessment*. New York: McGraw-Hill Book Company, Inc., 1967. A big, excellent, sophisticated, and expensive book of readings.

Kirkpatrick, James J., *et al.*, *Testing and Fair Employment*. New York: New York University Press, 1968. How tests sometimes predict job success differently for minority groups.

Lord, Frederic M. and Melvin R. Novick, *Statistical Theories of Mental Test Scores*. Reading, Mass.: Addison-Wesley Publishing Co., Inc., 1968. Excellent; highly technical.

Magnusson, David, *Test Theory*. Reading, Mass.: Addison-Wesley Publishing Co., Inc., 1967. Readable treatment of test theory by Swedish psychologist.

Nunnally, Jum C., *Psychometric Theory*. New York: McGraw-Hill Book Company, Inc., 1967. Good readable text.

Oetting, Eugene R. and George C. Thornton, III, *Exercises in Psychological Testing*. New York: Harper & Row, Publishers, 1969. Sample test materials for use in testing classes.

*Standards for Educational and Psychological Tests and Manuals*. Washington, D. C.: American Psychological Association, 1966. Recommended standards to be followed in publishing tests and manuals.

Super, Donald E. and John O. Crites, *Appraising Vocational Fitness by Means of Psychological Tests* (rev. ed.). New York: Harper & Row, Publishers, 1962. Long and dated, but good.

Thorndike, Robert L., *Personnel Selection*. New York: John Wiley & Sons, Inc., 1949. Old, but excellent.

Thorndike, Robert L., ed., *Educational Measurement* (2nd ed.). Washington D. C.: American Council on Education, 1970. A superb collection of articles of varying difficulty.

## *MONOGRAPHS*

The following set of monographs edited by Shelley C. Stone and Bruce Shertzer was published by Houghton Mifflin Company, Boston, in 1968. All are excellent and inexpensive:

Linden, Kathryn W. and James D. Linden, *Modern Mental Measurement: A Historical Perspective*.

Womer, Frank B., *Basic Concepts in Testing*.

Downie, Norville M., *Types of Test Scores*.

Bauernfeind, Robert H., *School Testing Programs*.

Lyman, Howard B., *Intelligence, Aptitude, and Achievement Testing*.

Cottle, William C. *Interest and Personality Inventories*.

Linden, James C. and Kathryn W. Linden, *Tests on Trial*.

Stoker, Howard W., *Automated Data Processing in Testing*.

Barclay, James R., *Controversial Issues in Testing*.

## *BOOKS OF READINGS*

Several excellent books of readings in measurement have been published in recent years. All are paperbacks and of moderate cost.

Barnette, W. Leslie, ed., *Readings in Psychological Tests and Measurements* (rev. ed.). Homewood, Ill.: Dorsey Press, 1968.

Chase, Clinton I. and H. Glenn Ludlow, eds., *Readings in Educational and Psychological Measurement*. Boston: Houghton Mifflin Company, 1966.

Flynn, John T. and Herbert Garber, eds., *Assessing Behavior: Readings in Educational and Psychological Measurement*. Reading, Mass.: Addison-Wesley Publishing Co., Inc., 1967.

Mehrens, William A. and Robert L. Ebel, eds., *Principles of Educational and Psychological Measurement*. Chicago: Rand McNally & Co., 1967.

Payne, David A. and Robert F. McMorris, eds., *Educational and Psychological Measurement*. Waltham, Mass.: Blaisdell Publishing Co. (A Division of Ginn and Company), 1967.

Wiseman, Stephen, ed., *Intelligence and Ability* (*Penguin Modern Psychology*). Baltimore, Md.: Penguin Books, Inc., 1967.

## *SELECTED MEASUREMENTS TEXTBOOKS*

As a general rule, those books which are *primarily educational* tend to be easier to read, but perhaps less thorough (except on achievement tests); those that are *primarily psychological* usually include more material on test statistics and personality testing, and give a wider variety of examples.

I have used (and like) the books by Anastasi, Cronbach, and Thorndike and Hagen; however, I believe that the others have merit, too.

**Primarily Psychological**

Anastasi, Anne, *Psychological Testing* (3rd ed.). New York: The Macmillan Company, 1968.

Cronbach, Lee J., *Essentials of Psychological Testing* (3rd ed.). New York: Harper & Row, Publishers, 1970.

Freeman, Frank S., *Theory and Practice of Psychological Testing* (3rd ed.). New York: Holt, Rinehart & Winston, Inc., 1962.

Helmstadter, G. C., *Principles of Psychological Measurement*. New York: Appleton-Century-Crofts, 1964.

Nunnally, Jum C., *Tests and Measurements*. New York: McGraw-Hill Book Company, Inc., 1959.

**Primarily Educational**

Adams, Georgia Sachs, *Measurement and Evaluation in Education, Psychology, and Guidance*. New York: Holt, Rinehart & Winston, Inc., 1965.

Ahmann, J. Stanley and Marvin D. Glock, *Evaluating Pupil Growth* (3rd ed.). Boston: Allyn & Bacon, Inc., 1959.

Baron, Denis and Harold W. Bernard, *Evaluation Techniques for Classroom Teachers*. New York: McGraw-Hill Book Company, Inc., 1958.

Bauernfeind, Robert H., *Building a School Testing Program* (1969 Impression). Boston: Houghton Mifflin Company, 1969.

Downie, N. M., *Fundamentals of Measurement: Techniques and Practices* (2nd ed.). New York: Oxford University Press, 1967.

Ebel, Robert L., *Measuring Educational Achievement*. Englewood Cliffs, N. J.: Prentice-Hall, Inc., 1965.

Gronlund, Norman, *Measurement and Evaluation in Teaching*. New York: The Macmillan Company, 1965.

Horrocks, John and Thelma Schoonover, *Measurement for Teachers*. Columbus, Ohio: Charles E. Merrill Publishing Co., 1968.

Lindeman, Richard H., *Educational Measurement*. Glenview, Ill.: Scott, Foresman and Company, 1967.

Mehrens, William A. and Irvin J. Lehmann, *Standardized Tests in Education*. New York: Holt, Rinehart & Winston, Inc., 1969.

Noll, Victor, *Introduction to Educational Measurement* (2nd ed.). Boston: Houghton Mifflin Company, 1965.

Nunnally, Jum C., *Educational Measurement and Evaluation*. New York: McGraw-Hill Book Company, Inc., 1964.

Remmers, H. H., *et al.*, *Practical Introduction to Measurement and Evaluation* (2nd ed.). New York: Harper & Row, Publishers, 1965.

——— *et al.*, *Measurement and Evaluation*. New York: Harper & Row, Publishers, 1966.

Smith, Fred and Sam Adams, *Educational Measurement for the Classroom Teacher*. New York: Harper & Row, Publishers, 1966.

Stanley, Julian, *Measurement in Today's Schools* (4th ed.). Englewood Cliffs, N. J.: Prentice-Hall, Inc., 1964.

Thorndike, Robert L. and Elizabeth Hagen, *Measurement and Evaluation in Psychology and Education* (3rd ed.). New York: John Wiley & Sons, Inc., 1969.

## *VIDEO TAPES, AUDIO TAPES, AND FILMS*

Audio-visual materials offer a different approach to teaching an understanding of testing. The video tapes listed are designed to demonstrate the characteristics of widely used individual tests of intelligence. The audio tapes and films are intended for use with either lay or professional groups.

The following video tapes, each 30 minutes in length, were produced by Sound Seminars for distribution by the McGraw-Hill Book Company Inc., New York.

Lyman, Howard B., *Administration of the Wechsler Intelligence Scale for Children: A Demonstration*, 1967.

————, *Administration of the Stanford–Binet Scales of Intelligence: A Demonstration*, 1967.

————, *Administration of the Wechsler Adult Intelligence Scale: A Demonstration*, 1968.

————, *Administration of the Wechsler Preschool and Primary Scale of Intelligence: A Demonstration*, 1968.

The following audio tapes were also prepared by Sound Seminars for the McGraw-Hill Book Company. They are the first tapes issued in what will be a longer set: Howard B. Lyman, ed., *Testing in the Schools*.

Lyman, Howard B., *Testing: Then and Now*, 1969.
Stone, Shelley, *How Standardized Testing Differs from Informal Testing*, 1968.
Miller, Elizabeth R., *Individual Intelligence Testing*, 1969.
Nunnally, Jum C., *Aptitude Testing*, 1968.
Katz, Martin, *Interest Measurement*, 1968.
Felix, Joseph, *Personality Testing*, 1968.
Lyman, Howard B., *How to Take a test*, 1969.

A series of five films, each about 15 minutes in length, has been produced by the Cooperative Test Division of the Educational Testing Service, Princeton, N. J. Each film centers on a single testing problem. The films may be borrowed or purchased from ETS.

# APPENDIX

**Glossary of Terms**

This Glossary of Terms, like the rest of the book, is intended primarily for those who have had little formal training in testing. Therefore, some of the definitions may not meet the more exacting requirements of professional measurements people. Because most of the terms are discussed elsewhere in the book, I have tried to keep these definitions brief. The designation of various derived scores according to Types refers to the classification scheme presented in Chapter Six. Most definitions in this Glossary come from my personal notes.

**accomplishment quotient (AQ).** A derived score (Type III D) is equal to the ratio between *educational age* and *mental age* (*EA/MA*); sometimes called "achievement quotient."

**achievement age.** See *educational age*.

**achievement battery.** A *battery* of *achievement tests*.

**achievement test.** A test designed to measure the amount of knowledge and/or skill a person has acquired, usually as a result of classroom instruction; may be either *informal* or *standardized*.

**adjustment inventory.** See *personality test*.

**age equivalent.** The chronological age for which a specified raw score is the average raw score.

**age norms.** *Norms* that give *age equivalents* for raw-score values.

**age score.** See *age equivalent*.

**alternate-form reliability.** A method of estimating test *reliability* by the *correlation coefficient* between two equivalent or parallel forms of the test; based on consistency of content.

**anchor.** A test or other variable which is used to insure the comparability of two or more forms or editions or levels of a given instrument.

**aptitude.** That combination of characteristics, both native and acquired, which indicates the capacity of a person to develop proficiency in some skill or subject matter after relevant training; usually, but not necessarily, implies intellectual or skill aspects rather than emotional or personality characteristics.

**arithmetic mean.** See *mean.*

**articulation.** Act or process of developing different *editions, forms,* and (especially) *levels* of the same test to yield results that are comparable.

**assessment.** Act or process of determining the present level (usually of achievement) of a group or individual.

**average.** A general term for any central tendency measure; most commonly used in testing are the *mean, median,* and *mode.*

**battery.** (1) A set of tests standardized on the same group, so that the results will be comparable; such a battery is called "integrated." (2) A set of tests administered at about the same time to an individual or group; e.g., an employment battery, a counseling battery, or an admissions battery.

**Buros, Oscar K.** Editor of the *Mental Measurements Yearbooks,* the "Bible" of testing.

***C*-score.** A *normalized standard score* [Type II B 4 (c)] of eleven units.

**chronological age (CA).** Any person's age; i.e., the length of time he has lived. The CA is used in determining *intelligence quotients* and is a factor to consider when interpreting certain types of scores, especially age scores.

**class interval.** The unit of a *frequency distribution,* especially when the unit is greater than one; a band of score values assumed to be equal for purposes of computation or graphing.

**coefficient of correlation.** An index number indicating the degree of relationship between two variables; i.e., the tendency for values of one variable to change systematically with changes in values of a second variable; no relationship $= 0.00$, a perfect relationship $= \pm 1.00$. [Although there are different coefficients for various purposes, the basic type is the Pearson product–moment correlation $(r)$, which is used when both variables are *continuous,* distributed symmetrically, etc.]

**cognitive factors.** Those characteristics of the individual that imply intellective ability, as contrasted with affective or personality characteristics.

**concurrent validity.** *Criterion-related validity* when both test scores and *criterion* values are obtained at about the same time.

**construct validity.** Test validation based on a combination of logical and empirical evidence of the relationship between the test and a related theory; concerned with the psychological meaningfulness of the test.

**content reliability.** The consistency with which a test measures whatever it measures; may be estimated by a *reliability coefficient* based on: (a) *split halves,* (b) *alternate forms,* or (c) *internal consistency.*

**content validity.** Logical evidence that the item content of a test is suitable for the purpose for which the test is to be used; concept is used principally with achievement tests.

**continuous variable.** A *variable* capable, actually or theoretically, of assuming any value—as opposed to a *discrete variable,* which may take only whole-number values; test scores are treated as being continuous although they are less obvious examples than time, distance, weight, etc.

**convergent thinking.**   Refers to a test that is scored for the "right" or "best" answer, used in opposition to *divergent thinking*.

**correction-for-guessing formula.**   A formula sometimes used in scoring objective tests to make an allowance for items that have been "guessed" correctly; general formula is: $X_c = R - (W/A - 1)$, where $X_c$ = corrected score, $R$ = number of items right, $W$ = number of items wrong, and $A$ = number of alternative choices per item. Although the underlying reasoning is dubious, the formula has considerable merit when examinees differ greatly in number of items left unanswered; use of the formula does not change order of scores when no one omits any items.

**correlation.**   Tendency for two (or occasionally more) variables to change values concomitantly. Note: evidence of correlation is not evidence of causation. See *coefficient of correlation*.

**creativity.**   See *divergent thinking*.

**criteria.**   Plural of *criterion*.

**criterion.**   A standard against which a test may be validated; e.g., grade-point average is an obvious criterion for a scholastic aptitude test.

**criterion-keying.**   The act or process of developing a test's scoring key empirically, through noting characteristic differences in answers made by different groups of individuals.

**criterion-related validity.**   Test validity based on data from practical situations; i.e., a correlation coefficient between a set of test scores and a set of criterion values. Syn. *empirical validity*.

**cross-cultural test.**   A test believed to be suitable for use in different societies because it is relatively free from cultural influences (such as language).

**cross validation.**   The act or process of verifying results obtained on one group (or one study) by replication with a different, but similar, group (or study).

**curriculum validity.**   See *content validity*.

**cutting score.**   The minimum passing score, usually determined through research, for some practical situation (e.g., college entrance or job selection). Syn. *cutoff score*.

**decile.**   Any one of the nine percentile points which divide a distribution into ten subgroups of equal frequency; e.g., the first decile $(D_1)$ is the same as the tenth percentile $(P_{10})$.

**decile rank.**   A derived score (Type II B 5) expressed in terms of the nearest *decile*; thus, a decile rank of 1 is given to any value between the fifth and fifteenth percentiles. Note: a decile rank of 0 is given to values below the fifth percentile; a decile rank of 10 to any value above the ninety-fifth percentile.

**derived score.**   Any type of score other than a *raw score*.

**deviation.**   The amount by which a score differs from a specified reference point (usually, but not always, the mean or other average).

**deviation IQ.**   (1) A standard score (Type II A 5) with a mean fixed statistically at 100 and standard deviation fixed according to the wish of the test's author; has advantages over the *ratio IQ*, which it is designed to approximate. (2) A normalized standard score [Type II B 4(e)] designed to resemble a *ratio IQ*, but possessing certain advantages. (3) A derived score (Type IV C) in which IQ is equal to 100 plus the amount by which an examinee's *raw score* deviates from the *norm* for his age.

**diagnostic test.**  (1) A test (usually of achievement) designed to identify specific educational and study difficulties. (2) Any test given in connection with counseling or psychotherapy as an aid to determining the nature of an individual's mental disorder, possible maladjustment, etc.

**difficulty value.**  A statement of a test item's difficulty, usually expressed as the percentage of individuals in a given group answering the item correctly.

**discrete value.**  A value obtained through counting rather than measuring; thus, can take only whole-number values—e.g., number of employees in each plant, number of books in school libraries, number of students in each classroom, etc.; unlike *continuous* variables, which can assume any value.

**discrimination value.**  Any of several statistics used to express the extent to which a test item shows a difference between high-ability and low-ability examinees.

**distracter.**  Any incorrect alternative in a multiple-choice item.

**distribution.**  See *frequency distribution; normal distribution.*

**divergent thinking.**  Refers to a test in which novel or creative responses are desired; contrasts with the more-common *convergent thinking* items.

**educational age.**  A derived score [Type II D 1 (b)] in which the examinee's performance on an achievement test is stated as the age for which his performance is average; analogous to *mental age* scores on an intelligence test.

**empirical validity.**  See *criterion-related validity.*

**equivalent form.**  Any of two or more forms (or versions) of a test, usually (but not always) standardized on the same population and published at the same time—these forms are designed to be similar in item content and difficulty, so that scores on the forms will be similar.

**error.**  A generic term for those elements in a test and testing situation that operate to keep a test from giving perfectly valid results: (a) *constant errors* have a direct adverse effect on validity, but may not affect reliability (e.g., having arithmetic items in an English test); (b) *variable* (or *random*) *errors* reduce reliability directly and validity indirectly (e.g., nonstandard conditions of test administration, chance passing or failing of items, ambiguous wording of test items, etc.). Note: errors are inherent in all measurement, but mistakes are not; we can estimate the amount of *variable error* present, but not the amount (or the presence) of mistakes.

**essay test.**  See *subjective test.*

**expectancy table.**  Any table showing class intervals of test scores (or other predictor variable) along one axis, and criterion categories (or similar information) along the other axis; entries show number or, more typically, percentage of individuals within specified score intervals who have achieved at a given level on the criterion variable.

**extrapolation.**  The act or process of estimating values beyond those actually obtained; e.g., extreme values for both age and grade-placement scores have to be established in this manner.

**face validity.**  Superficial appearance of validity; i.e., test looks as if it should measure what is intended (regardless of the presence or absence of data indicating that it is actually valid for some purpose).

**factor.**  (1) Strictly and technically, an element or variable presumed to exist because of its ability to help explain some of the interrelationships noted among a set of tests. (2) Equally properly, the ability or characteristic represented by a *factor* (def. 1). (3) Loosely, anything which is partially responsible for a result or outcome (e.g., "study is an important factor in obtaining good grades").

**factor analysis.**  Any of several complex statistical procedures for analyzing the intercorrelations among a set of tests (or other variables) for the purpose of identifying the *factors* (defs. 1 and 2), preferably few in number, that cause the intercorrelations; widely used in efforts to understand the organization of intelligence, personality, and the like.

**frequency.**  The number of individuals obtaining any specified score or falling in any specified class interval.

**frequency distribution.**  Any orderly arrangement of scores, usually from highest to lowest, showing the number of individuals (i.e., the frequency) making each score or falling in each class interval.

**frequency polygon.**  A type of graph used commonly to portray a distribution of test scores (or values of some other continuous variable).

**grade equivalent.**  See *grade-placement score.*

**grade norm.**  The average test score obtained by pupils with a specified grade placement.

**grade-placement score.**  A derived score (Type II D 2) expressed as the grade placement of those pupils for whom a given score was average; e.g., a grade-placement score of 7.3 indicates average performance for pupils in the third month of the seventh grade.

**group test.**  A test designed to be administered simultaneously to a group of examinees by one examiner.

**heterogeneity.**  Possessing a great deal of variability; thus, in testing: a test with a great variety of content, or a group that varies considerably in the attribute tested.

**homogeneity.**  Having little variability; thus, in testing: a test composed of items that vary little in type, or a group that varies little in the attribute tested.

**individual decision.**  A term used by Cronbach and Gleser to describe the situation in which a choice must be made by the individual (or, sometimes, on his behalf) rather than by an institution; e.g., the choice of a career.

**individual test.**  A test that usually, if not always, can be administered to only one examinee at a time.

**inferential statistics.**  Statistics used to test hypotheses, establish confidence limits, etc. (e.g., $t$, chi square, or analysis of variance).

**informal test.**  Any test intended primarily for the use of the test constructor; used in opposition to *standardized test.*

**institutional decision.**  A term used by Cronbach and Gleser to describe the situation in which a choice must be made on behalf of an institution (a school or company) rather than by the individuals tested; e.g., which applicants to select and which to reject. Tests can almost always be more helpful in situations requiring institutional decision than in situations demanding *individual decisions*.

**intellectual status index.**  A derived score (Type III B) used by the California Test Bureau; similar to a *ratio IQ* except that the average chronological age of pupils with his same grade placement is substituted for the child's actual chronological age.

**intelligence.**  An abstraction variously defined by various authorities; in general, that capacity or set of capacities which enables an individual to learn, to cope with his environment, to solve problems, etc.

**intelligence quotient (IQ).**  See *deviation IQ; ratio IQ*.

**internal consistency.**  A term referring to any of several techniques for estimating the *content reliability* of a test through knowledge of *item analysis* statistics.

**interpolation.**  The act or process of estimating a value that falls between two known or computed values; this practice is often followed in establishing age and grade-placement scores, so that the norms table will cover all possible ages or grade-placements (e.g., samples of children aged 7–0 and 7–3 may have been tested and their average scores established as being 7–0 and 7–3, respectively; intermediate scores would be assigned values of 7–1 and 7–2 by *interpolation*).

**inventory.**  (1) Most commonly used to describe a *paper-and-pencil* test of personality, interest, attitude, or the like. (2) Less commonly used to describe an achievement test designed to "take an inventory" of student or class knowledge or skill on a specific task.

**item.**  (1) Any individual problem or question on a test. (2) Usually, but not always, the basic scorable unit of an *objective* test.

**item analysis.**  The act or process of examining a test item empirically to determine: (a) its *difficulty value*, and (b) its *discrimination value*. Note: such values will differ somewhat from group to group and from time to time and according to the particular statistic used.

**key, scoring.**  (1) The collection of correct answers (or scored responses) for the items of a test. (2) The device or sheet, containing the scored responses, which is used in scoring the test (e.g., see *stencil key; strip key*).

**Kuder-Richardson formula.**  Any of several formulas developed by Kuder and Richardson for the estimation of *content reliability* through an *internal-consistency* analysis.

**machine-scoring.**  The act or process of scoring a test with the aid of a mechanical or electrical device that counts and may record the scored responses of a test (or subtest); the most common machines involve one or more of these processes: (a) *mark-sensing*, (b) *punched-hole*, or (c) electronic scanning.

**mark-sensing.**  Descriptive of a system of *machine-scoring* tests that uses an electrical contact to "sense" responses to be scored.

**maximum-performance test.**  Any test on which the examinee is directed, at least implicitly, to do the best job he can; e.g., intelligence, aptitude, and achievement tests. Used in opposition to *typical-performance test*.

**mean.**  Most widely used measure of central tendency; equals the sum of scores divided by the number of examinees.

**median.**   Next to the mean, the most common measure of central tendency; the point on the scale of score values which separates the group into two equal sub-groups; the fiftieth percentile ($P_{50}$), second quartile ($Q_2$), and the fifth decile ($D_5$).

**mental age.**   A derived score [Type II D 1 (a)], used on intelligence tests only, which is expressed as the age for which a given *raw score* is average or typical; e.g., a mental age of 12-4 indicates intelligence test performance that is average for children of twelve years four months of age.

**modal age.**   The chronological age that is most typical of children with a given grade placement in school.

**modal-age norms.**   Norms based only on those pupils near the modal age for their actual grade placement; such norms are used on most school-level *achievement batteries* as a presumed refinement in establishing *grade-placement scores*.

**mode.**   A measure of central tendency; that score value which has the highest *frequency;* i.e., that score obtained by more examinees than any other.

*N.*   Symbol used in this book to represent number of examinees in any specified group.

**norm.**   Average, normal, or standard for a group of specified status (e.g., of a given age or grade placement).

**normal distribution (curve).**   A useful mathematical model representing the distribution expected when an infinite number of observations (e.g., scores) deviate from the mean only by chance; although a normal distribution can never be attained in reality, many actual distributions do approach this model. The curve drawn to portray the normal distribution is a symmetrical bell-shaped curve whose properties are completely known.

**normalized standard score.**   Any of several scores (Type II B) which resemble standard scores (Type II A), but which make the obtained distribution conform more closely to a normal distribution through the use of percentile equivalents.

**norms.**   A set of values descriptive of the performance on a test of some specified group; usually shown as a table giving equivalent values of some *derived score* for each *raw score* on the test.

**objective test.**   A test for which the scoring procedure is specified completely in advance, thereby permitting complete agreement among different scorers.

**omnibus test.**   A test, usually of intelligence, in which items of many different types are used in obtaining a single over-all total score; usually has one set of directions and one over-all time limit.

**paper-and-pencil test.**   Any test which requires no materials other than paper, pencil, and test booklet; most group tests are paper-and-pencil tests.

**parameter.**   A summary or descriptive value (e.g., *mean* or *standard deviation*) for a *population* or universe; i.e., a parameter is to a *population* as a statistic is to a *sample*.

**percentage-correct score.**   A derived score (Type I A) expressing the examinee's performance as a percentage of the maximum possible score; frequently over-looked is the fact that such scores are more a function of item difficulty than a true measure of an examinee's absolute performance.

**percentile (P).**   Any of the ninety-nine points along the scale of score values that divide a distribution into one hundred groups of equal frequency; e.g., $P_{73}$ is that point below which fall 73 per cent of the cases in a distribution.

**percentile rank (PR).**   A derived score (Type II B 2) stated in terms of the percentage of examinees in a specified group who fall below a given score point.

**performance test.**   An ambiguous term used variously to mean: (a) a test involving special apparatus, as opposed to a *paper-and-pencil* test; (b) a test minimizing verbal skills; or (c) a work-sample test. All of these uses are unfortunate, because the term "performance" already means "the behavior of an examinee on a given test," "the score of any specified examinee on a test," etc.

**personality test.**   A *typical-performance* test, questionnaire, or other device designed to measure some affective characteristic of the individual.

**population.**   Any entire group so designated; i.e., the total group that is of interest or concern. As commonly used in testing, refers to the totality about which statistical inferences are to be made and from which a *sample* is taken.

**power test.**   Any *maximum-performance* test for which speed is not an important determinant of score; thus, a test with no time limit or with a very generous time limit.

**predictive validity.**   *Empirical validity* where criterion values are obtained subsequent to the determination of the test scores.

**probable error (PE).**   A measure of variability, rarely used today, found by multiplying 0.6745 by either the *standard deviation* (to obtain the probable error of a distribution) or the *standard error* (to obtain the probable error of some statistic). In a normal distribution, one-half the cases lie within $\pm 1\ PE$ of the mean.

**profile.**   A graphic representation of the performance of an individual (or, less commonly, a group) on a series of tests, especially the tests in an integrated *battery*.

**prognostic test.**   A test used to predict future performance (usually, success or failure) in a particular task.

**projective technique.**   Any method of personality measurement or study that makes use of deliberately ambiguous stimuli (e.g., ink blots, incomplete sentences, etc.) into which the examinee must "project" his personality when responding.

**punched-hole.**   Descriptive of a system of *machine-scoring* tests; utilizes holes punched into cards (e.g., IBM cards).

**quartile.**   Any of the three points which divide a frequency distribution into four groups of equal frequency. The first quartile $(Q_1)$ equals the twenty-fifth percentile $(P_{25})$; $Q_2 = P_{50}$ = median; and $Q_3 = P_{75}$.

**r.**   Symbol for Pearson product–moment *correlation coefficient*.

**random error.**   See *variable error*.

**random sample.**   A sample drawn from a *population* in such a manner that each member has an equal chance of being selected; samples so drawn are unbiased and should yield statistics "representative" of the population.

**range.**   The difference between highest and lowest scores made on a test by a specified group.

**ratio IQ.**   A derived score (Type III A), being used less and less commonly, found by the formula: 100 $(MA/CA)$, where $MA$ = mental age determined from a test, and $CA$ = chronological age (an adjusted chronological age being used for older adolescents and for adults).

**raw score.**   The basic score initially obtained from scoring a test according to directions given by the test maker; usually equal to number of correct responses, but may be number of wrong answers or errors, time required for a task, etc.

**reliability.** Consistency or stability of a test or other measuring instrument; necessary for, but not sufficient for, *validity*. Commonly expressed as a *reliability coefficient* or a *standard error of measurement*.

**reliability coefficient.** A *coefficient of correlation* designed to estimate a test's *reliability* by correlating: (a) scores on equivalent forms, (b) scores on matched halves (corrected for length), or (c) scores on two administrations of same test.

**reproduce-ability.** See *reliability* (pages 25–32).

**rho ($\rho$).** Term (sometimes) and symbol (commonly) used to denote a Spearman rank-difference correlation coefficient.

**sample.** A general term referring to a group, however selected, assumed to represent an entire *population*.

**scaled score.** (1) Loosely, any derived score. (2) More technically, any of several systems of scores (usually similar to *standard scores*) used in: (a) articulating different forms, editions, and/or levels of a test; or (b) developmental research.

**selection ratio.** The ratio of number of persons selected to number of persons tested; other things being equal, lower ratios (i.e., more people tested in order to select a given number) result in a higher proportion of those who succeed among those selected.

**sigma.** Greek letter widely used in statistics. Capital sigma ($\Sigma$) means "to add" or "find the sum of." Lower-case sigma ($\sigma$) is often used to mean *standard deviation*, especially of a *population;* however, *s* has been used in this book, rather than $\sigma$.

**skewed (distribution).** A noticeably asymmetrical distribution of scores. A distribution with many high scores and very few low scores is said to be "skewed to the left" or "negatively skewed."

**Spearman-Brown (prophecy) formula.** A formula designed to estimate the reliability that a test will have if its length is changed and other factors remain constant; most commonly used in "correcting" *split-half reliability coefficients*.

**speed test.** (1) A test on which an examinee's speed is an important determinant of his score. (2) A test on which the score equals the time taken to complete it.

**split-half reliability coefficient.** An estimate of content reliability based on the correlation between scores on two halves of a test; usually, the odd and even items are scored separately to provide these two half-test-length scores.

**standard deviation ($s$ or $\sigma$).** A measure of variability preferred over all others because of its soundness mathematically and its general usefulness as a basis for: (a) standard scores, (b) standard errors, and (c) various statistical tests of significance.

**standard error.** An estimate of what the *standard deviation* of a statistic would be if successive values were found for that statistic through repeated testings (usually on different, but similar, samples drawn from the same population).

**standard error of estimate.** A *standard deviation* based on differences between obtained scores and scores predicted (from knowledge of correlation between a predictor variable and a criterion variable), rather than differences between scores and the mean.

**standard error of measurement.** An estimate of the *standard deviation* that would be found in the distribution of scores for a specified person if he were to be tested again and again on the same or a similar test (assuming no learning).

**standard score.** Any of several derived scores (Type II A) based on number of standard deviations between a specified raw score and the mean of the distribution. See also *normalized standard score.*

**standardization.** The act or process of developing a *standardized test;* many stages are involved in careful standardization, among these: tryout of items, item analyses, validation studies, reliability studies, development of norms, and the like.

**standardized test.** An empirically developed test, designed for administration and scoring according to stated directions, for which there is evidence of validity and reliability, as well as norms.

**stanine.** A *normalized standard score* [Type II B 4 (b)] of nine units, 1–9; in a normal distribution, stanines have a mean of 5.0 and a standard deviation of 1.96.

**sten.** A *normalized standard score* [Type II B 4 (d)], similar to the more common *stanine*, but having five units on either side of the mean; the mean sten (in a normal distribution) is 5.5, and the standard deviation is about 2.0.

**stencil key.** A *scoring key* made for placing over the answer sheet, the examinee's responses being visible either through holes prepared for that purpose or through the transparent material of the key itself; the IBM 805 Test Scoring Machine uses a scoring key of this type.

**strip key.** A *scoring key* prepared in a column or strip which may be laid alongside a column of answers on the examinee's answer sheet or test paper; when several columns of answers are printed on the same scoring key, it becomes a "fan" or "accordion key."

**subjective test.** A test on which the personal opinion or impression of the scorer is one determinant of the obtained score; i.e., the scoring key cannot be (or is not) prescribed in advance of scoring.

**survey test.** A test designed to measure achievement in one or more specified areas, usually with the intention of assessing group understanding of the concepts, principles, and facts—rather than individual measurement.

**test security.** The act or process of insuring that only authorized people have access to tests and test supplies.

**T-scaled score.** A *normalized standard score* [Type II B 4 (a)] with a mean of 50 and a standard deviation of 10.

**T-score.** A *standard score* (Type II A 2) having a mean of 50 and a standard deviation of 10.

**temporal reliability.** Test stability over a period of time, estimated through a test-retest *reliability coefficient;* i.e., a coefficient of correlation based on scores made on the same test at two different times.

**true score.** A theoretical concept never obtainable in practice, an error-free score; usually defined as the average of the scores that would be obtained if a specified examinee were to take the same test an infinite number of times (assuming no learning).

**truncated.** Term used to describe a distribution of scores that is cut off artificially or arbitrarily at some point, whatever the reason; e.g., a distribution of test scores in which many examinees receive the maximum possible score, thereby not enabling these examinees to score as high as they could have if the test had a suitable ceiling.

**typical-performance test.**    Any test designed to measure what an examinee is "really like," rather than any intellective or ability characteristic; category includes tests of personality, attitude, interest, etc.; used in opposition to *maximum-performance test.*

**universe.**    See *population.*

**validity.**    The extent to which a test does the job desired of it; the evidence may be either empirical or logical. Unless otherwise noted, *criterion-related validity* is implied.

**variability.**    A general term relating to the amount of scatter or dispersion there is among a set of scores.

**variable.**    (1) Any trait or characteristic that may change with the individual or the observation. (2) More strictly, any representation of such a trait or characteristic which is capable of assuming different values; e.g., a test is a variable.

**variance.**    A statistic, equal to the square of the standard deviation ($SD^2$); widely used in research.

**variable error.**    Any deviation from a *true score* attributable to one or more non-constant influences, such as guessing, irregular testing conditions, etc.; always has a direct adverse effect on reliability; by definition, *variable errors* are uncorrelated with *true scores.*

**work-sample test.**    A test on which the examinee's response to a simulated on-the-job problem or situation is evaluated; e.g., a pre-employment typing test.

**z-score.**    The basic standard score (Type II A); widely used in test-related research; $z = (X - \bar{X})/s$, where $\bar{X} =$ mean score, and $s =$ standard deviation.

# INDEX